Contested Truths

CONTESTED TRUTHS

Keywords in American
Politics Since Independence

DANIEL T. RODGERS

Basic Books, Inc., Publishers

NEW YORK

Library of Congress Cataloging-in-Publication Data

Rodgers, Daniel T.
  Contested truths.
  Bibliography: p. 253.
  Includes index.
  1. United States—Politics and government—Terminology
—History.   2. Political science—United States—
History.   3. Political oratory—United States—History.
I. Title.
JK39.R654   1987   320.5′0973   87–47522
ISBN   0–465–01415–1

For Oliver and Dorothy Rodgers

CONTENTS

Contents

ACKNOWLEDGMENTS

Books are shaped by accidents, occasions, and, not the least, generosity. The occasion which first turned my thoughts in the direction of political language was an exceptionally stimulating series of discussions on "Ideology and Power" which took place among the participants in the Davis Seminar in Historical Studies at Princeton University from 1980 to 1982. New colleagues opened new dimensions of the historical domain, jolted not a few thoughts out of their slowly rusting grooves, sparked ideas by the sheer, joyful multiplicity of their own. If the results have merit, a good deal of the credit belongs to the intellectual environment my Princeton colleagues continue to foster and sustain.

As the inquiry took shape, I was fortunate in being able to try out my working hunches farther afield. Through the lively and critical reactions of graduate students and faculty members at the Columbia University Seminar in American Civilization, the University of Pennsylvania, the University of North Carolina, Harvard University, and the Free University of Berlin, the project began to take on form and focus. The major part of the manuscript itself was written during a Fulbright year in Frankfurt, West Germany. To my colleagues in the Institute for English and American Studies for a pleasant, quiet environment in which to work I remain grateful.

But above all books need engaged, critical readers. From those with whom this manuscript has been blessed I have swiped ideas, corrections, warnings, and inspiration, in what I can only hope are the right proportions. Stefan Collini, Stanley Katz, Arno Mayer, John Murrin, Dorothy Ross, Jerrold Seigel, John A. Thompson, and

Acknowledgments

Sean Wilentz all read sections of these pages with wit, care, and a willingness to argue back. Other friends—Daniel Czitrom, David Hollinger, Louis Masur, James Oakes, David Peeler, and Donald Worster—read virtually the entire manuscript and through their encouragement and sharp, critical objections strengthened it immensely. At Basic Books, Steven Fraser not only trusted the manuscript but gave it once again a smart and critically helpful reading. Out of acts of extraordinary intellectual generosity like these are ideas engaged and the dream of a community of scholars brought a step closer to tangible realization.

Finally wisest, most generous, and most demanding of all these readers has been, as always, my wife, Irene Rodgers. Compounded in so many ways over so many years, my obligations to her dwarf every effort to put them in words, even into metaphor.

Princeton, New Jersey
January 1987

Contested Truths

Prologue

Words and Acts

This is a book about political words—an inquiry into the language of argument in the American past through a handful of the key-words which have boomed and rattled through American politics since independence. It is a commonplace to ask what our political tradition *means*. I have tried, to the contrary, to ask how certain of the central words in our putative political creed were *used*: how they were employed and for what ends, how they rose in power, withered, and collapsed, how they were invented, stolen for other ends, remade, abandoned. For the history of political talk in America—if I have it straight—is not the story of a slowly unfolding tradition but of contention, argument, and power. Yet language is commonly supposed to be ephemeral material, the stuff of ornament, perhaps, or logic, but not of power and not always easy to take seriously amidst the clash of harder historical forces. It may be best, then, to start with words themselves.

"If you want to know what a politician is up to," Marvin Meyers cautioned years ago, "watch his feet, not his mouth."[1] As first lessons in political wisdom go, a better one than this is hard to imagine. Under the flimflam of evasive political noises, someone is certain to have interests at stake, a covert agenda in mind, a hand in the till. It is one of the functions of political rhetoric to cover up acts of this sort, to hide the policy of the day behind the popular slogans of the moment. Political words mystify. They screen political acts, obscure them behind a cloud of rhetoric so dense that most of us are left to play fools' parts, trying to guess what is really going on. When we dismiss the verbal guff of politics as "mere rhetoric," a veil drawn over the hidden games of politics, we are onto an important truth.

But clearly political words do more than mystify; they inspire, persuade, enrage, mobilize. With words minds are changed, votes acquired, enemies labeled, alliances secured, unpopular programs made palatable, the status quo suddenly unveiled as unjust and intolerable. Through words, coalitions are made out of voters who, stripped of their common rallying cries and slogans, would quickly dissolve into jarring fragments. Words make mass actions possible. With words ringing in their heads, masses of men have made revolutions and crusades, flung themselves into war, savaged other human beings who refused to give up some contrary form of talk. Through words some of the most potent forces of modern politics are wheeled into motion.[2]

Perhaps in some of the small, tightly closed political societies of a distant past, where the political actors all knew each other, took each other's measure over a flagon of beer and wasted no words about it, political language carried fewer consequences. But in modern societies, stretched over vaster territories and far more diverse citizenries, a politics stripped of powerfully expansive words is virtually inconceivable. Mystify as they may, they are the stuff that holds political coalitions and political movements together. "The last thing a political party gives up is its vocabulary," Tocqueville concluded. "This is because, in party politics as in other matters, it is the crowd who dictates the language, and the crowd relinquishes the ideas it has been given more readily than the words it has learned."[3] But not without reason. For it is largely through a string of words—be they "freedom," or "equality," or the "sanctity of property," or the claims of race—that individuals separated from normal sight of each other are shaken into consciousness that their grievances, ambitions, angers, and desires are not peculiarly theirs but, at some slightly altered level of generalization, the material of politics. Abstract, generalizing talk makes private matters public. The bigger, the more sonorous the words, the more private desires they can bind together, the more new desires they can create.

But if words unify and mobilize, they have a still greater, hidden power as well. Words legitimize the outward frame of politics; they create those pictures in our heads which make the structures of authority tolerable and understandable. Thus human beings come to talk of the sacredness of the king's body, the sovereignty of the people, or the destiny of nations—word pictures all, tissues of metaphor, but essential to their reconciliation with realms of power beyond their reach. Many of the most powerful words in the lexicon of politics are of this sort. "Fictions," Edmund Morgan has called them: acts of political make-believe.[4] But of all the functions of political talk, the superimposition of some believable sense and endurable legitimacy on top of the chaotic motions of day-to-day power is the least dispensable. Let the citizens believe that the law is a thing of logic (rather than the whim of men called judges), that their government is a democracy (though only a fraction of the people rule), that human beings were born with rights (though it is plain that they are born to the powerlessness of infancy), and their words have consequences. Let such words shift, let a part of the citizenry suddenly read new meanings into the reigning political figures of speech, let the self-evident truths undergirding the structures of power be open to doubt and contest, and the event is momentous indeed.

If the words work. For the making of words is indeed an act, not a business distinct from the hard, behavioral part of politics but a thing people do. So, by the same token, are the acts of repeating other people's words, rallying to them, being moved by them, believing them. The old dichotomy between behavior and ideas, intellectual history and the history of politics, shopworn with use, never in truth made much sense. Political talk is political action of a particular, often powerful, sort.

The attempt to divide words and acts was not a cavalier distinction, but it hinged from the first on a peculiar kind of essentialism. Did one know a person down to his roots through his talk or through his actions? Did ideas move history or did some putatively nonideational force called interests? Rhetoric or reality? Feet or mouth? As if one were bedrock, the other mere motion. But surely the psychological assumptions back of those distinctions were so thin that we would barely recognize them if applied to everyday life. We act and speak, in and out of politics, with many ends in view. Some ways of talking we try on for a lark, some for company, some to cover our tracks. From others—those in which we have invested our keenest longings and faiths—we will not be moved, cost what it may. Our repertoire of words, running the octaves from taunt to rallying cry to hypocrisy to prayer, is astonishingly large. Taken in their right sense, we mean them all and know what each is good for. We *use* words, and we are used by words. To be wise to the forces of politics is not only to keep one's eyes peeled but one's ears open.

It is in that spirit that I have tried to look again at what is commonly (though all too neatly) called the American political tradition. The result is, frankly, an inquiry. Out of the huge variety of political talk in the American past—the slogans, pieties, and epithets, the coded talk of backroom dealers, the public oratory of the stump—I have extracted only a sliver. The thread of inquiry I have tried to run, however, leads through a handful of the political words which Americans constructed on a scale bigger than the rest. Immense and changeable as the American political vocabulary was, a few of its terms seemed to the talkers somehow fundamental. Let one ask about the purposes of political life; let one ask what a citizen owed his country or ought to get from it; let one ask what governments were, what they were good for, how far their powers reached, or where indeed they got the powers they wielded, and the political talkers fell back on a relatively small number of words. With these they legitimized public life, explained their governments to themselves, invested their political institutions with big words and generous symbols, mobilized voters, and fought over their political future. Without that kind of expansive political talk, politics atomizes. Where it flourishes, all kinds of political arguments will be funneled through its categories; the keywords will be, literally, everywhere.[5]

Nowhere has this been more true, it seems to me, than in America. Our manifestoes have boomed with abstractions; our political bodies have run awash in high-principled loquaciousness. In the nineteenth century, Americans made political giants out of men we would now call consummate windbags. Even now the national equivalent to the crown jewels, sealed in lead and helium, watched by sentries at arms, is the Declaration of Independence: pure words.

To stress this side of American politics runs against the grain of a great deal of historical and political writing. It has been one of our boasts since the beginnings of this century that Americans did not go in for abstract thinking. "The most distinctive American theory of government is not to theorize," Harvard's leading political historian wrote with some pride in 1907. Our political theorists have singled out our Revolution as a wonderfully untheoretical upheaval, in contrast to the revolution in France, where the citizenry (so the assumption runs) took ideas too seriously. A nation of practical tinkerers, plain Henry Fords who make things work, we have left the high-wire risks of theory making to other folks. We were pragmatic, it is said, centuries before pragmatism was invented, utilitarians without needing to read Jeremy Bentham. In a world swept by ideologies, we have often taken pride in having none.[6]

But ideologies we have had in abundance, and big, impractical words to go with them, often at the expense of a level of talk closer to everyday life, out of which less shallow sorts of political communities, closer to the skin of commonplace dreams and desires, might possibly have been made. So broad an assertion is clearly beyond proof. But that there has been a peculiar expansiveness to American political talk, an unmistakable appetite for powerfully resonant and powerfully abstract words is beyond doubt. That demonstration is the burden of chapter 1, an exploration of the vocabulary of utilitarianism, which eighteenth- and nineteenth-century Americans were exceptionally loath to swallow and whose absence long framed the legitimate boundaries of political argument in America. Lay the language of American politics alongside its English cousin, as I have tried to do at the outset of this inquiry, and there is no mistaking which political culture was the more wordy, the more word obsessed.

"I find that the people of this country are strangely at a loss to determine the nature of their government," Washington Irving wrote in 1807. "Some have insisted that it savors of an aristocracy; others maintain that it is a pure democracy; and a third set of theorists declare that it is nothing more nor less than a mobocracy. [Yet] the simple truth of the matter is, that their government is a pure unadulterated *logocracy,* or government of words."[7] There is a truth to that even now, in a political culture which has otherwise all but obliterated the one Washington Irving knew. Ronald Reagan's America, our America, swinging back and forth from the crassest sort of interest politics to harebrained political metaphysics is not a new thing under the sun. It has a history worth unraveling.

Tools and Paradigms

Not so long ago it was a commonplace to remark that political talk in America, in contrast to political talk elsewhere, ran down strikingly narrow channels. "We have debated fiercely," Clinton Rossiter reaffirmed the point in 1962, "but as men who agreed on fundamentals and could thus afford to sound more ferocious than we really were. We have all spoken the same political language; we have made the same political assumptions; we have all thought the same political thoughts." One could bind our major political writers (Adams, Jefferson, Lincoln, the two Roosevelts, even John C. Calhoun) within a common tradition, a consensus, a common frame— or so it seemed. The most powerful argument in this vein remains Louis Hartz's *The Liberal Tradition in America* (1955), a brilliant, scorchingly critical portrait of a political culture without exits, without critics, imprisoned in one dimensionality.[8]

Merge Hartz's method with a more vivid sense of social power, and the argument comes out as a case for the hegemony of a single, class-based worldview over all its rivals.[9] Yet neither consensus nor hegemony seems to me to do justice to the deep, continuous elements of conflict in our political talk. Critics we have had in abundance (though not always with handy access to printing presses) and deadly serious arguments over precisely the assumptions Hartz and the historians of hegemony have tended to see at every turn. Vying for control of a common vocabulary, stealing each other's terms in hopes of investing them with radically altered meanings, political opponents have often left behind an illusion of consensus. But contemporaries knew better. When the Socialist Labor party wrapped itself in the mantle of Thomas Jefferson, when artisan radicals pleaded for a man's rights to property, when abolitionists

insisted that law-abiding persons could not in good conscience recognize the lawfulness of slavery, the process was not mimicry but
struggle of a deadly serious sort over the basic symbols of legitimacy.

To most historians in recent years, to be sure, our past has looked
far more fractured than it did to Rossiter and Hartz. Like unity,
however, dualisms have a powerful attraction on the mind, and for
simplicity's sake recent historians of political culture have increasingly tended to narrow the messy, roiling conflict they have found
to a collision of two distinct worlds and worldviews: an old one,
now lost, called "republicanism," and a newer one, the one that
preoccupied Hartz, called liberalism. Paradigms they are called: logically incompatible ways of imagining the world of politics, so
clearly at odds that one could no more hold both in the mind than
an astronomer could hold simultaneously to Ptolemy and Copernicus. To see politics from within the liberal, individualistic, Lock-
ean frame was to see the world in private terms: the private self,
private property, a wealth of private accumulations held together by
the orderly hand of the competitive market and (when the market
failed) the second-best efforts of the state. To see the political world
in republican terms, in contrast, was to think in public terms: to talk
seriously of the public good, to distrust the haggling individualism
of the market, to value self-restraint, to prize that active commitment to the commonweal men called "virtue." In a land born republican, so the story goes, that worldview died, and liberalism was
shoved into its place. Out of an angry clash of incompatible paradigms in this twice-born land, the political culture of modern capitalist America was born.[10]

That modern America—capitalist, individualistic, hitched to the
careening fortunes of private property—is the result of a long series
of angry, anguished clashes of value seems to me incontestable. We
are hardly through with them yet. But the notion that the history
of political argument in America can be shoehorned into a massive
paradigm shift seems to me no more convincing than the older
assumptions of consensus. In tight intellectual communities (departments of physics, perhaps), people may indeed think in those
peculiarly coherent systems of words we call paradigms. But in
socially complex societies, political argument proceeds in far less

tidy ways. Public commitments and private preoccupations have vied with each other in America in constantly shifting ways at least since independence. We are still full of conflicting feelings about competition, partisans by turn of the detached self and the militant nation, committed to a dozen incompatible notions of the word "freedom." To hunt through our words and arguments for systems of belief fashioned out of logics as tight as Adam Smith's or Copernicus's is to fall into what can only be called a fallacy of misplaced coherence. Political talk in America has roiled with too many voices, too many groups struggling too hard to find words for their desires and claims of justice, to serve it well by clamping either consensus or paradigms over it.

We use political words, most of the time, not as signs of hidden intellectual systems but as tools. We *do* things with words; William James was never more profoundly right than in that assertion. Out of them we fashion arguments; we persuade, maneuver for space and advantage. Political words take their meaning from the tasks to which their users bend them. They are instruments, rallying cries, tools of persuasion.

Political words are, to be sure, complicated, often recalcitrant tools. Not every conceivable word—or meaning—is available when one might imaginably want it. The stock of arguments and assertions with life to them has its limits; the cupboard is a product of culture and history. That was what Karl Marx meant when he complained that "the tradition of all the dead generations weighs like a nightmare on the brain of the living. . . . Just when they seem engaged in revolutionising themselves and things, in creating something entirely new, precisely in such epochs of revolutionary crisis they anxiously conjure up the spirits of the past to their service and borrow from them names, battle slogans and costumes in order to present the new scene of world history in . . . time-honoured disguise and . . . borrowed language."[11] Words come to us in clusters, trailing associations and meanings we may not intend. Born into political languages we did not invent, we are never able to talk any which way we might want.

But though words constrain their users, hobble political desires, nudge them down socially worn channels, they are in other circumstances radically unstable. Let enough persons repeat a cant phrase (all men are created equal, for example), and there is a chance that they will suddenly charge the words with new meaning—take them literally, perhaps, or apply them to circumstances where their inventors never imagined they belonged. That is one of the reasons why the cant phrases are important, why Americans should have fought so intensely over mere words and transparent fictions. They are all double-edged, profoundly radical or profoundly conservative, depending on who has hold of them. Assertion, co-optation, formalization, reinvention—this is the basic stuff of political argument. We get closest to the language of politics not by looking for paradigms nor by stringing our best writers together in traditions but by noticing what the talkers and scribblers are doing with the big words at their disposal. Words are tools, often weapons; the vocabulary of politics is contested terrain and always has been.

Keywords

Utility, Natural Rights, the People, Government, the State, Interests, Freedom. The handful of words I have picked out of the din of argument in our past hardly begins to exhaust the vocabulary of American politics. They are, at one level, simply exemplars; what the talkers would do with this handful of political words, they would do with all the rest. There was nothing static about any of them, no consensus about their meaning. They rose and fell in spectacular arcs, pushed hard and as deeply resisted, their uses open and contested. For those accustomed to thinking of the language of American politics as the logical unfolding of a few bedrock, self-evident truths, this part of the story may come as some surprise. Yet these shifts and reversals, these contests and discordancies, these struggles for legitimacy and advantage are, even now, the central dynamic of our political talk. To unravel the histories of this handful of words is to begin to fathom the processes out of which political language is made.

But there is a second rationale for the words I have chosen: together they offer entry into a series of historical moments when the basic metaphors of politics were up for grabs. It was out of these words that Americans fashioned the language of political authority: the verbal tools one seized when the issue at stake was the nature, the origins, or the legitimacy of government itself. Was the fundamental purpose of politics to restore to men their natural rights or to set the people's unrolling will in motion? To maximize happiness? To mirror the government of God? To fulfill the higher destinies of the State? Or to balance the claims of the vested social interests? These were no idle figures of speech but keywords in the construction and reconstruction of legitimacy. Their moments of currency and collapse were critical moments in the social history of politics. Lay those half-dozen words, and moments, in a chronological line, and the roiling course of argument falls into patterns—often surprising ones.

Utility, to begin with, was a keyword of a peculiar sort—until the twentieth century not a strong word at all. In eighteenth- and nineteenth-century America it was a vulnerable word in a political culture which was drawn strongly toward the abstract; and therein lies at once its surprise and submerged importance. For though Americans have had a love affair with many kinds of utility, the language of political utility was, for a long time, suspect and controversial. When utilitarianism's prophet, Jeremy Bentham, showered the Americans with entreaties to think first of happiness, to abandon their figures of speech for a calculus of consequences, they responded with a century-long shudder. Why they did so, why the language of utilitarianism planted such shallow roots in nineteenth-century America is the burden of chapter 1. Readers impatient with the story of a failure may wish to begin directly with chapter 2, Natural Rights. But the long, agitated quarrel with the language of utilitarianism is not simply the story of the hazards of an imported jargon. To talk of mere "expediency," at the expense of what Bentham denounced as the "metaphysics" of politics, was to violate a vigorously defended boundary of legitimate argument in post-Revolutionary America. In the puzzling absence of Jeremy Bentham in a society he seemed to fit so well, one begins to fathom the uses of the bigger, booming abstractions that so dominated American political culture in its formative years.

Natural Rights and the People were abstractions of precisely that sort. Natural Rights was the central radical political slogan of the Revolution, an ancient phrase suddenly fashioned into a tool of defiance. The cry of "rights" has always been double-edged: radical in the hands of those with novel claims to establish, profoundly defensive in the hands of those with vested privileges to protect. It was one of the unexpected results of the search for a Revolutionary argument that the subversive edge of the word "rights" should have been honed so sharply—or joined to so volatile an adjective. In America, Natural Rights became a tool for those on the margins of power: dissident colonists, workingmen, the opponents of slavery or of domestic paternalism. It was they who kept the language of Natural Rights alive in pre–Civil War America against the determined, nervous efforts by those at the center of power to trim and co-opt it. One of the most powerfully subversive phrases of the early republic, it was never again fully extinguishable from political argument: a phrase whose very abstractness left it permanently open to new meanings, new grievances, new users.

The People was an outsiders' word of a different sort: the key-word of majoritarian democracy in its first, aggressive phase. Its moment of power came later than that of Natural Rights. Though the sovereignty of the people was a commonplace of the Revolution and the early years of the republic, the phrase rose to full pitch only in the 1830s and 1840s, when more common sorts of men than had ever ruled before seized it to wedge open the machinery of government for the many. With it antebellum Democrats pushed the claims of majoritarian democracy as far as they have ever gone in America, tried their tongues around talk of the revolutionary majority and the general will. But if the career of Natural Rights illustrates the ability of an abstraction to absorb recurrent waves of new meanings, the history of the People is an example of the brittleness of the bonds between a political metaphor and its political moment. For the rhetoric of popular sovereignty, its initial occasion passed, proved a set of words desperately hard for its users to hold in check. As their new, white, male democracy skidded toward sectional crisis and civil war, even the People's partisans began to scramble nervously away from a figure of speech the times had suddenly made ambiguous and unstable.

Natural Rights and the People's sovereignty were among the most highly charged political words to come out of the Revolution. To turn from these to Government and the State is to turn to phenomena of a very different sort. For they were counterrevolutionary words. They rose out of a counterassault on the verbal heritage of the Revolution—far bigger, more ambitious, and far more successful than our histories have fathomed. Forged in repudiation, they took form in opposition to the claims of extralegal rights and majority rule. Struggle over the metaphors of legitimacy, to be sure, there had been since the beginning. But in the second half of the nineteenth century, with the political character of the new democracy up for grabs, those spilled over into every aspect of politics. The result was to blunt badly the Revolutionary rhetoric which had served the outsiders so well and inject a new set of keywords into the language of politics.

Government was the first of these, a word which rolled out of the early nineteenth-century Protestant revival, part of an intense hunger for law and political obligation. A tool of cautious Whigs and aggressive Protestants, the term pitted those who talked of governments as consciously constructed (hence reconstructable) devices against those who talked of Government as the gift of God or the inevitabilities of history. Rising to a pitch during the Civil War, the word marked an attempt to shift the locus of political authority upward into the lap of society or divine law. Dramatically successful as a wartime rallying cry, it likewise dramatically complicated the debates over freedom when, with slavery finally brought to its knees, obfuscation had powerful political consequences.

The State was the term the professional political scientists tried to paste over the conceptual raggedness that was left. It was a word of professional political authority, part of a concerted effort to wrest political argument out of the hands of the people. With it in the 1890s the first generation of political scientists gutted remnant talk of rights, tried hard to push the People to the margins, and did their best to stretch a mantle of legitimacy over the new, raw order of industrial capitalism. The most abstract, contorted, and (so it has usually seemed) the least American of our political words, it stood for an extraordinary piece of intellectual patchwork by a profession eager for authority and a class and generation desperate to make the social chaos of the late nineteenth century whole. The State was a term of reassurance and not a little outright mystification—an example of the coherence-making functions of political language pushed to their utmost.

And then, after so long a quarrel with Bentham, a language of calculus and utility suddenly swept into the twentieth century. The wholistic abstractions, taut and overextended, collapsed. There was no State, the political scientists concluded, no People, no common will. By the end of the 1930s, realistic political talk had come down to Interests: dozens of interest groups looking out for their own advantages. An epithet of the turn of the century became the keyword of realist political science. That, it seems to me, is still the dominant way we talk about politics in America at the trailing edge of the twentieth century. After an intense fling with the word Freedom in the generation after 1940, we have come back once again to interests—though not without massive ambivalences and a few regrets. Interest fuels the machinery of politics; let interest groups more or less balance out, so that no one contending group swipes the whole sack of marbles, and public life is said to be as healthy as reasonable persons have a right to expect. The route from the rights-filled manifestoes of the 1770s to the marketplace metaphors of pluralism had been no gradual unfolding of some basic Americanisms but a twisted, conflict-strewn road.

Every powerful political metaphor has a long and active half-life. That is what distinguishes a keyword from a passing phrase of the moment. Each of the half-dozen words at issue here worked its way deeply into the fabric of political argument. Never fully suppressed even by their most determined repudiators they endured, open to revivals and new employments. I have been less interested in echoes (or anticipations), however, than in moments of dominance: those historical moments when a word first breaks out of the political theorists' texts into power and political authority. The chapters which follow nest, accordingly, in a rough chronological order. From Bentham's first salvos of the 1770s, through the rights-filled rhetoric of the Revolution, the mid-nineteenth-century contests over popular government, the language of late nineteenth-century political science to the interest-group realism of the New Deal, I have tried to set these words where they belong: in the context of sharp reconfigurations in rhetorical authority and political power. A more comprehensive story might deal more fully with persistence and reverberations. But if we are to comprehend the shards and fragments all around us, the tools we use and those used upon us, there is a fundamental advantage in knowing the circumstances in which we came upon them.

This route through the tangled language of our politics is not a comprehensive one. From declarations of rights through the oratory of constitutional conventions to political science texts, I have tried to match these keywords with the forums of expression which carried and characterized them. But I have slighted many of the talkers—from political theorists like Calhoun to the immense tribe of partisan stump orators. I have not attempted to canvass all the things Americans talked about in politics nor even those issues about which they talked most deeply and heatedly. It would take a different set of words to begin to do justice to the language of political economy, for example, or the rhetoric of international destiny or the complicated ways in which all these languages merged and intertwined. These are at best examplars of the ways in which a certain, powerful class of words have functioned in our political culture. Taken at that, however, there is something to be said for a serious look past the gauze of scholarly and popular myth at a few of the most potent tools and expansive political metaphors we have possessed.

It is not my aim, let me finally repeat, to pin down with a lexicon's timeless precision what we have meant by this handful of our keywords. "A word is not a crystal, transparent and unchanged," Oliver Wendell Holmes wrote; "it is the skin of a living thought."[12] My intent is not to describe a creed, not even a shifting set of common faiths. The words we use, the words the speech writers still zing through the air, counting on something in us to nod in assent, have been made, remade, repudiated, fought over. Should someone try to sell you a piece of political goods as an authentic encapsulation of the American political faith, the wise course is to run for cover. We have been too conflict-ridden a church to have a creed. The keywords, the metaphors, the self-evident truths of our politics have mattered too deeply for us to use them in any but contested ways.

1

Utility

The Puzzling Failure of Jeremy Bentham

Utility was one of the glittering words of the Enlightenment. In the capitals of eighteenth-century Europe, wherever knots of inventive men gathered to talk, to wrangle over the mysteries of religion, or to debate the new discoveries of science, one could hardly help stumbling over the word. Men made moral systems out of usefulness; they founded societies for the promotion of useful knowledge; they let their imaginations run free with useful inventions. When toward the end of the eighteenth century Jeremy Bentham seized upon the term Utility and set it up in capital letters, his achievement was not to invent a philosophy but to codify a powerful, cosmopolitan enthusiasm. That is why the deeply controversial career of Bentham's term in America presents, at the outset, such a puzzle.

Utility began as an inventors' and promoters' word, shoved into the center of eighteenth-century talk by men with a tremendous variety of gadgets on their minds: steam engines and street designs; pumps and penal codes; electricity, eye glasses, encyclopedia. Yet there was no mistaking, at the same time, the sharp, aggressive edge of the word. Talk of useful knowledge was a tool with which the contrivance makers of the Enlightenment hoped to undermine the prestige of the merely verbal sciences. Metaphysics, scholasticism, the casuistry of the natural law scholars, the metaphors which clouded the study of politics and history—whole empires of abstractions promised to come tumbling down at the test of their practical consequences.

It was Jeremy Bentham's lot to gather these passions for improvement, these distrusts of mere verbal labels, these hard-headed preoccupations with consequences into a system. In an inventive age, he was a tinkerer of extraordinary versatility. So close were the projects of political and mechanical invention in his mind that for a long time he could not decide whether his life's task lay in the writing of books or as the engineer of an all-purpose architectural contrivance he called the Panopticon. But in his political writings he clung to the test of utility with unswerving consistency. The only question that mattered, he maintained, the only line of inquiry that did not veer back into a maze of abstractions and conundrums was simply this: did a law or a political institution contribute to—or diminish—the sum of human happiness?

Bentham codified a way of talking which, if the conventional wisdom has taken their measure correctly, his American contemporaries should have rushed to embrace. Practical and calculating as we have taken late eighteenth- and nineteenth-century Americans to be, equipped with a tin ear for metaphysics and a sharp eye for effects, capable of sizing up a wilderness for its timber values, of buying and selling human beings by shrewd estimates of their labor value, equipped (as Frederick Jackson Turner wrote) with "coarse" but "practical" habits of mind, they should have dashed pell-mell to plant Utility at the center of their political talk. That they shared in the passion for invention is hardly to be doubted: witness Tom Paine's love affair with iron bridges, Jefferson's consuming zeal for plows and architectural proportions, and Franklin's inexhaustible stream of projects for the improvement of himself and his countrymen. Did not the genius of their politics (as Daniel Boorstin once put it) lie in that very practicality? In the Americans' isolation from the philosophical talk of the European salons? In their refusal to take abstract ideas too seriously? "This is a utilitarian country," their intellectual in politics, Woodrow Wilson, wrote for them soon after the turn of the twentieth century. "We are proud that we know what is useful and what is useless. We are proud that we are a practical people who do not waste their time upon matters of mere fancy which do not set their lives forward." Utilitarianism was a philosophy for persons skeptical of mere philosophy, a set of words for the pragmatic and the present minded. It should have struck a deep, instantaneous response in America.[1]

And yet when Jeremy Bentham offered his work to the Americans, proclaiming himself an American in spirit, they rejected it virtually out of hand. In nineteenth-century America, his books gathered a handful of ineffectual disciples and a mountain of excoriation. By the end of the century, it was a commonplace among observers of English politics that Bentham's influence had cast its beam over every cranny of their political life; one could not open a serious book on politics without being pulled into yet another discussion of the merits and limits of utilitarianism. In America at the same moment, Bentham's way of talking about politics was only beginning to emerge from under an immense heap of repudiations and rebuke. We start, then, with a puzzle, and no simple one at that. No one applied the notion of utility to politics with more energy and concentration than Bentham. Yet when they learned what he had done, the Americans wanted none of it.

Part of the trouble lay with Bentham, so full of quirks and heresies. Still more, however, lay in depths and appetites in the American political culture that we have barely begun to measure. For the puzzling failure of Jeremy Bentham in America is larger than a mere quandary in the history of ideas and influence. Cultures do not, as a rule, dismiss the words that allow them to say what they mean. To follow Bentham's reputation across the Atlantic is to find ourselves not at the center of legitimate political talk but on its margins, watching a form of political talk being declared out of bounds, where we were hardly prepared to find so vigorously defended a boundary at all. But in truth the practical turn of mind we have vaunted so often conjoined with a deep, antipodal desire for abstractions of precisely the sort Bentham had hoped to silence with his calculus of utilities. To watch Bentham's way of talk, controversial and unloved, sputter out in the first century after independence is to begin to sense the pressure of the powerful, half-hidden rules which governed the language of politics in America.

In time, to be sure, some of the rules would change. Soon after the turn of the twentieth century, in many quarters of the polity, the long, stubborn resistance to Bentham's vocabulary collapsed in a phenomenon no less momentous and startling than the resistance itself. But in eighteenth- and nineteenth-century America, in the formative years of American political talk, Bentham's animus against abstractions could not breast the demand for broader, more abstract words than mere Utility or consequence. In America, abstractions were essential to the vocabulary of politics; they were the crucial levers of argument. They obscured and they empowered, but the need for them framed the language of politics. As an initial measure of that frame and the words it bound so long, there is no better place to begin than with the sort of language eighteenth- and nineteenth-century Americans found illegitimate: with Jeremy Bentham and the implications of his failure.

Antimetaphysics

Political discourse in Bentham's London, like Franklin's Philadelphia, remained a thicket of metaphors in the eighteenth century. Where political writers argued over the "body politic" as if the term were a literal fact, where the law was so full of fictions that only lawyers could figure it out, to talk of measuring justice by a scrutiny of its consequences could not but be startling and provocative. Let loose in political discourse, the language of Utility invited men to see the realm of politics as nothing other than a mass of practical, improvable contrivances, albeit more complicated and more clumsily built than most. It invited men to throw to the winds their metaphors, their fiction-clogged talk of the origins of kings and rights and parliaments and ask what (if anything) their political associations might be good for.

That, at bottom, was Bentham's project. For though no human being has ever managed to get along without metaphors, more than most persons Bentham tried. At heart he was a lawyer whose legal education didn't take. Sent up to Oxford in the 1760s, where he heard Blackstone lecture on the majestic principles of English law, established by his ambitious father in an office in the legal warrens of Lincoln's Inn in London, Bentham never managed to get over his first impression that the subject he had taken on was a morass of deliberately confused and mystifying words. He never brought himself to practice law. He contracted instead the ambition to reform it: to clearcut its metaphors and semantic confusions, to demystify wholesale and with a vengeance the language of politics.[2]

Blackstone's suave and complaisant *Commentaries,* just off the press in the 1760s, stuffed with the hackneyed political slogans of the day, was an obvious target for a young man of such ambitions. Bentham went after it in a pamphlet which reads, at first glance, like an unguided salvo of quibbles, until the magnitude of Bentham's project becomes clear. He wanted, if he could, to clear every whiff of metaphysics out of the common jargon of politics. The Whig notion of a sacred "contract" between rulers and ruled, the countervailing Tory talk of "sovereignty," the shibboleth that the distinctive virtues of monarchies, aristocracies, and democracies found their carefully balanced reflection in king and Parliament, even the distinction between natural societies (which had no governments) and civil societies (which did)—Bentham would admit none of them. They were all fictions, false on a moment's reflection, clouds of words designed to keep men from asking what laws and governments really did.[3]

It was a point Bentham never tired of making. The central chapter of his most widely circulated book bore the wonderfully revealing title "False Methods of Reasoning on the Subject of Legislation." To reason from figures of speech, like constitutional "balance," was a form of false reasoning. ("Leave that," Bentham wrote, "to Mother Goose and Mother Blackstone.") To reason from historical fictions, like the social contract of Locke's imagination, was false reasoning. To reason from big and sonorous words, like "rights" or "right reason" or the "laws of nature" was to mistake a set of pompous, "passion-kindling appelatives" for the hard stuff of results and consequences.[4] Men might "bawl till their lungs be spent," his disciple, John Austin, wrote for him; they might mouth "of 'the rights of man,' or 'the sacred rights of sovereigns,' of 'unalienable liberties,' or 'eternal and immutable justice'; of 'an original contract or covenant,' of 'the principles of an inviolable constitution' " and think they were engaged in principled debate. But all it amounted to was mere "sounds" to dispute about. "The language of error is always obscure, and indefinite," Bentham himself argued; the language of clarity was the language of consequences.[5]

So much of the customary vocabulary of politics having been savaged in this fashion, what words remained with which to describe or measure consequences? To that question Bentham, despite his labors, never found a very good answer. General Utility, he soon realized, was far too indeterminate. "Happiness," "public happiness," "the greatest possible happiness of the community," or, striving always for a precision that eluded him, "the greatest happiness of the greatest number"—these were improvements. But the expressions he confessed he really understood were "pleasure" and "pain." Given Bentham's hatred of intangibles, given the amount of thought he put to that complicated prescription of pain called the penal code, this was an understandable resting place. It pinned the potentially elusive term "happiness" to a calculable entity. "In this matter we want no refinement, no metaphysics," he wrote. "It is not necessary to consult Plato, nor Aristotle. *Pain* and *pleasure* are what everybody feels to be such—the peasant and the prince, the unlearned as well as the philosopher."[6]

Demonstration of the crudity of this psychological and moral reductionism kept alive generations of philosophers, who ultimately reduced Bentham himself simply to a hedonist of a peculiarly mathematical variety. But Bentham never thought of himself as the founder of a psychological school. What was central to Bentham was his insistence on a calculus of effects. "I asked myself," he later wrote, *"how* this or that institution contributed to the greatest happiness?—*Did* it contribute?—If not, what institution *would* contribute to it?"[7] It was his ambition not to create an ethical philosophy but a political science out of linguistic skepticism, invention, and arithmetic.

The creation of a political method was not, to be sure, the same thing as the formulation of a politics. Bentham tacked and veered through the crisis-filled turn of the nineteenth century like every other Englishman. He detested the American campaign for independence and, still more, the French Revolution. By the second decade of the new century, however, he was avidly ransacking news from the United States to demonstrate to his own corruption-mired countrymen what sorts of happiness cheap and simple government could produce. He was a Tory as a young man; in his seventies he became what in contemporary Britain was called a Radical, a savage opponent of the unreformed Parliament, publishing tracts in advocacy of "virtually universal" suffrage and scribbling away in private on a constitutional code which would have replaced the "Corrupter-General," as he called the king, with a corps of trained civil servants.[8]

Just as he changed his mind about the organization of government, Bentham was never very consistent about what it was the function of governments to do. He had as deep an instinctive dislike of taxes and legal restrictions as the average eighteenth-century American colonist. "Every law is an evil," he wrote, for every law restrained, and every restraint, however counterbalanced by gains in happiness, could not but add to the total social sum of pains and punishments. He made a fetish of cheap, economical government, and tinkered repeatedly with the suggestion that a good deal of its work could be let out to private bidders to everyone's advantage. In the 1780s he took Adam Smith to task for being what we would now call "soft" on laissez-faire, and he left behind a string of disciples devoted to the natural harmonies of the unimpeded economic market. When Karl Marx denounced Bentham as the "pedantic, leather-tongued oracle of the ordinary bourgeois intelligence of the nineteenth century," he had his reasons.[9]

But though the libertarian streak was strong in Bentham, he had so little fondness for liberty in the abstract that he declared it yet another of the words he failed to understand. He acknowledged no limits to government's omnicompetent authority, no "rights" beyond the sphere of legislation. The idea of inquiring in the abstract into the legitimate sphere of the state, had it occurred to Bentham at all, would have struck him as a return to barren metaphysics. He preferred to concentrate authority in a few responsible hands rather than divide and disperse it, and when his followers in the administration of India had a chance (as Eric Stokes has shown), they did precisely that. He proposed to cut through the "Gordian knot" of English poverty, not by leaving the poor to the incentives of the free market but by gathering them into a system of workhouses built on the panoptical plan, where they might be fed, clothed, housed in tiers of cells set in a great circle around a central observation post, and put to productive labor. For economy's sake he proposed that the whole system be farmed out to a quasi-private contractor to make what returns it could on the system.[10] Statist and antistatist strains swirled together in these schemes. "The community is a fictitious *body*," he wrote early in his career; it possessed no other interest than "the sum of the interests of the several members who compose it."[11] And yet he never struck the word "community" from his vocabulary, as he struck so many others, nor a notion of the "universal interest."

Those who have tried to shoehorn these proposals and prejudices into one or another of the ordinary boxes of political thought have not surprisingly had a hard time of it. Bentham has been called an individualist and an authoritarian, an apologist for market capitalism and an early architect of the welfare state.[12] His deafness to so much of the political sloganeering of his day, his shifts of interest and of mind, his hopelessly disjointed mode of writing have left him a curiously fractured figure in the historical record. But the key to the man was surely the one John Stuart Mill ultimately saw so clearly: his obsession with specificity and practical detail. He was by temperament an inventor and contrivance maker, who yearned to break up the sacramental expressions of his day into more useful materials. What made him the great "subversive" of his age, as Mill put it, was not the largeness of his ideas but his inability to think long about any institution without imagining how vastly it might be improved by practical tinkering. That was what Mill meant, finally, in calling Bentham's mind incomplete, limited to the practical realms of life.[13] The fundamental questions of politics were not for Bentham live questions at all. He cared not a wit for the origins of governments or for their nature or their legitimacy. He tried to make a political philosophy out of a single-minded concern with effects, and he was certain that the world—and the Americans in particular—would be the happier for the effort.

Influence

Practical political philosophers do not always lead practical lives. Bentham's, in truth, soon settled into a pattern so eccentric and untidy that it is a wonder that his ideas ever gained a hearing, much less a shred of influence, beyond the household of clerks he employed to keep his fragmented papers in order. Before he had reached middle age, something had begun to go wrong with Bentham's sense of the connection between writer and audience. His first general formulation of the utilitarian method, *An Introduction to the Principles of Morals and Legislation* of 1789, struck Bentham as so incomplete and unsatisfactory that he never tried to wrest his ideas into systematic form again. Financially sustained by a fortunately timed inheritance, he devoted himself to writing fragments instead, compiling mountains of scraps and pieces to clarify whatever problem happened at the moment to be uppermost in his mind, leaving it to his assistants to file the bundles away under the appropriate headings. After 1789, virtually nothing published under his name was in the conventional sense his own work but was rather the effort by one or another of his small circle of disciples to bind a sheaf of the master's scraps together. Thus it came about that the most influential statement of his philosophy was a free translation into French of that part of Bentham's accumulating pile of manuscripts which an admirer, Etienne Dumont, thought the best of Bentham's writings of the 1780s and 1790s, translated back into English in 1840 by an American, Richard Hildreth, to be picked up by British publishers as the standard introduction to the man for the rest of the nineteenth century.[14]

Bentham's lapse into this solipsistic mode of writing coincided with a deepening personal eccentricity. By the time fame finally caught up with him in his own country, Bentham had settled into the life of a hermetic philosopher, encased in a protective shell of private habits which left visitors to his London "hermitage" shaking their heads in bewilderment. He affected a quaint, vaguely Quaker style of costume, grew his hair down to his shoulders, and talked in a vocabulary so saturated with his own improvements on common English that it cost his apprentices a good deal of effort to comprehend the dialect which this savager of jargon had himself invented.[15]

His ultimate eccentricity, however, was surely his own notion of himself as a man of influence. He spent most of his final years working "like a dragon" on a universal constitutional code for all "progressive" nations, playing simultaneously the part of legal inventor and philosopher king. He offered to codify the laws of imperial Russia, Spain, Greece, and the new republican states of South America. He volunteered to sweep aside the rotting corpus of common law in the United States with a body of civil, constitutional, and penal law of his own devising; and when President James Madison failed to reply, he repeated the offer in a circular letter to the governors of the American states. He felt the excitement of Andrew Jackson's election strongly enough to send him a long argument for the utility of abolishing the United States Senate. To the governor of Pennsylvania, in a moment of tragicomic hubris, he wrote, "Join hands with me, you and I will govern the world. Sir, I will show you how we will govern it."[16]

So saturated was Bentham's life with the ridiculous that it should all have come to naught. And yet by the end of the nineteenth century English writers all across the political spectrum were agreed that Bentham had somehow stamped a significant part of nineteenth-century Britain with his vocabulary and his way of thinking. Not until the mid-1820s, when the aging Bentham put his remaining financial resources into the publication of a utilitarian journal, did he begin to make a name for himself among his countrymen. By the end of that decade, however, the stock of claims and phrases he had launched had already become a major irritant in British intellectual life. For English romantics, abuse of utilitarianism became a formal badge of membership. Disraeli skewered Bentham's journal as a "Screw and Lever Review"; Carlyle thundered imprecations at Bentham's head; Dickens concentrated his hatred of utilitarianism into a savage cartoon named Thomas Gradgrind.[17] Closer to church and chapel, defenders of moral intuitionism and the conscience poured so much energy into rebuttal to Bentham's equation of goodness and happy effects that by the middle of the century it was hard to begin to talk about moral philosophy in any other terms than that of a great controversy between the doctrines of intuition and of utility. When a piece of Bentham's writings finally made it into the required examination reading at Cambridge in 1867, it was in precisely that controversial fashion, as part of a four-way debate between Kant, the intuitionist William Whewell, and the Scottish moral sense philosopher Dugald Stewart.[18] So fiercely rebutted, so savagely lampooned, so frequently dismissed and yet somehow indismissible, utilitarianism was edged by its opponents into a central place in British controversial life.

But if Bentham gathered critics easily, he somehow gathered disciples as well. In the 1820s and 1830s the circles and subcircles around the old man had begun to fill with persons of exceptional force and energy: James Mill at the East India Company; Thomas Southwood Smith at the new commission to investigate the conditions of factory labor and, later, the new General Board of Health; James Kay of the public education movement; Rowland Hill at the reformed postal service; Edwin Chadwick, who in the formative years of the new British administrative state contrived to be everywhere at once, full of statistics, contrivances, and administrative energy; and John Stuart Mill, who grew from Bentham's amanuensis into a colossus among mid-Victorian men of letters. When the first reformed Parliament met in 1833, the year after Bentham's death, his partisans were numerous enough to form a small but aggressive parliamentary faction. In the new agencies of administration—the fact-finding commissions, administrative boards, and statistical bureaus, imposed after 1832 on the old political fabric of patronage and favoritism—men of utilitarian sympathies enjoyed a still greater prominence.[19]

So striking were the legislative innovations set in motion in the 1830s and 1840s, so closely did the new mechanisms of governance seem to follow the designs Bentham had sketched that those who presumed to keep track of British opinion began to look to Bentham with newly respectful eyes. By 1880 the Cambridge political philosopher Henry Maine was telling his students that Bentham's followers had "suggested and moulded the entire legislation of the fifty years just passed." By 1905, when Maine's counterpart at Oxford, A. V. Dicey, swept together the entire legislative period 1825–70 as "The Period of Benthamism," the hermit of the first quarter of the century, the irritant of the second quarter had taken on yet a third life as the preeminent political philosopher of Victorian Britain.[20]

The puffing of Bentham's reputation by dons like Maine and

Dicey had, as was only to be expected, its partisan advantages. Dicey's Bentham was an "individualist," inextricable from Dicey's desire to bring the Liberal party back from its recent experiments in social legislation. Yet nothing more strikingly demonstrated the way in which Bentham's words had worked their way into the fabric of British political discourse than the fact that Dicey's "collectivist" opponents had equally begun to herald the man as their own. To trim the individualistic branches out of Bentham's thought required a bit of work. One needed to scrap his mechanistic psychology, replacing Bentham's inner calculator of pleasures and pains with a psyche capable of more generous and subtler notions of happiness. One needed to sever the ties James Mill had worked so hard to forge between the calculus of utilitarianism and laissez-faire economics and to stir into the Benthamite phrase "the greatest happiness of the greatest number" a more vigorous sense of the common good than Bentham himself had possessed.

But by the 1880s, helped along by the criticism of writers like T. H. Green and the sobering revelation of the extent of late-Victorian poverty, both operations had proved possible to contrive. Joseph Chamberlain in 1885 defended his apostasies from Gladstonian liberalism by appealing to Bentham's greatest happiness principle. To Chamberlain's left, the Fabian Society was chock full of contrivers of the general welfare who, like Sidney Webb, thought of Bentham as their intellectual godfather. When in 1882 W. Stanley Jevons, at the forefront of the economists' challenge to the shibboleths of laissez-faire, was asked to define the justifiable boundaries of state action, he assumed Bentham's antimetaphysics had done its work: "The State is justified in passing any law, or even in doing any single act which, without ulterior consequences, adds to the sum total of happiness." Twenty years later, the publicists of the "new," socially conscious Liberalism routinely began their case by getting straight with Bentham.[21]

No thinker makes an age. Dicey's notion of an era of Benthamism was as feeble as the notion might be of an era of Kant or Calvin Coolidge. Political language is inherently too full of argument for any person to shape the times to a single way of talking. In parts of British society, definition of one's convictions via ridicule of Bentham remained a lively business all through the nineteenth century. A census count of out-and-out utilitarians at any time in the century would have resulted in a thin and meager showing. But somehow a way of talking about politics as a business of consequences, a sense of laws and administrative forms as contrivances for happiness—all this sank deeply into the fabric of British political debate.

Perhaps the man was simply fortunate in his disciples. Without James Mill's political ambitions and Chadwick's energy, without John Stuart Mill's smoothing off of so many of utilitarianism's rough edges, Bentham's language of Utility surely could not have cut the figure in nineteenth-century British intellectual life that it did. John Stuart Mill's role was in some ways the most important. It was he (in *Considerations on Representative Government*) who deliberately cut the tie between utilitarianism and the democratic majoritarianism of Bentham's old age; who (in *On Liberty*) labored to inscribe a clear and precise circle of immunities around the individual in a manner Bentham had never acknowledged; who (in *Utilitarianism*) stirred so large a dash of feelings and poetics into utilitarian psychology that other Benthamites shook their heads at Mill's lapse into German mysticism; who, in all these ways, softened and naturalized utilitarianism for middle-class British readers and in so doing helped keep it alive in the middle years of the century, between the death of Bentham's converts of the 1820s and 1830s and the late nineteenth-century Benthamite revival.[22]

Still, a dozen John Stuart Mills and a dozen Chadwicks could not have worked Bentham's words and slogans so firmly into nineteenth-century British political discourse had it not been that that way of talking had struck a set of responsive chords in important parts of British society. Among administrators like Mill and Chadwick, in the statistical societies and in parts of the civil service, in the new technical colleges set up to provide the practical learning and technical expertise that Oxford and Cambridge failed to provide, among businessmen who had made a way of life out of foresight and calculation Bentham's style of talk made its quiet headway. In the Britain he thought inextricably mired in antique words and conundrums, this antimetaphysical political philosopher, this man of practical facts and consequences, ultimately found a measure of the influence he dearly wanted.

Quicksands of Expediency

In hard-headed, practical, nineteenth-century America, however, utilitarianism was virtually stillborn. Not until the very end of the century did Bentham's writings gain more than a handful of followers in the United States. When American reviewers bothered to take notice of Bentham's work, it was to pillory him as the author of a "despicable and repulsive" philosophy. On the subjects of tobacco prices and steam engines, railroads and tariffs, the Americans filled their talk with facts and practical reasons with an enthusiasm that would have done credit to a tribe of Gradgrinds. But when it came to talk of politics, the straightforward language of Utility, stripped clean of metaphysics, seemed too bare and inadequate. The abstract words Bentham hoped to consign to the rubbish heap were, in America, indispensable.

Bentham's failure in the land he had come so much to admire never ceased to puzzle him. His essential phrases were not by their nature strange or terrifying. He had himself appropriated them from the pages of Cesare Beccaria, Claude-Adrien Helvetius, Joseph Priestley, and Francis Hutcheson—writers who cast as long a shadow in late eighteenth-century America as in eighteenth-century England. "All speculative politicians" were agreed that "the divine science of politics is the science of social happiness," John Adams wrote in 1776, well before he could have drawn the words from Bentham. "The form of government which communicates ease, comfort, security, or, in one word, happiness, to the greatest number of persons, and in the greatest degree, is the best."[23] Ten years later, the same point could be found lodged in what was to be the most widely used of the antebellum college moral philosophy texts, William Paley's *Principles of Moral and Political Philosophy*—a spectacular success as a textbook on both sides of the Atlantic, its utilitarian ethics generally held suspect by the American teachers who employed it, but so ubiquitous a presence in the college curricula as to have planted the seeds of dozens of native varieties of utilitarianisms had the political culture offered them a modest degree of nourishment.[24]

As for Bentham's own writings, though never popular in the

United States, they made headway enough. American printers in the late 1770s and 1780s had far too many pressing demands on their type fonts to bother bringing out Bentham's first manuscripts. But Dumont's Bentham, widely read on the Continent, was known in the United States as well. By the mid-1840s, one could buy not only a good American-made translation of Dumont's *Traités de législation* but a treasury of selected Bentham quotations, hawked by a Philadelphia publisher.[25] Twenty years later, with John Stuart Mill's reputation at its height, the utilitarian style of argument could hardly be said to have been unfamiliar. But familiarity only deepened the suspicion and contempt.

Utilitarianism's trouble in finding a foothold in the United States came clear first in the matter of disciples. During the early years of the century, a surprising number of Americans found their way into Bentham's "hermitage." Aaron Burr showed up in 1808 to talk about the usefulness of tattooing and, more vaguely, of translating Bentham's works back into English. John Neal, a journalist, worked his way into Bentham's circle of editorial assistants. John Quincy Adams sought Bentham out for several long walks around London. But Burr was in disgrace, Neal a scamp, and John Quincy Adams quickly shed his first, charitable impressions of the man as he began to sense the depths of Bentham's political and religious impieties.[26]

With time the ranks of Bentham's admirers widened a bit. Jacksonian Democrats, drawn to Bentham's angry jibes at the complexities and burdens of the law and to the democratic radicalism of his old age, made a passing hero of the man, appropriating "the greatest good of the greatest number" as a radical, workingmen's majoritarian slogan. But the Jacksonians' Bentham, his words mixed into sweepingly abstract talk of rights, represented so thin a slice of Bentham's opinions as hardly to be Bentham at all. A far more consistent utilitarianism could be found in the South, where Thomas Cooper, a onetime English radical, whom chance had deposited in a professorship at South Carolina College, used Bentham's work to grease his way from Paine's *Rights of Man* to an open, rights-denying, utilitarian defense of slavery. Yet Cooper's labors started no school of southern utilitarians, and South Carolinians more pious than he rewarded his philosophical conversion by trying hard to hound him out of his teaching chair.[27] John Stuart Mill attracted his own circle of mid-nineteenth-century admirers. For a moment in the 1860s, E. L. Godkin imagined turning the new organ of advanced Republican party opinion, *The Nation,* into a counterpart to Mill's *Westminster Review.* But Godkin's backers, repelled by a politics bare of higher claims than utility, squelched the idea, and Godkin eventually moved on from utilitarianism. Mill's closest friend in the United States, Charles Eliot Norton, prudently kept his utilitarian sympathies confined to his private letters.[28]

Bentham's isolated, ineffectual disciples had reasons for their caution. From the first reviews of Bentham's writings in the 1830s through the end of the century, through every stage, that is, of Bentham's English reputation, magazine reviewers in America swamped utilitarianism in a powerful tide of rebuke. The *Southern Review* set the tone in 1831: Utilitarianism was a "repulsive" philosophy, designed to "chill enthusiasm, to extinguish sensibility, to substitute wary and even crafty calculation, for the native goodness of an uncorrupted heart." Utilitarianism was cold, materialistic, mechanical; morally it was but another name for expediency or, worse, mere selfishness. It denied all ideals, all moral sensibilities, all appeals to conscience, the moral sense, divine law, even to right itself. This response to utilitarianism was in no way peculiar to the American side of the Atlantic. Bentham's most vociferous English critics had hounded him in precisely this manner. What was remarkable in America was the endurance of the anti-utilitarian animus and the one-sidedness of the contest. The great English debate between the champions of intuitional and utilitarian moral theories, carried on salvo upon salvo in the reviews, was washed out in America by the overwhelming weight of utilitarianism's critics. Southern slaveholders grumbled their dislike of utilitarianism in private letters; Wendell Phillips, the tribune of abolitionism, proclaimed his opposition from the rooftops. Even Bentham's champions at the *Democratic Review* admitted Bentham's radical defect as a moralist; the heirs to their freethinking, democratic impulses at the turn-of-the-century *Arena* turned openly on the Benthamite creed to denounce its blindness to every shred of moral idealism.[29]

The game of denouncing Bentham did not necessarily imply, of course, wholesale repudiation of Bentham's method. Perhaps, as Bernard Crick once suggested, the Americans failed to be moved by utilitarianism because they already knew so much of what the man had to say.[30] A culture capable of spawning a Benjamin Franklin simply may have had no need to take on a Bentham and all the more reason, accordingly, to recoil from his quirky vocabulary and (as the reviewers correctly suspected) his religious heterodoxy. Perhaps the opposition to utilitarianism was a matter of timing and association. In England, Bentham's mid-nineteenth-century reputation borrowed massively on the role his allies had played in the dramatic political innovations of the 1830s and 1840s: parliamentary reform, the new poor law, public health legislation, the first effective factory inspection and education acts. In the United States, in contrast, utilitarianism had to make its way on its bare propositions alone. Entering the American scene in the midst of the great religious revivals of the second quarter of the century, moreover, utilitarianism had a profoundly difficult time shaking off its initial reputation as a queer and dangerously amoral church for nonbelievers.

Still, the resistance to Bentham—like the resistance to Paley before him—ran too long, too hard, and through too many corners of the American political culture to be successfully explained away by emphasis on Bentham's quirks alone. Follow the pommeling of Bentham's words long enough, and it is difficult to avoid the conclusion that their liabilities lay deeper than that—in a suspicion of bare talk of expediency and happiness, in a hunger for abstractions, for more metaphysical and expansive arguments than Bentham, in calling himself an American at heart, ever fathomed.

The transatlantic contrast may not be stretched too far. Late eighteenth- and nineteenth-century Americans did their obvious share of political contrivance making. Within the proper sphere of the words, they were as fond as anyone else of the language of advantage and Utility. In the early years of the nineteenth century, the state governments pushed their way into large-scale projects of economic promotion—financing canal systems, founding banks, showering private railroad undertakings with grants of land and credit—with very little argument except that of practical advantage. During the contraction movements that followed hard on the century's recurrent economic crises, when the states scrambled to get out of these same businesses, to drastically narrow the practical sphere of government, and to heap up new constitutional barriers to debt contraction, they did so (on the whole) with precisely the same arguments.[31] Touring the United States in the 1880s, when the economists' debates over the theoretical limits of the state were winding up to their sharpest pitch, James Bryce found himself amazed at the amount of piecemeal, untheoretical interventionary legislation the states were writing, heedless of the laissez-faire pieties in the air. A language of practical benefits and economic calculation found a ready home in the legislatures, the courts, and the constitutional conventions.[32]

By the same token, the Americans knew just as keenly as Bentham himself how to employ the words "speculative" and "philosophical" to deflate a political argument couched in dangerously expansive terms. Jefferson caught the tarry end of this brush with particular force; among Jefferson's antagonists nothing was more common than to debunk Jefferson's political opinions as the abstractions only to be expected of a man of his "theoretical and speculative disposition in politics," who flirted with French philosophers and fed potatoes to his horses. "Governments are instituted for practical benefit, not for subjects of speculative reasoning," Daniel Webster insisted early in his career, backed into a narrow corner in the Massachusetts constitutional convention of 1820.[33] Apologists of southern slavery often bore down on the same argument. By experience and expediency one could defend a lot in nineteenth-century America: railroad lines, property, industrialism, slavery, the federal union, the complex beauty of the common law, or the peculiar inequities of the Massachusetts constitution.

It was Utility bare and alone that made the trouble: Utility yanked out of rhetorical relationship with the bigger, more abstract words which lay just below the surface of late eighteenth- and nineteenth-century political talk, like the core of a massive iceberg. The rhetoric of the law is a case in point. Hard as nineteenth-century lawyers worked to shovel instrumental reasons into the law to the benefit of their favorite economic enterprises and general economic growth, they were enormously reluctant to admit, even among themselves, that they were doing anything of the sort. To the contrary, jurists and law writers fell over themselves (as Perry Miller noted) in their haste to declare the law "sublime," to insist that the stuff of every pettifogging lawyer and the law of nature itself were part and parcel of the same thing. Blackstone had pasted an appeal to natural law into his *Commentaries,* conspicuous enough to spur Bentham to savage rebuttal. But this was a mere rhetorical figleaf in comparison with the seriousness with which the American law writers insisted on the point. From James Wilson's "Lectures on Law" of 1790–91 through the rhetorical formulas of late nineteenth-century bar association orations, in the legal opinions of Supreme Court justices and the edicts of scores of local magistrates equipped with a smattering of statutes, a dose of common sense, and strong convictions of natural justice, the congruence of ordinary, man-made law with natural law formed one of the staples of legal talk.[34]

Hard cases, to be sure, were rarely decided solely on principles of natural justice. Talk of this sort was essential to the rhetoric of the law, not necessarily to the processes of decision. Thus in 1845 when New Jersey abolitionists appealed to the state supreme court to overturn the state's surviving vestiges of slavery on the grounds that the revised New Jersey constitution had declared all men by nature free, the court dismissed the argument on the grounds that such "general phrases of abstract natural right" appealed "to the feelings [rather] than to the legal intelligence of the court."[35] But through the end of the century and beyond, lawyers faced with troublesome precedents were not above appealing to the legal "feelings" of the courts; nor were the judges, when they had an unpopular opinion on their hands. Bentham had argued that the law was nothing more or less than a set of commands, issued by whatever body the people accepted as their lawgivers. But in late nineteenth-century America, Oliver Wendell Holmes's conclusions to the same effect were a mere chip of dissent on a tide of more exalted, principled legal talk.

If the language of the law was saturated with appeals to first principles, so equally was the language of politics. Political orators often chafed at "abstractions," but they spat the word "expediency" at each other with the force of a powerfully charged epithet. Andrew Jackson wielded it in that way at those who spoke for broad constitutional construction. Antislavery orators heaped the word on their opponents. Let a delegate to any nineteenth-century constitutional convention rise to blast an argument as abstract, and another was sure to respond that the country had been founded on "the very abstraction of abstractions." To reason from mere "expediency" was amoral and "jesuitical." Start from these beginnings, a Virginia constitutional convention delegate maintained angrily in 1829, and men would find themselves drifting "without star or compass to guide us, veering about to every purpose, on the great deep of expediency."[36]

So formulaic were the words, so deeply a part of the structure of political argument did they become, that they reemerged in all manner of contexts as if repeated by a company of itinerate actors, their lines memorized, flitting from stage to stage. "Shall our government be founded on principles or expediency—on the solid rock foundations of fixed principles, to which wise and patriotic freemen have every where assented, or on the shifting quicksands of expediency?" a delegate pleaded at the next Virginia convention, twenty years later:

Expediency! How often, in religion and in politics, has a short-sighted man, abandoning the principles of eternity, been led astray by the expediency of the moment! The light of expediency is that of the will-o'-the-wisp, the *ignis fatuus,* that beguiles the deluded sons of men from the ways of principle, of truth, and of virtue, into devious paths of error, falsehood and crime.

Let a government depend upon expediency, and "the rain will descend; the storm will come; [and] that government must fall." Let men desert the "hard pan of principle" (the words now came from New York in 1867), and they would find themselves "afloat upon a boundless sea, without chart or rudder."[37]

The savaging of expediency and the grumbling at abstractions arced back and forth, in dialectical fashion. Let a speaker talk of practicality, and another voice would immediately cry out for the justice of the thing. Let an orator talk merely of justice, and another would demand to know if he had the wit to think through the potential results of his high-sounding abstractions. Was not an abstraction, as a Virginian put it in the debates of the 1850s, "the stewed down essence of facts?" Was there not by "chance," a Pennsylvanian countered in the midst of an objection to woman suffrage in the 1870s, "a principle involved in the very thing called 'expediency?' "[38] Persons skilled in political argument learned to appeal first to the one, then the other, with a formality as consistent as the rules of parliamentary procedure: inventing tangible economic advantages for justice and undergirding convenience with right reason and principle. "In a country full of schoolmasters, legislatures, newspapers, talking men—a measure without a principle to bear it up is like a single twig of willow cast out on a wooden floor," Theodore Parker observed, eyeing the increasingly elaborate proslavery arguments of the 1850s; without a principle "for it to grow by, it will die."[39] Close calculation and extraordinarily sweeping abstractions—the unspoken rules of political argument required them both.

By the end of the nineteenth century, British observers of the United States could hardly contain their bemusement that a people so wedded to inventive material improvement could have created a public life so full of dogmas and political generalities. Beatrice Webb, who visited the United States in the late 1890s, eventually concluded that the American mind and her own were, on some deep level of tolerance for verbal abstractions, fundamentally different. George Bernard Shaw remembered that in his first encounter with Henry George in London in the 1880s, even as George swept Shaw off his feet and into the cause of socialism, Shaw knew him for an American

because he pronounced "necessarily"—a favorite word of his—with the accent on the third syllable instead of the first, because he was deliberately and intentionally oratorical, which is not customary among shy people like the English; because he spoke of Liberty, Justice, Truth, Natural Law, and other strange eighteenth-century superstitions; and because he explained with great simplicity and sincerity the views of the Creator, who had gone completely out of fashion in London in the previous decade and had not been heard of since.

"The late Mr. Lloyd," the *Fabian News* observed in a similar vein in a notice of Henry D. Lloyd's last book, "being an American, was, of course, eager to discuss any political question which had an abstract side." Self-serving these observations were, but they harbored a germ of truth.[40]

The abstract, metaphysical words which Bentham so abhorred lay deep in the formulas of American political argument. The result was to pull political discourse hard toward the axiomatic, the self-evident, and the fundamental. Often, to be sure, smaller caliber words sufficed. But where Americans opposed each other with deadly seriousness—not over economic promotion but over slaves or property or their forms of government—talk of mere Utility and happiness did not meet the buried, half-acknowledged criteria of legitimacy. Crass as political argument was in America, those who earned their fame as talkers—the country's Jeffersons, its Websters, its Lincolns, its Bryans, or its Wilsons—knew they must be prepared to produce on demand something approaching a political theory. Utilitarianism, in short, had stumbled not merely over the prejudices of the reviews, the taint of Bentham's religious heterodoxy, or the vagaries of his disciples but over the unwritten grammar of legitimate political talk.

The Frame of Political Argument

A practical, often crassly materialistic people, hell-bent on results, who learned to calculate and commodify across vast stretches of American life—all this, let there be no doubt, the Americans were. Their philosophers were few, and as a rule undistinguished. They nailed their frames of government together like carpenters trussing a complicated barn. They assented to the calculus of capitalism— despite their doubts and internal divisions, despite the wrench in values it entailed—with only a fraction of the protest Marx predicted for them. Early in the twentieth century, when those charged with the articulation of the science of politics finally cast aside the scruples of their fathers and began to talk of politics in terms of effects and efficiency, they did so with an eagerness, a sense of release, that one might mistake for the mood of parched travelers coming finally on a desert spring. But we must be wary of the image. Americans had known the location of that utilitarian well for a long time, and they had circled past it as tainted, unsafe. Why should that have been so? What pressed such a people for well over a century toward a style of argument which, in its antipodal impulses toward material calculation and metaphysical wordiness, was so different from utilitarianism?

Clearly no single answer will suffice. Perhaps a part of the explanation lies in the peculiar pressures words may acquire in consciously contrived nations. Where governments stretch back time out of mind, the need to sustain symbols of their legitimacy is considerably less intense than in newborn nations, where the citizens can still remember the feeble, conflict-filled infancy of the state. Legitimating devices, to be sure, come in many sorts. A hero (like Washington) will do; so will a historical myth or a delusion of destiny; but so will words and first principles. Where the governments the heroes serve remain weak, moreover, where the nation's history trails off into a dozen particular histories glued together none too securely, words may do best of all; and certain phrases mined from the nation's founding documents may be made to carry extraordinary importance.[41] In America, born (as even the participants would choose to remember it) not in the shrewdly managed anticolonial war launched in 1775 but in the manifestoes of 1776, the keywords of the Revolution proved extraordinarily difficult to budge from political talk—despite herculean efforts to trim, supplant, or repudiate them. Even now the myth that the nation's mission and purpose were written down at birth, retrievable by whatever snatch of the founders' writing strikes the strongest chord with the needs of the moment, has a symbolic and rhetorical power of no mean utility.

Whatever the weight of Revolutionary circumstance, however, the symbolic pressures on words were quickly multiplied by the Americans' decision to bind their governments by written constitutions. The haste with which they turned to constitution drafting— as if a set of words, carefully chosen and jealously guarded by the citizens, could restrain the brute ambitions of power—and the speed with which they learned to argue within the terms of those documents left an enduring imprint on political talk. Their constitutions concentrated an enormous number of political arguments into contests over a small number of highly general terms. Immense antagonisms of region and class came to a head in definitional wranglings over a handful of words like "rights" or "sovereignty." The presence of written constitutions helps explain why, in Grant Gilmore's terms, "American formulation of a legal rule has always tended to be more rigid, more abstract, more universal, than the English formulation."[42] As the political talkers grasped for constitutional legitimacy, their arguments were pressed in the same direction. By Bentham's death virtually no one in Britain doubted Parliament's unconstrained legislative authority. British politicians labored for influence, not for constitutional authority. But in America, it was hard to talk seriously about politics without recourse to the peculiarly abstract vocabulary of constitutional exegesis.

Finally, if written constitutions encouraged a peculiarly juridical style of political argument, that style was, in its turn, egged on and exaggerated by the tremendous preponderance of lawyers in American politics. From the Revolution on, the lawyers were literally everywhere. Half the members of the federal constitutional convention of 1787 were lawyers; almost half the signers of the Declaration of Independence were lawyers as well.[43] It was they who channeled so much of the intellectual energy of the Revolution into the construction of written responses to the royal governors, legal briefs against the jurisdictional rights of Parliament, declarations, and constitutions. It was they who sustained the oratorical extravagances of the nineteenth century: the two- to three-hour senatorial speeches, carefully rehearsed, stuffed with rhetorical devices and yards of quotation, for which political lawyers like Daniel Webster and Rufus Choate were famous.

In the British Parliaments of the nineteenth century, lawyers were vastly outnumbered by landowners, by a ratio of seven to one in the first reformed Parliament of 1833 and by not much less a generation later. Influence lay in property, tenants, and dependencies. But even in the American plantation South, it was not land but a smattering of the law that offered the broadest, most heavily traveled highway to political office in America. On the eve of secession, well over half the members of the Alabama lower house had started their careers as lawyers; in the Virginia constitutional convention of 1850, about three-quarters of the delegates listed themselves as lawyers. In the nineteenth-century United States Senate, some two-thirds of the seats were regularly filled with lawyers.[44] Similar figures can be cited almost endlessly. If the language of politics bristled with abstractions, a good deal of the responsibility was owed to the law-

yers' peculiar skill with words, their need for arguments transcend-
ing the particulars of the case, and their glib and ready way with
principles.

None of these circumstances by themselves propelled political
argument in America away from straightforward debate over utilities. It was not simply the pressing need for symbols, for a string
of words on paper is not necessarily the best means of reconciling
a people to its governments. Nor was it the construction of written
constitutions; for the writing of a constitution does not preclude
rewriting it so often (as in revolutionary France) to desanctify the
words and strip them of all but instrumental meanings. Nor was it
merely the social weight of lawyers; for ultimately the lawyers
would learn to think of themselves not as enunciators of principle
but as skilled manipulators of a desacralized system of rules. Two
more factors surely were at work.

Beatrice Webb thought she scented one of them in the political
arguments of her American acquaintances: a "Protestant metaphysics" as old and, in her mind, as antique as Cromwell.[45] And on a
certain level, she was almost surely right. There is no doubt that in
both Britain and America the anti-utilitarian argument was saturated with an explicitly Protestant animus. In this matter, little separated the two nations. Church membership boomed in both Britain
and the United States in the late eighteenth and early nineteenth
centuries; revivalists and reformers crisscrossed the Atlantic as
agents of a common Anglo-American evangelical culture; in both
countries church-going citizens grasped hard for the levers of politics at the front of assaults on slavery, prostitution, sabbath breaking, and drunkenness.[46] Were we to issue prizes for serious, conspicuous piety in high political office, the medal would go, hands
down, to William Gladstone. But during the era of Protestantism's
hegemony, the Americans may have had something else: a more
deeply biblical, verbal style of Protestantism, a sharper and more
widely distributed appetite for theology, for religious dispute, for
wrangling with the Word and (hence) with words of every sort.

Some of this open zeal for first principles was fueled in the American colleges. Oxford and Cambridge, filled with clergymen's sons
and clergymen on the make, guarded until the 1850s by religious
test acts, never took half the pains of the American colleges to drum

into their students a view of the world as a logically consistent whole, shot through with divinely created, generalizable laws.[47] Even more of it, however, must have derived from the multitude of competing churches in America, jostling with each other for authority and members, separated by theological differences a hairsbreadth in width but crucial enough to attract crowds of amateur disputants to their defense. The dominant religious style was (in British terms) not merely that of Protestantism but of Dissent; and it carried with it a reluctance to identify faith merely with day-to-day piety, an eagerness to second-guess the designs of God, and a broadly diffused appreciation of metaphysical argument.

Not only did Protestantism bear down peculiarly hard on words in nineteenth-century America, it was also peculiarly difficult to escape. Utilitarianism, despite the large number of former members of the dissenting churches in its ranks, was an aggressively secular political creed; it drew its strength from persons loosed from traditional forms of religion, ready to trade metaphysical certainty for statistical inquiry. But in nineteenth-century America, where religiosity was so broadly diffused, where the inheritances and sinecures which sustained so much of secular British intellectual life were so much harder to come by, persons handy with ideas had relatively few choices other than journalism or the piety-dominated colleges. Those who increasingly fell out of church allegiances in England— the working class and the intellectuals—stuck more tenaciously to their old creeds in the United States. The biblically charged rhetoric of a Lincoln, a Theodore Roosevelt, or a Woodrow Wilson reflected not merely a personal bent but a massive sociological fact.

Yet if the expansive, abstraction-filled rhetoric of political argument reflected the pressures of a peculiarly powerful and wordy Protestantism, it reflected, no less importantly, the pressures of popular politics as well. Protestant and democratic ways with words sometimes reinforced each other, sometimes stood starkly opposed; but in the making and remaking of the vocabulary of politics both played a part. Bentham had dreamed of finding patrons; Beatrice Webb counted on her ideas and allies to permeate the British decision-making establishment. The keywords of American politics, in contrast, were words for the open air. From the Revolution on, American political writers knew the imperative of words big enough to mobilize the broad mass of citizens upon which their experiment in a kingless government depended. Their arguments were forged not in anterooms or parliamentary halls but in manifestoes, rallying cries, school texts, and public oratory. The result, as in revolutionary France, was a style of political talk thick with mobilization devices, utopian visions, and abstract promises.

But a language *for* the people was also a language open to repeated transformation *by* the people. Many of the biggest, most open words—words, so Tocqueville complained of the new democratic style, "like a box with a false bottom," in which "you may put in . . . what ideas you please, and take them out again without being observed"—were sustained from below, by a people who knew their multiple uses.[48] The abstractions of the Revolution, in particular, were to be an extraordinarily versatile tool for those outside the structures of power, a popular, unstable, controversial rhetoric of powerful consequence. The Americans took their keywords big, in part, because so many of them were words for the *demos,* shaped in a politics which, despite its glaring inequities, was never as closed a shop as politics in eighteenth- or nineteenth-century Britain.

All these circumstances, then—the need for symbols, the pressures generated by written constitutions, the preponderance of lawyers, the cultural dominance of a Protestantism peculiarly wedded to words, and the force of popular politics—combined to push to the fore precisely the vague and sounding words the utilitarian method was designed to supplant. These circumstances framed political argument in America in the century after independence, sustained its unwritten rules, lent it its central rhetorical power and its distinctive circumlocutions.

If the Americans escaped Bentham's quirks and rigidities, however, that came with certain costs. Of what conceivable use was the state? Oxford's professor of jurisprudence wrote in the early 1880s, in an elaboration of the point on which Bentham and his heirs had labored so hard. "What is sovereignty for, if it is not there to be directed by every light of reason towards the attainment of the common happiness?"[49] Their skill at words notwithstanding, the Americans had no easy time putting Bentham's question this directly. Start on this line, and someone was sure to shunt their talk onto more metaphysical tracks. Off into the origins of the state, the grounds of legitimacy, or the basis of rights the arguments would veer. Hence the survival of Natural Rights talk, long after it gave out in Britain. Hence the Americans' sweeping talk of the People's sovereignty, in comparison to which even the Chartists' claims for the people were but a feeble chirp. Hence the extraordinary intensity with which Americans frightened of this sort of talk worked to root out such words, to wrest from their political opponents not only power but language.

Yet if the political talkers took eagerly to abstractions, it was, finally, because they knew their uses. In a hard place, they grasped for bigger words than effects or happiness. With them they fought, quarreled, and struggled for advantage. They made out of their keywords, their axioms, their definitional wrangles not a political consensus but the tools of debate. So full of liberating potential and handy obscurities, such words had their own utility.

2

Natural Rights

Declarations

To Jeremy Bentham nothing revealed the folly of the American Revolution more clearly than the Americans' defense of it. Copies of the Declaration of Independence had barely reached London late in the summer of 1776 before Bentham sat down to scribble out a rejoinder in an effort to dissipate the "cloud of words" with which the Americans had tried to disguise "the enormity of their enterprises." Although in time Bentham changed his mind about the American Revolution, the opening arguments of the Declaration never struck him as anything other than ridiculous. Rational persons, he was convinced, did not waste their time puzzling like children over the origins of governments or wrestling their desires into something called Natural Rights. Rights talk he thought in itself vague and dogmatic enough; to prate about Natural Rights was to set one unintelligible word on top of another so that nonsense strutted about on stilts.[1]

And yet of all the big and booming terms to come out of the American Revolution, the most powerful and least containable was Natural Rights. In other nations in momentous times, citizens have counted up their rights and nailed them boldly to their church doors. But in none but the United States did the act of declaring and redeclaring rights ultimately work its way so deeply into the basic tools of politics. Scholars, law writers, judges, and bookmakers lent a hand in the process, trying hard (as a rule) to corral the appeal to Natural Rights within precise and limited bounds. From the beginning, however, the term was made for declarations, sustained by the uses the declaration drafters would put it to.

Had the Americans merely discovered the rights of human beings once and contented themselves with periodic redeclarations of what they had found, their enumerations of rights would quickly have hardened into settled, stabilizing forms. From the outset there were many Americans who devoutly wished as much. But out of the slogan makers' compounding of the words "right" and "nature" emerged a way of talking about politics far less predictable than that. Set the words together in the manner forged in the heat of the Revolutionary agitation of the 1760s and 1770s, and they invited inquiry, not simply into the rights which human beings possessed but into those rights which, given their nature, they *ought* to possess. More pointedly still, lest one founder in the deep waters of philosophy, it invited human beings to imagine what rights must once have been theirs, long ago, in the first moment of natural creation. "I say RIGHTS," John Adams exploded at the outset of the Stamp Act crisis in 1765: rights "antecedent to all earthly government,—*Rights, that cannot be repealed or restrained by human laws—Rights, derived from the great Legislator of the universe.*"[2] It was this retrospective use of the words, this open enticement to leapfrog across custom, institutions, and history into a nick of time, a state of nature antecedent to all human governments, and to repossess whatever claims had been left behind—it was this that made the words so volatile, the rights themselves so expandable, the act of declaring them so repeatable.

Such an appeal to a state of nature was, from the beginning, intensely contested terrain. The declaration writers of the early 1770s happened on it slowly, hesitantly, pushed by circumstances of controversy and politics, resisted by the more cautious among them. The framers of the early bills of rights chose their phrases with the nervousness of persons aware that words were weapons, and double-edged at that. From an inquiry into man's natural rights one might emerge, like John Locke, with a refurbished defense of existing property relations. But inquiry into a forgotten, original fund of rights was full of subversive possibilities; those who took the idea of natural rights seriously in America often ended up, not where Locke would have wanted them, but elsewhere: dumping tea cargoes overboard or decrying the unnatural privileges of banks and corporations or as critics of the ancient notion of a man's ownership of his wife or his slaves. To talk of rights was to employ the language of courts and barristers. To talk of Natural Rights, on the contrary, was to talk of rights which had somehow slipped out of everyday law. It was a tool whose uses those on the margins of politics and power could not but be particularly quick to see.[3]

For all these reasons, there was nothing static or consensual about the language of Natural Rights in America. The words were used and evaded, aggressively championed and earnestly rebutted. The term was injected into the center of political argument by the crisis over Parliament and taxes. But independence was still far from secure before many of the patriots rushed to lock up their words and trim their implications. Formalized in the new century, encased in rituals and constitution drafters' boiler plate, the slogan of Natural Rights erupted once more when it was seized by those most deeply out of sorts with Jacksonian America: workingmen, land reformers, slavery opponents, and feminists. Finally at this juncture, those with deeper stakes in the status quo turned against the words and the mode of argument they represented and tried their best to bury them altogether.

There is another, more familiar way of describing the career of the term, in which Locke, Jefferson, and the modern advocates of human rights join hands in a great liberal tradition stretching across the centuries. But intellectual traditions are the convenient inventions of intellectual historians. Talk of Natural Rights was a tool, sharp with subversive possibilities, and always controversial. What Bentham overheard was not the enunciation of a political creed but an argument: words big enough for men to fight over their possession.

A State of Nature

It was Thomas Jefferson's assignment in 1776 to sweep together a dozen years of angry, extrapolated argument into a self-evident whole, as if the axioms of the Declaration of Independence had been all along, as Jefferson was later to claim, simply the "common sense" of the matter.[4] But Americans angry at Parliamentary taxes and impositions had not set out at the beginning to talk about their "inherent and inalienable rights." Only with vastly more effort than the Declaration admitted had they begun to talk about the natural, original rights of man at all.

Much of the time, as Bernard Bailyn and others have made clear, they had used a language very different from this. They had responded to the succession of British efforts to integrate them into the imperial tax system in many ways, but none more important than with angry, morally charged talk of power and corruption. Taking all they knew (and the worse they surmised) of late eighteenth-century Britain, swarming with a multiplying horde of assessors, tax collectors, and excise men, and fusing those fears with a deep-seated suspicion of court corruption and concentrated authority, the leaders of the resistance efforts concocted a nightmarish rhetoric of grasping, always unsatisfied power. They tried to rouse their countrymen, not with a precise enumeration of their rights but by unveiling a secret design which put *all* the colonists' liberties and possessions in danger: a plot so immense that the Declaration's talk of "an absolute Tyranny" seemed none too strong. The fears (and the words) were common coin in the eighteenth-century English-speaking world, ripe for appropriation. With them, the patriot leaders stoked the crowds with their own fierce urgencies, mobilized the boycotts, the letters of remonstrance, the correspondence committees, the extraordinary protest congresses, the mobbing of tax collectors, the taunting of soldiers. To sustain the movement of resistance the slogans were indispensable.[5]

The language of rights, however, had its own vitally important uses. Charges of plots and corruption, indispensable as they were at home, were not likely to change many ministry officials' minds or win many allies in Parliament. Here the leaders of the resistance needed a soberer language of charter precedents, implicit constitutional guarantees, and rights. To the task of transmuting the colonists' nightmares into formal declarations of rights, dozens of lawyer-pamphleteers were eager to lend a hand. But during the opening crisis over stamps and import duties in 1764 and 1765, when the penmen of the nascent resistance began to salt their work with the term Natural Rights, it is not clear that the adjective added much to their arguments.

In its most common eighteenth-century employment, the word "natural" amounted to hardly more than a fashionably resonant term of emphasis. To insist on the natural rights of British Americans was, in this sense, simply to insist, more strongly than usual, on the rights inherent in the colonists' formal relations to the crown and empire. This was clearly the intention of the Massachusetts House of Representatives in 1764, for example, in insisting that "the allegiance of British subjects being natural, perpetual, and inseparable from their persons, let them be in what country they may, their rights are also natural, inherent, and perpetual."[6] A handy term to plaster onto virtually any assertion, the word's vagueness and its versatility were part and parcel of each other.

More philosophically inclined writers, to be sure, employed the word in a second, more precise way: to appeal to the rules and relations God had etched as the Laws of Nature in the universe itself. This was the way the term was taught in the colonial colleges, and it did not take the manifesto writers long to yoke it to their declarations, first to double the rhetorical force of their legal arguments and eventually (as the escalating stakes of the contest pushed them past the bounds of chartered rights and constitutional precedents) to rest a wing or two of their case on natural law principles alone. There were rights, the declaration writers began to insist, which the lawyers had never written down: rights "founded in the Law of God and Nature" (as the Massachusetts Stamp Act resolves put it in 1765), which were "the common Rights of Mankind." Our rights, John Dickinson declared in the same vein a year later, "are not annexed to us by parchments and seals. They are created in us by the decrees of Providence, which establish the laws of our nature. They are born with us; exist with us; and cannot be taken from us by any human power without taking our lives. In short, they are founded on the immutable maxims of reason and justice."[7]

The pamphleteers grasped hard for the words; but as a rhetoric of resistance, much less of revolution, the language of natural law had its limits. It was one thing to appeal, as the patriot leaders continued to do well past 1776, to laws written in the frame of human nature, but it was another to gather much agreement on the rights that frame entailed. As for society, generations of natural law glosses and compromises had managed to stretch the maxims of right reason over virtually every imaginable arrangement. Slavery, war, despotism (of a marginally enlightened sort), coercions of every kind, all had their powerful natural law defenses.[8] Were not kings part of God's natural creation? And the prerogatives, taxes, and tax collectors which made kings possible? Was not the grand, historically evolved edifice of powers and obligations binding the British empire together just as natural as any of the supposed immunities the tax-resistant Americans were defending? To read the edicts of natural justice from the frame of God's creation, given how many contradictory things he managed to contrive, was no straightforward piece of work. Of the major figures of the Revolution, Jefferson was one of the few to stick with the task over the long haul. One might call the policies of the king an affront to the laws of nature, but where the most telling thing conservatives found to say about the rebellion in America was that it was profoundly "unnatural," the rhetoric of natural law was not particularly tractable stuff to put to the service of open disobedience.

It was in its third, though at the outset least common, meaning —as a description of rights inherited from an original state of nature —that the word "natural" was capable of genuinely unsettling uses. To talk in this way was not (in truth) to appeal to nature at all but to slip past the existing arrangements of nature one knew all too well, past the centuries of natural law casuistry, past history itself, to a vision in the mind's eye of the world as it must once have existed, fresh from the hands of its creator. Here was a device to impel human beings to imagine an age older than kings and governments, older than property and oppression, older than political society itself. To talk in this way was to induce men to ask what rights human beings must originally have possessed and could conceivably have agreed to surrender when, out of nothing but their free consent, they had brought governments into being; and to imagine all this so vividly that the subsequent loss of any of those unsurrendered rights should loom as an ugly, massive injustice. To talk in this way was to talk retrospectively, utopianly, and (in the sense that the game of reimagining the terms of creation was one at which anyone, not simply the natural law jurists, could play) democratically. Here, in short, was a meaning for the term Natural Rights powerful enough to knock the pins out from the smooth assertion of a Tory like Blackstone that, in the nature of things, king and Parliament had "the supreme disposal of every thing."[9] But it was not a way of talking that the colonists came to easily or self-evidently.

The trouble with state of nature reasoning was that by the last third of the eighteenth century, just when the patriot writers needed it, it had fallen sharply into disrepute. It is true that Locke had written in this way, in lines that still enjoyed currency in colonial America, and that Rousseau (just beyond the colonists' ken) was beginning to do so once more. As for the simple point that human beings had hoisted themselves out of an individualistic, prepolitical state of nature into a state of civil society by contracting with each other to behave as a political whole, that could be found, cursorily but unmistakably treated, in virtually all the great compendia of natural law. But the intricate, guarded reasoning of the reigning natural law authorities—of a Pufendorf, a Burlamaqui, a Vattel, or a Hutcheson—was all but impossible to press into a legitimation of open political resistance. Locke's style of argument was considerably stronger. But among the eighteenth-century British writers whose lines the colonial pamphleteers were pillaging for usable arguments, the flight from Locke's state of nature notions was all but complete.[10]

Open attack on the fiction of a reservoir of rights retrievable from the past was the work of the Scots political philosophers. The hatchet man, not surprisingly, was David Hume, who in an essay, "Of the Original Contract," in 1748, had ridiculed the notion that eighteenth-century British subjects, born into civil society in full flood, were somehow usefully conceived as immigrants from a state of nature, carrying with them an ancient satchel of rights. The emphasis of the Scots writers was on history and change, not on a mythic past. "If we are asked, therefore, Where the state of nature is to be found?" Adam Ferguson wrote in 1767, the answer was not at the beginnings of creation but "here," wherever men now found themselves and put their natural talent for "improvement" to best use.[11]

The Americans wrote for English, not Scottish ears, to be sure, and among English Whig and opposition writers an older tradition of retrospective argument still carried massive weight. Where Tories talked of Right, opposition spokesmen talked of rights which were theirs by ancient possession. But by the middle of the eighteenth century they too had cautiously cut their ties to Locke's strategy of reimagining the terms of original creation. When mid-eighteenth-century Whig writers wrote of the "original contract," what they usually had in mind was the constitutional settlement of 1689. And when they pushed deeper into the past than that, it was not to the indistinct and speculative ground Locke had tried to naturalize for them, where all things—law, monarchy, even property itself—were in a dangerously ambiguous state but to a soberer myth they called the Ancient Constitution, that collection of Saxon rights which the Norman tyrants were said never legally to have obliterated. The scholarly game of whittling down John Locke's influence has had its moments of excess; Locke remained a presence both in England and its colonies. But it is nonetheless clear that Locke's endeavor to imaginatively reconstruct the state of nature was something of a sport, closer to the intellectual enthusiasms of the seventeenth century than to the more tangible, material ways in which eighteenth-century Englishmen were inclined to talk about their rights and liberties.[12]

In the stock of political slogans available to the colonists in the 1760s—in the collection of words lying on the shelf, as it were, sharp and ready for employment—there was, then, very little from which to predict that the Americans would end up talking seriously, heatedly, of rights passed down unimpaired from something so fantastic as a state of nature. The patriot writers groped for their words throughout the 1760s and 1770s under the shift and stress of circumstances, inventing lines of argument and backing away from them. Even as state of nature claims began to edge their way into their resolves and pamphlets, the force of the appeal was at first severely limited. James Otis, at the head of the first stirrings of protest in Massachusetts, had brought up Locke's speculations in a pamphlet of 1764, only to dismiss them as not particularly useful to the patriot cause. Two years later in Virginia, Richard Bland took them up more seriously to buttress a passing claim that the freedom of emigration was an inviolable right; but Bland's effort went largely unread and unreprinted.[13] It is in Massachusetts in the 1770s, in a cultural soil peculiarly deep in politico-theological speculation and under the pressure of particularly intense conflict between patriot leaders and royal officials, that one suddenly begins to find stronger uses of the words. By 1771 Samuel Adams was deep into a reading of Locke on the origins of property and government. A year later, partly under Adams's prodding, the Boston Town Meeting suddenly blazed up with talk of those essential rights which men "at the entering into [civil] society" had never renounced and, indeed, could not permanently renounce even if "fear, fraud or mistake" should cause them for a time to let them go. The Continental Congress of 1774 settled, after sharp debate, for a far more cautious appeal to natural law. But by 1776 the claim that men were by original nature free and independent of each other ("created equal and independent" were the words that first came to Jefferson's pen), possessed of a fund of natural, original rights which their descendents could turn back to and reclaim whenever the scales fell from their eyes—all this (to the alarm of many of the more cautious patriots) reverberated up and down the colonies.[14]

None of the penmen of the Revolution later sat down to describe how the word "natural" had been wrenched out of its ordinary tracks, how Natural Rights had become retrospective rights, how that palpable abstraction called the state of nature had become real enough for men to imagine they could wring rhetorical advantage from it. In the middle years of the 1770s, as the colonists moved from boycotts and remonstrances to armed resistance and, finally, independence itself, the pressure of circumstances on their words was far too intense to make their choices logically tidy.

A hint of the multiplicity of those pressures came to the surface in Virginia in June 1776, when the telltale phrases of the state of nature were first wedged into a statement of fundamental law. "All men are by nature equally free and independent, and have certain inherent rights, of which, when they enter into a state of society, they cannot, by any compact, deprive or divest their posterity"—

so the Virginia Convention boldly began its Declaration of Rights, in phrases which electrified readers far beyond Williamsburg. The Virginians themselves, however, had chosen their words with the hairsplitting sophistry of men with a dangerously hard case on their hands—groping for lines bold enough to justify their rebellion against king and Parliament and yet cautious enough so that no inadvertent phrase would compromise the logic by which they themselves held several thousand of those naturally free and independent persons as slaves. The phrase, "when they enter into a state of society," had not been part of George Mason's original draft. It was slipped in at the end of several days' nervous debate over words and slavery in order to draw a line, tortured, to be sure, but distinct enough that no constitutional lawyer would be in danger of mistaking it, between those persons within political, civil society, whose rights were being declared to the world, and those who, being slaves, stood outside the compacts and rights of Virginia altogether.[15] From the outset the terms of the state of nature were elastic —verbal contrivances open to men in all sorts of hard places.

But the overriding exigency, which pushed the declaration writers where the Scots and the English Whigs were no longer willing to go, was the need for precedents. Claims of power demanded counterclaims of precedent. That much every country Whig and every colonial lawyer knew. The patriot writers filled their briefs with precedents of all sorts, appealing to a hodgepodge of "natural, ancient, constitutional, and chartered Rights" (as the Virginians did in 1774) in arguments that were deliberately thick and jumbled rather than thin and carefully focused in hopes that a few of their assertions would meet their mark.[16] But as the colonists searched back in time for an American equivalent to the Ancient Constitution, they found only a patchwork of diverse charters and, back of that, nothing at all but British subjects on the outposts of a ramshackle empire. Still if the demands for precedent were urgent enough, one might begin to imagine that the first American colonists had regained something strikingly akin to the state of nature itself: that the conjectural territory which the natural law writers had placed beyond the grasp of men at the beginnings of time was a land the colonists had in sober fact reclaimed.

None of the manifesto writers pushed the half-acknowledged

reifications of the state of nature all the way to these conclusions, where the claims would surely have broken on the ridicule of the court historians and lawyers. The point is a more subtle one: that as the patriot writers turned back upon their histories, ransacking them for legal precedents which with each escalation of their resistance grew more tortuous to invent, the temptation grew to reimagine their histories along lines which mirrored—and, in doing so, made increasingly real—the theoretical origins of civil society itself.

One of the hints of the ways the words grew in weight was the tightness with which speculation about original rights stuck to discussions of emigration. The patriot writers had insisted almost from the first that the right to quit the land where birth and chance had deposited them—"to retire from Society, [and] to renounce the Benefits of it," as Richard Bland put it in 1766—was no mere privilege, as virtually all the big natural law textbooks on their shelves maintained, but a natural right. Even Franklin, who used the term Natural Right with the parsimony of a man deeply suspicious of abstract political argument, insisted on the point; his fellow Pennsylvanians wrote it into their bill of rights in 1776. But what if such persons should find themselves, not in another part of the realm, but (as the Pennsylvanians put it) in "vacant countries?" Was that not tantamount to having leapfrogged back to the prepolitical state of man? What possible meaning lay hidden in the words Samuel Adams pushed through the Boston Town Meeting in 1772, as part of the clause on the right of emigration, that "all Men have a Right to remain in a State of Nature as long as they please"—wildly abstract and seemingly gratuitous words for men with control of their governor's salary on their minds—other than that the state of nature and the wilds of America were being rapidly fused for the urgent purposes of argument. The colonial charters became not grants but *contracts*—here, too, even Franklin insisted on the point —though that was scarcely the way they had been conceived in London by those who had promulgated them. Memories of the complex corporate machinery of the Virginia Company and the Plymouth Adventurers gave way before a strikingly different image of men, originally free and independent of each other, creating political society out of nothing but their common will and consent. As the stakes of the conflict escalated faster than the lawyers could keep pace, the boldest of the patriot writers pumped more and more reality into the state of nature, merged it with their remembered past, and pressed it into the void where the Ancient Constitution should have been.[17]

Not all the champions of colonial resistance were willing to follow this string of conflations all the way down the line. Among those who valued stability, state of nature talk chafed a sensitive nerve. When Richard Henry Lee, pleading with the delegates to the Continental Congress in 1774 to rest their defense of the American cause "upon the broadest bottom, the ground of nature," tried to clinch his case by reminding them, "our ancestors found here no government," his opponents dismissed the idea as a "feeble" conceit.[18] Most of the patriot writers, indeed, never contended that the Americans had been anything but British subjects from the start. For many of them the state of nature was a synonym for fearsome anarchy. Even Jefferson, pressed by claims that the Revolution had brought Virginia law back to a tabula rasa, was to complain of the "most mischievous tendency" to force the social contract idea "from theoretical to practical use." But so deep had the words sunk into the vocabulary of resistance that in 1774 and 1775, when the institutions of imperial authority began to unravel—as the colonial assemblies were prorogued, the courts closed, and the governors put to flight—there were manifesto writers in some of the angrier corners of the colonies ready to declare that it was time to go the whole way, to "fall into a State of Nature until our Grievances are fully redressed."[19] Such a deed was by Locke's lights, by Rousseau's, too, an impossibility. For Locke the disintegration of a government could not unhinge the underlying civil contract or let loose the primordial rights of man. For Rousseau, too, there was no return to a state of nature. But in America, the state of nature had been yanked out of the beginnings of time and into imaginable history, as a reservoir of continuing claims vis-à-vis political society.

Tom Paine, long after the fact, set down the underlying dynamic of the argument. "The error of those who reason by precedents drawn from antiquity, respecting the rights of man, is that they do not go far enough into antiquity. They do not go the whole way. They stop in some of the intermediate stages of a hundred or a thousand years, and produce what was then done as a rule for the present day." But each precedent had its forerunner to contradict it. "It is authority against authority all the way till we come to the divine origin of the rights of man at the creation. Here our inquiries find a resting-place, and our reason finds a home."[20] By a process something like this, pressed hard for arguments, lured by the resemblance between the patently abstract and the imagined historical facts, the Americans had rediscovered the state of nature. Take the words of the declaration writers seriously and a riot of original claims had suddenly sprung into being. The question, heavy in the air in 1776, was what to do with them.

Delimiting Rights

Prudent men, having come this far, would have locked the argument up. A style of reimagining the bases of politics, subversive enough to undermine king and empire, was unlikely to treat authority more gently simply because its seat had been transferred to Boston or Williamsburg. Let persons go on mining a myth of political origins for new rights, and there was no telling what would become of the fragile arrangements the patriot leaders were now bent on consolidating. For those on the inside of the new governments in 1776, the pressing task was the containment and employment of power. From talk of Natural Rights the patriot leaders turned quickly to the construction of constitutions and alliances, cashing in their pre-independence citations of Locke for the soberer maxims of Montesquieu.[21] In this setting the centripetal impulses in the language of Natural Rights became a liability. If the words had grown too popular simply to be shoved aside, they could at the least be defined and formalized, the invitation to new rights making cut off, the state of nature abandoned, before talk of it should pull their polities apart. In the first dozen years after independence, in response to a flood of rights talk from below, the leaders of the new republic went a long way toward doing precisely that.

When the first bills of rights were hastily pieced together in 1776, the word "rights" was still a word of quicksilver fluidity, open to all sorts of uses. Only five of the thirteen new states produced bills of rights in the first flush of independence; a decade later, almost half had yet to do so.[22] The most famous of the first declarations, those of Virginia and Pennsylvania, bristled with expansive political claims; others were cut far more cautiously and legalistically. Wherever the Americans wrote bills of rights, however, they threw into them claims of an almost bewildering diversity. The rights of individuals and the rights of the people as a whole; the immunities of citizens against their governments and the imperatives of the common welfare; old grievances honed on the abuses of royal officials and new assertions of the proper frame of government; natural rights, legal and procedural rights, and pious injunctions—all these were stirred together without nice theoretical distinctions.[23]

Nothing indicated more clearly the flexibility of the term than the fact that it could be attached to so many different sorts of possessions. Many of the rights spelled out in 1776 inhered in individuals. But if persons had rights, nations, communities, and majorities had rights as well. The framers of the Declaration of Independence, assigned the task of justifying a rebellion, might write that governments were instituted to preserve the inalienable rights of men; but the more common bill of rights claim was that governments were instituted for the "common benefit," the "public weal," "solely for the good of the whole."

The immediate intent of such words was to insure that no new, homegrown set of governors would dare (like the royal placemen) milk the state for their own private profits and advantages. But the notion of collective rights and the public good ran still more deeply than this. Behind it lay a suspicion of mere private desires and a dream of active, public virtue, whose lineage J. G. A. Pocock has so brilliantly reconstructed. "The social compact or state of civil society, by which men are united and incorporated, requires that every right or power claimed or exercised by any man or set of men be in subordination to the common good," a committee of Philadelphians, organized to enforce compliance to the wartime price controls, declared in 1779. The right "for every man to do what he pleases [is] a right, which . . . is repugnant to the very principles on which society and civil government are founded."[24]

Rhetoric of this sort erupted with the collapse of government in

1774 and flourished during the war. With it the committees of safety and fragile assemblies beat back the challenges to their authority, wrung taxes and economic sacrifices out of those who had no appetite for either, drove persons loyal to the empire into exile, auctioned off their land to men of nationalistic sentiments and ready cash, silenced presses, and in general did the dirty work that even as tame a revolution as the American entailed. In this context, we should hardly be surprised that the Virginia Declaration of Rights, which opened by proclaiming men "by nature equally free and independent," should have ended with a series of urgent, self-denying injunctions: to justice, moderation, temperance, frugality, virtue, forbearance, love, and charity. Out of the cultivation of virtue and (still more) the science of constitutional mechanics—out of frames of government so designed that power would be divided, balanced, harnessed to the common good—the patriot leaders sought to consolidate the resistance movement and shore up their new political entities against the tendency of every republic known to them to collapse into squabbling pieces.[25]

Outside the new arrangements of power, however, it is clear that the Americans were still getting their tongues around the term "rights." If the eclectic character of the early bills of rights reflected the awkwardly balanced commitments of the framers, it was equally a sign of the unexhausted ferment of Natural Rights talk below the patriot elites. Through the end of the 1770s there were Americans ready to insist that the old, obnoxious imbalances of representation and power, having been dissolved in the colonists' fall into a state of nature, could not simply be reestablished by the wave of a legislature's hand. Others groped for still stronger words for rights. Within two years of independence, in the town meetings of Massachusetts—to which the legislature had incautiously submitted a constitution, without a bill of rights, for popular ratification—men had begun to talk seriously of a distinction between two sorts of natural rights: alienable rights, which the makers of a social contract might exchange (if the bargain were good enough) for their equivalent in social benefits, and rights so precious that no fair price could be put on them but were, by their nature, unexchangeable, "inalienable."[26]

And everywhere out of serious talk of rights erupted new assertions of rights. Religious dissenters up and down the colonies seized on the rhetoric of inalienable rights to demand new immunities of religious conscience. The Tory charge that men who brayed so loudly about Natural Rights had best begin by abolishing slavery found echoes in scores of petitions—many of them from black Americans—that enslavement, no matter what its cause and origin, was a violation of an inalienable right. Where the popular record is best preserved, in the returns of the Massachusetts town meetings of 1778, men were talking about inherent rights with breathtaking inventiveness: the right to absolute property in oneself and one's earnings (though it meant the death of slavery), the right (even of poor or black men) to vote, the right to cashier one's public officials once a year and make them stand for annual election, the right engraved in "human nature" to a fairly apportioned legislature, the "unalienable right" to a constitution ratified by a popular vote. As long as the words gave men license to look backward, past the screen of law and custom to the origins of political justice, the rhetoric of rights was bound to be unstable and unpredictable.[27]

Only a fraction of this sort of talk, exploding so rapidly in the late 1770s, gained a place in the first bills of rights. Outside of New Hampshire, the constitution drafters contrived to keep even a clear distinction between alienable and inalienable rights out of their documents. Instead the constitution writers made their own rough distinctions. The members of the body politic were surrounded by all sorts of procedural guarantees and legal privileges; the coercive powers of governments were splintered, divided, and hemmed in; but only a few sorts of rights were distinguished as "natural," "inherent," or "inalienable." The drafters of the Virginia Declaration of Rights opened with the most fundamental of these, "the enjoyment of life and liberty, with the means of acquiring and possessing property, and pursuing and obtaining happiness and safety." To this they added only one other "indubitable, inalienable, and indefeasible" right: the collective right, inherent in "a majority of the community," to "reform, alter, or abolish" its government "in such manner as shall be judged most conducive to the public weal." The drafters of the Pennsylvania constitution, three months later, added a handful more: the natural right to protect (as well as acquire and possess) one's property; the natural right of

expatriation; and finally, in words more sweeping than the Virginians had been prepared to stomach, the "natural and unalienable
right to worship Almighty God according to the dictates of their
own consciences and understanding." All the other rights pronounced so boldly in 1776—of elections and representation, of war-
rants and jury trials, of free assembly and a free press—were, by
implication, lesser rights, strong claims but immune neither to
change nor (where the safety and happiness of the whole was at
stake) outright invasion.

Even the inalienable rights were not really absolute. Life and
liberty were forfeitable by crime or treason. The right to worship as
one's conscience dictated was not incompatible, in the minds of
most eighteenth-century Americans, with the countervailing right
of the majority to promote its own articles of faith, to tax dissenters
for the support of public preaching, or to bar holders of publicly
obnoxious religious beliefs from assuming political office. As for
property, no one doubted that a person's goods were alienable,
taxable, condemnable, "subservient to public uses" (as the drafters
of the Vermont constitution of 1777 declared) "when necessity
requires it." What the bills of rights designated as inalienable was
not every last farthing a person owned but a set of verbs—acquiring,
possessing, and defending—surrounding the word "property," porous enough to allow public necessity and the public weal their
legitimate shares.[28]

Here—ambiguous and compromised as the words were—was a
stopping place of no mean attractiveness to men made uneasy by
the ferment of rights invention from below. Now that a handful of
natural rights had been declared, one might have expected such men
to try to haul rights and obligations back into more normal balance,
to bring the ransacking of the state of nature to a close, to turn men's
minds from an ancient fund of rights to the soberer instruments of
laws and constitutions. There were several ways to turn the trick,
none of them beyond the imagination of the patriot leaders in the
early years of independence. One might have halted further construction of bills of rights before the enterprise became entrenched
and customary, leaving the rights of men where Edmund Burke
thought them safest, discernible but not defined.[29] One might have
balanced off the existing bills of rights with equally solemn declara-

tions of men's duties, along the lines of the Thermidorian constitution in France in 1795. One might have turned on retrospective talk of Natural Rights altogether, silenced those like Paine who talked incessantly of origins, and tried to drive the mischievous adjective out of currency. In one way or another, a style of argument, its usefulness over, might have been locked up before men grown accustomed to reasoning from an imagined state of nature should discover too many novel rights and new injustices.

The British course was outright repression. The rhetoric of original, natural rights, rare in the eighteenth century, erupted in England in the 1770s, 1780s, and 1790s. Revived in large part by the debate over American policy, fed through the connections between radical English Whigs and radical colonists, the phrases met a political culture already deeply worked by anger at official corruption and Parliamentary rottenness. From admirers of the American resistance, like Richard Price, Joseph Priestley, and John Cartwright, from younger artisan radicals, from the new, politically conscious crowds in the streets, and from the mushrooming correspondence and constitutional societies, the cry of rights thundered with extraordinary power. Still faster than their American counterparts, the pamphlets and broadsides of British radicalism spun off a stream of new rights: the rights of suffrage and representation, of annual Parliaments and genuinely popular governments; the rights of dissent; the rights of women; the right to restore the land to its original state of common ownership, before a tribe of gentlemen had dared to fence it in; the right of the people (if they chose) to cashier the king and frame a republic for themselves. The last and greatest of these manifestoes was Tom Paine's *The Rights of Man* of 1791–92, in which, with furiously concentrated energy, Paine compelled his readers to imagine an age back of the musty talk of Saxon rights and the Ancient Constitution, when there were no kings, gentlemen, land engrossment, or anything but the pure, equal birthrights of men.[30]

The counterattack on popular English radicalism, when it was unleashed in the 1790s, was thorough and savage. The constitutional societies were broken up, their leaders jailed or mobbed, Paine hanged in effigy, and bonfires stoked with *The Rights of Man*. By the end of the decade the back of the movement had been broken and its slogans repressed. The words of the victors were

Burke's. The British constitution—king, Parliament, corruption, and all—went back time out of mind. To hunt before that for the rights of man, "in all the nakedness and solitude of metaphysical abstraction," was (Burke warned) destructive of every sort of political society.[31]

Efficient as the repression was, it did not fully succeed in eradicating talk of Natural Rights from British political life. Paine, outlawed and execrated, continued to be read and to cast a formidable shadow over the next generation of artisan radicals. At Chartist rallies in the 1830s and 1840s men toasted his birthday and reiterated his slogans. Through Herbert Spencer a severely amputated remnant of the radical language of the 1770s came to lodge on the conservative side of the political spectrum in the vocabulary of late nineteenth-century antistatist individualism. Even as late as the 1890s, J. A. Hobson could still remark on the presence in his lectures of "a certain little knot of men of the lower-middle or upper-working class, men of grit and character, largely self-educated, keen citizens, mostly nonconformists in religion" who talked of land reform as a "natural right."[32] But this was the language of the backwaters and eddies, not of the mainstream of British political life. In 1885, when Joseph Chamberlain lapsed briefly into an appeal to the natural rights of man, John Morley, the Liberal centrist, professed himself as dismayed as if he had seen a dinosaur "shambling down Parliament Street."[33] No British Thermidor could extinguish the grievances or hopes on which popular radicalism flourished. But repression could blunt some of its rhetorical weapons, devalue its rallying cries, strip its slogans of a measure of legitimacy, and leave them crippled as the dialect of a class or cultural fragment.

Thermidor in America was a gentler affair. But in America, too, even before Paine's *Rights of Man* was put to the torch in England, the framers of constitutions and governments were working hard to contain the expansive rhetoric of rights, not by silencing the words but by defining and delimiting them, severing state of nature speculation from the soberer, legal word "right." The movement to consolidate the terms of the Revolution took time to gather force. In Massachusetts in 1780 and New Hampshire in 1784, the continued thrust of popular political theorizing from below produced bills of rights in which the language of rights, virtue, and original contracts swirled together in a mixture headier than one could find anywhere else in America. But after that, the quantity of abstract constitutional rhetoric into which one could thrust an unsettling, novel claim rapidly diminished.

Bills of rights proliferated in the 1790s, but none of them tried to pin down with half the theoretical precision of the Massachusetts and New Hampshire drafters the origins, the theory, or the aims of government. Nor did any of them expand the list of "natural" or "inherent" rights beyond the handful enumerated in Virginia and Pennsylvania in 1776. In 1790, when a new, conservative majority rewrote the Pennsylvania constitution, the inherent rights of man were indeed reduced by one, as the convention scrubbed the adjective "natural" from the right of expatriation. Even the injunctions to piety and justice fell sharply out of fashion as men pulled the constitutional teeth from terms as open as "virtue." After a decade of invention and efflorescence, the theoretical parts of the American state constitutions began to shrivel into sparer formulas.

The seriousness of the effort to wriggle away from the dangerously indefinite words of the 1770s was most clearly revealed not at the state level but in 1788–89 in the controversy over the formation of a federal Bill of Rights. That the men who convened in Philadelphia in 1787 to draft a federal constitution rejected the addition of a declaration of rights scarcely needs to be said—though George Mason had offered to concoct one on the spot for the purposes. When the convention's work was submitted to the Continental Congress, Richard Henry Lee tried again to engraft a bill of rights onto the document, though again without success.[34] For those who feared the creation of any new supragovernment, who sensed in the secret assembly in Philadelphia yet another cabal of power-hungry men, the absence of a declaration of rights grated hard on already inflamed suspicions.

By the time the ratification debate reached Virginia the antifederalists had begun to demand not only a substantial diminution of the national government's powers but the addition of a declaration of rights placed at the head of the constitution, distinct from that document and clearly superior to it. But in revising the Virginia Declaration of Rights for the purposes, George Mason and his antifederalist allies inadvertently revealed how much more tender men had become of the rhetoric they themselves had thrown in the teeth of the British. The Virginians now discovered, as they had not before, the rights of petition, speech and assembly, the people's right to instruct their representatives, and the right of conscientious objection to war. Pressed by the rising force of religious dissent, they elevated the free exercise of religion to a natural and inalienable right. But the insistence that the people recur frequently to "fundamental principles" was quietly abandoned. So, more dramatically, was the opening claim of 1776 that "all men" were "by nature equally free and independent," victim of the Virginians' mounting fears of antislavery talk. By the time the ratifying convention itself was through with the document, the community's right to alter or abolish government had vanished as well. The new Virginia list of rights was a consolidation of the hasty, exuberant inventions of the mid-1770s: longer, more precise, less dangerous.[35]

It fell to James Madison, though he was no friend of the effort to contain power through mere "parchment barriers," to smooth the still-contested waters by introducing a radically cut-down version of the Virginia demands into the new Congress in 1789. The bill he proposed (as "highly politic for the tranquility of the public mind, and the stability of the Government") began with a clear acknowledgment, to be placed at the very head of the Constitution, that governments derived their powers solely from the people, existed for the benefit of the people, and could be reformed or changed whenever the people chose to exercise their inalienable right to do so.[36] But most of Madison's words died in the drafting committee, and the remnant of social contract theory that survived was excised by the Senate. What came out of the first Congress of 1789 as the first ten amendments was a document, trailing at the rear of the Constitution, stripped methodically bare of every speculation about the origins of rights or the legitimacy of governments. The carefully chosen, lawyerly words have turned out, at times, to hold more power than Madison had conceived possible. But the federal Bill of Rights was hardly a manifesto comparable to the first declaration of the Virginians, much less to that other construct of 1789, hammered together in revolutionary Paris: the Declaration of the Rights of Man and the Citizen.

Yet it is an indication of how much men's minds had turned from declarations to governance that even the antifederalists, though they had labored hard for bolder words, did not greatly mourn the failure. In Congress, Aedanus Burke had complained of Madison's work as a dish of mere "whip-syllabubs, frothy and full of wind." "Rights, without having power and might, is but a shadow," Patrick Henry protested, when news of the amendments reached him.[37] To know the mechanics of power, to know how to frame an uncorruptible machinery of government was more important than to worry through the distinction between alienable and inalienable rights or to vex one's imagination with the terms under which human beings, in the fullness of their original liberties, would have consented to give up some of their natural rights for the security of laws and governments. By the 1790s, even Jefferson, the collector of so many of the sweeping political discontents of that decade, had learned to talk constitutionally, to pin even as crucial a political argument as his case against the Alien and Sedition Acts not to the rights of man but to the words of the Constitution.

Down such legal and constitutional tracks the ordinary talk of politics would flow, running roughshod where it might over claims that those still on the outside of politics had not somehow managed to wedge into the law. The notion of a reserve of *extralegal* rights had been a tool for the occasion, a crowbar to throw in the tracks of the empire. Americans in 1789 possessed vastly more rights than a quarter-century before, and they could point to them with far greater clarity. But in formalizing rights, the consolidators of the 1780s had done their best to close down the style of argument most fertile of further rights production. Men were to be induced to think, once more, soberly and legally. The state of nature, only recently discovered, was already being abandoned.

Certain Political Rituals

Shoved out of the center of political talk, however, the words were not yet exhausted. Wherever admirers of France gathered to toast the fortunes of the revolution, the term "natural" could still be found, clinging to rights as an expansive modifier. Jefferson never dropped it from his vocabulary nor ceased to wring inventive meanings from it. With much more single-minded concentration, the lawyers quickly began to mine the language of uninvadable rights for tighter defenses of private property than lay at hand in the common law. By the end of the 1790s, in a pair of judgments challenging the authority of legislatures to change their minds about property grants once having made them, the justices of the Supreme Court had granted property holders a handful of powerfully expansive dicta for the purposes. In other corners of post-Revolutionary America, the small core of rights declared in 1776 remained the focus of seriously contested argument. The rights-charged movement to abolish slavery in the northern states did not reach its climax until the turn of the nineteenth century. Definition of the inalienable rights of conscience continued to be a conflict-swept terrain long afterward.[38]

Finally there were the documents of the Revolution itself. Big with extravagant talk of rights beyond the ken of law, freighted with symbolic weight, the manifestoes of the 1770s were not easy to ignore. And yet nothing showed more clearly the force those at the center of post-Revolutionary politics sensed still smoldering in the words than the caution with which they approached the documents of their independence. The manifestoes of the 1770s endured. The public documents of the early nineteenth century are filled with lines and fragments borrowed from the first bold declarations of rights. But they endured only with their hardest parts lopped off, their Natural Rights talk whittled down to terse, laconic formulas. The radical slogans of the Revolution were reduced to rituals.

The Declaration of Independence is a special case, a document which grew in stature after the fact. Jefferson's Declaration had, in truth, cut no very large figure in 1776. Though the members of the Continental Congress took Jefferson's phrases seriously enough to debate them and to excise his remarks on slavery—interrupting the much more pressing business of the war, then a year old, to do so —the surviving letters of the delegates wasted not a word on the occasion. Even Jefferson himself did not get around to setting down the history of the Declaration until almost half a century after the fact. Unlike the state declarations of rights, Jefferson's Declaration was a legally impotent document: a declaration of rights and grievances, a document of explanation, not terribly different from all the other manifestoes on which other patriot drafting committees had worked so hard. As a political document of extraordinary power, the Declaration of Independence was constructed not in 1776 but after the fact, by uses other men would make for it.[39]

The Declaration's first active employers were the partisans of Jefferson himself. In the late 1790s, when the Declaration began to be pulled out of the mass of patriot writing as a document of much more than ordinary significance, its most avid readers were Jefferson's political allies. Eager to boost his reputation as a Founder of comparable weight to Washington and Adams, they began to magnify the importance of the Declaration and to insist on its reading at Independence Day rallies. But a consensual symbol is not easily fashioned out of a party document, and where Jefferson's political opponents were in ascendancy in the heatedly partisan climate sustained by the European wars, the Fourth of July planners took equal pains to keep the Declaration out altogether.[40]

Only in the 1820s, some fifty years after independence, as part of a hunger for tangible connections with the revolutionary past, now slipping very fast from living memory, did the Declaration finally begin to take on a life larger than the partisan rivalries of politics. With a passion as much antiquarian as political, the Americans set about resuscitating Jefferson's document, inventing for his words an importance they never had in life. John Trumbull got up a dramatically fictionalized portrait of the Declaration's signing, which toured the cities in the early 1820s. The United States government helped fuel the process by marketing facsimiles of the Declaration in preparation for the fiftieth anniversary of independence—though all of these efforts were upstaged by Providence's arrangement of the deaths of both Jefferson and Adams for sesquicentennial day itself. Drummed now into the heads of schoolchildren, read at Independence Day gatherings, distributed as keepsakes, inserted at Jefferson's own insistence into the curriculum of the University of Virginia, parodied or solemnly reenacted (as the South Carolina nullification convention contrived to do in 1832), Jefferson's document had been lodged in a position where—given the right circumstances—it might be used to make the language of Natural Rights explosive once more.[41]

Still, ritualizing the Declaration and taking its words seriously were two different matters. Even after 1826, the political centerpiece of Fourth of July celebrations was not the reading of Jefferson's Declaration but the grand oration. The giants of nineteenth-century oratory threw their most carefully polished efforts into the occasion. But as a rule they steered wide of Jefferson's Natural Rights talk. The heroics of the war, the poignant sacrifices of local heroes, the general blessings of liberty, the sanctity of the Constitution, and the promises of prosperity—these were the ritual themes. If the orators quoted Jefferson at all, they did so with the ingenious ellipses of men who recognized the Declaration for the troublesomely unpredictable instrument it was. Not until 1844 did a national political party—and at that the tiny Liberty party—try to bolster its platform slogans with a piece borrowed from the Declaration. And not until seven years after that did a state, in search of an appropriately eloquent introductory clause for its bill of rights, slip Jefferson's words into the spot.[42]

The more powerful, less easily avoidable words in the first half of the new century were George Mason's. It was the Virginia Declaration of Rights which had caught men's imaginations in prerevolutionary Paris and which, in the first half of the nineteenth century, continued to set the style for bill of rights drafting at home. In the state constitutions written between the turn of the new century and Civil War, the philosophical nakedness of the federal Bill of Rights was rarely imitated. Closer to the currents of popular political talk, the constitution drafters rarely felt their work complete—or legitimate—without an opening declaration of the origins of political authority or a restatement of the natural, original rights of man. There were exceptions, to be sure. Louisiana, steeped in its own peculiar, French-derived political traditions, came into the union with a constitution bare of any references to natural rights or original contracts; so did Minnesota (where the Democratic and Republican delegates to the constitutional convention had found so little to agree upon that they had refused to sit in the same hall together) and Michigan. In New York, lawyers fighting over the legal implications of every phrase and adjective repeatedly reduced all abstract statements of rights to rubble. In South Carolina and Georgia, nightmares of slave revolt accomplished the same result. But everywhere else the rituals of constitution making demanded the incorporation of a shred or two of the language of the Revolution in some appropriately sonorous form.

In this work familiarity was wanted, not originality. Men quarried and requarried a few of the early bills of rights for fittingly resonant formulas, passed their favorite fragments from convention to convention, altering them rarely, carrying them along the sectionally marked paths of westward migration. The preamble to the Massachusetts constitution of 1780 had a particular currency in states settled by New Englanders. Lines carved out of Mason's work were carried deep into the South and (by way of their early incorporation into the Pennsylvania constitution) the Middle West. But if the pattern of borrowing was predictable, the pattern of omissions— once one lays the trite, formulaic words out on a map to find it— is a dramatic sign of the unsettling power the words retained. Lopping off what frightened them most in the language of the 1770s, the constitution writers produced not a consensual creed but two strikingly different formulas—rent down the line of section.

The process began with the South's headlong retreat from the assertion with which the Virginia Declaration of Rights had opened: that men had inherent rights to life, liberty, property, happiness, and safety. Spread through its reiteration in the Pennsylvania bill of rights, the formula became a commonplace of northern constitutional rhetoric. But outside a broken rim of border states—Delaware, Florida, Arkansas, and Virginia itself—fear that the words might endanger slave property caused southern constitution drafters to shy hard away from any such open, general statements of natural rights.[43] In the slave South, the inherent rights of man were almost immediately cut down to two: the right of conscience and (still more prominently) the right of revolution. The rest of Mason's rhetoric was snuffed out in quick, barely disguised panic.

While southerners clamped down on loose talk of rights, in the North it was revolution—the notion that the state was a mere contract, voluntarily made and (when necessary) abolished—that made the constitution writers nervous. John Adams had written the point eloquently into the Massachusetts constitution of 1780. But after the 1780s, northern references to the "social contract" shriveled so fast as to leave the term an exclusive mark of southern bill of rights writing. Still more revealing was the speed with which the northern constitution drafters, starting with the redrafting of the Vermont constitution in 1786, began to squirm away from such hard words as the right to "abolish" or (as Adams had put it) "totally change" their governments. In the South, the dream of dissolving political society into its constituent atoms whenever its (free, white) contractors deemed it oppressive remained live enough to make the constitution drafters cherish the word "abolish." But in the vast majority of the northern states organized after 1789, the conventions retreated to such words as "alter" or "reform"; and after the Missouri crisis of 1820 loosed the specter of national disintegration, no new northern state risked calling even the right of reforming one's government a "natural" or "inalienable" right.[44]

For anyone with a sensitive ear for the accents of section, these events were reason for worry. In North and South a common rhetoric was being stretched over increasingly divergent purposes. In the North, if the formulaic, constitutional clauses were to be believed, natural rights inhered in the citizens as individual liberties. In the South, the hard core meaning of Natural Rights was a collective right: the revolutionary right to begin political society over again. Down the lines of slavery and section the phrases of the Revolution were rent.

But North and South, the common phenomenon was a skittering for safer verbal contrivances. Public documents and ceremonies like these caught only a sliver of the common talk of politics, to be sure, but they tell their own revealing tale. Unwilling on such occasions to let the words go, men chopped them up, encased them in formulas, wedged apart talk of rights and talk of social contracts, and amputated the phrases that smelled most strongly to them of anarchy; they memorized the words, incorporated them into the rituals of patriotism, bowdlerized them. Not until the words escaped the constitution drafting committees and the Independence Day orators, not until they met a new set of grievances, far from the ken of the political elites, did the language of Natural Rights gain its second wind.

Revival

The revival of Natural Rights talk, when it occurred, came once more from below and outside the mainstream of politics. This time the users of the words were not patriot writers at the rims of an empire but persons on the margins of power at home: slavery opponents, feminists, and, most importantly, workingmen. In the second quarter of the nineteenth century they broke the language of Natural Rights out of its encasements and made it once more the stuff of manifestoes—protean and inventive.

Through what threads of repetition and memory the claims of natural rights were sustained in artisan America between the collapse of the French Revolution and the revival of workingmen's politics in the 1820s is a story still waiting to be told. But by the late 1820s, when workingmen's organizations began to spring up once more in the cities, it is clear that artisan radicals were at the forefront of the revival of the radical language of the Revolution. When Alexis de Tocqueville reached Albany, New York, on July 4, 1831, it was the printers who had hoisted a handpress onto a wagon to make copies of the Declaration of Independence for the crowd, most of them mechanics themselves. Everywhere the new spokesmen for artisan politics insisted on rights, *equal rights,* rights earned on the battlegrounds of the Revolutionary War only to be stolen away by new-style moneyed despots and the new-style tyranny of wage labor. As Edward Pessen wrote, with only slight exaggeration, "To read the many statements made by the Jacksonian labor leaders is to be back in the world, not of the nineteenth, but of the eighteenth century," when men still talked as if the doctrines of Jefferson, Locke, and Paine "were original with them or, at the least, of recent origin, put forth only yesterday or the day before." In antebellum America, this was where talk of the rights of man was in strongest ferment.[45]

The old words took their force in the 1820s and 1830s from an economic world that was painfully new. In every commercial center of considerable size, unfamiliar sorts of middlemen, equipped with a hold on the supplies of raw materials and loans of capital, had begun to elbow their way into the economics of production. The old relations between journeymen and master craftsmen—never easy, full of tension over the masters' claims to paternal authority, but made tolerable partly by familiarity, partly by the journeymen's hopes of eventually starting up as master craftsmen on their own —gave way to a greater subdivision of tasks, a deeper cleavage between the possessors of capital and the possessors of mere labor, and increasingly blatant manifestations of the assumption that labor, priced now by wages, was a market commodity like any other. To these injuries were added insults of another sort: a sudden proliferation of banks, where men fortunate enough to have gotten hold of cash, connections, and a legislative charter were able to make money out of the mere possession of influence and money; and an unstable credit network already extensive and fragile enough in 1837 to give working-class Americans their first taste of a full-scale economic depression. Add to that, finally, the extension of the vote to men without property, so that the enhancement of one's political status and the degradation of one's economic lot came hard upon each other, like bumper-riding events, and the result was a volatile one.

Little wonder, then, that in the seaboard cities the newly organized artisans' and journeymen's organizations began to boil over with manifestoes. Nor that the manifesto writers should have taken over the stock formulas of the Fourth of July to describe themselves as common men, beset once more by a horde of distant, rapacious aristocrats. The language of eighteenth-century "republicanism," charged as before with angry talk of unchecked power and moral corruption and stoked with outrage at the chasm between the interests of the few and the commonweal of the many, flourished once more in the workingmen's movement.[46] With no other set of words in post-Revolutionary America could one talk about inequality and exploitation with a better chance of wringing sympathy from beyond one's trade and class. Power, luxury, betrayal of republican principles—this was the rhetoric of outrage. But, as in the 1770s, the language of *demands* was that of rights.

Being new sorts of persons, the artisan radicals could not but make the language of rights new in appropriating it. The cry of *equal rights* was an example: a slogan as old as the assault on special privilege that it encapsulated, a staple of radical Painite oratory worn trite enough for even John Quincy Adams to drop it into his inaugural address in 1825.[47] But within a decade, fueled by Jackson's bank war, workingmen's groups were using the words to assail the economic institutions so dear to Adams—banks, paper money, and chartered corporations—on the grounds that their privileged legal status could not stand up against the principle of equal rights. Where property barriers to the suffrage still endured, workingmen's orators turned the slogan into a demand for the equal right of men to vote. Land reformers pushed the cry still further into a demand for *"equal means"* to rights—equal access to the "rightful means of sustenance, education and happiness"—in phrases that were to rattle through the platforms of late nineteenth-century socialism.[48]

For the moment, however, the most volatile claims spun off from that outwardly most sober and conservative of the natural rights: the rights of property. The leaders of the colonial resistance had employed the words to defend their goods against the depredations of tax collectors and customs men; the lawyers had picked them up to defend vested property rights against the whims of legislatures. Now in the face of exploitation of a radically different sort, the phrase was transformed into a cry *for* property: for a man's birthright share of the common land and the full value of his labor. Thomas Skidmore, the tribune of thoroughgoing property redistribution, never forgave Jefferson for substituting something so ephemeral as the pursuit of happiness for the harder, specific right of human beings to property, in the equal shares in which mankind had first received it. Closer to everyday artisan experience, working-class radicals used the language of Natural Rights to assail the power of employers to dictate the terms of wage labor. Did we not, a Boston manifesto of 1835 declared, have a "Natural Right to dispose of our own time in such quantities as we deem to be most conducive to our own happiness, and the welfare of all those engaged in Manual Labor?" Did not "all who toil have a natural and unalienable right to reap the fruits of their own industry?" Time and labor power were the workingman's property. How in justice could he be required to give them up except under terms that would ensure their fair equivalent? Like Paine's progeny in England, working-class radicals raked over Locke's notion of the natural, prepolitical status of property for its subversive elements, seeking to wrest the claims of right from the holders of unnatural property and make them their own. "The *personal* exertions of each individual of the human race are exclusively and unalienably his own," Skidmore insisted. When land was monopolized and labor sold for a pittance, a person was not simply poor; he was not a victim of natural economic laws; he was a man dispossessed.[49]

In the late 1820s and 1830s, when the antebellum labor movement was at the peak of its intellectual energies, only a few of the manifesto writers joined explicit appeal to the state of nature to their fusillade of natural rights. Tom Paine's axiom that "the condition of every person born into the world, after a state of civilization commences, ought not to be worse than if he had been born before that period," already had a musty, antiquated sound.[50] But the underlying retrospective theme of dispossession was little changed. What gave the adjective "natural" its power was, as before, the workingmen's sense of massive contradiction between what now was, and what, in the infancy of God's design, must have been. Poverty was an artifice, a cruel mockery of the original largesse of nature. The point lay at the very heart of the land reformers' creed that God had given the earth, not to a few, but to "the great community of men," as a collective commons open to all. Skidmore ultimately concluded that there was "no remedy but by commencing anew," voiding the lines men had scratched on the "great estate of . . . the Supreme Being," and dividing property up, into its equal, original shares, all over again. More conventional Jacksonian radicals talked of restoring "the simple order of nature."[51] In their minds' eye they constructed a world prior to wage labor and poverty, a world of equal rights and reasonably equal wealth, uncorrupted by banks, wage slavery, moneyed aristocrats, or chartered privileges—a state of nature in all but the name.

Antebellum society was too deeply saturated with racism for most of the authors of the working-class declarations of rights to recognize the much more massive dispossession entailed in outright slavery. Open attack on the southern institution of slavery— still no bigger than a hand against the sky in the 1830s—came from a different quarter. But it, too, reverberated with a reborn rhetoric of rights. Swept as abolitionism was by the mandates of divine governance, its relationship to the rhetoric of the Revolution was always (as we shall later see) strained and unstable. But the abolitionists rarely missed a chance to assail slavery as a violation of a person's inalienable right to liberty, to the products of his labor, to the possession of his very self. If they harbored an enduring distrust of Jefferson—for his infidelity, his slaves, and his politics—they took Jefferson's Declaration as inspired writ. The workingmen's borrowings from the rhetoric of the Revolution had been eclectic and inventive. The abolitionists, in contrast, concentrated on the Declaration of Independence with the intensity of scriptural literalists. No other political movement of the nineteenth century worked more zealously to break Jefferson's words out of their ritualized frame, to insist on their superiority to ordinary law, even to the Constitution itself—to slip them into the emptiness where a genuinely philosophical bill of rights should have been.[52]

That the Declaration was legally superior to the Constitution was, to be sure, a historical fiction, as wild and subversive as the fiction of a state of nature. But to the abolitionists, badly in need of tools with which to hack away at the protective coil of ordinary law wound around slavery, the transcendent status of the Declaration was an indispensable point of faith. "We plant ourselves upon the Declaration of our Independence and the truths of Divine Revelation, as upon the Everlasting Rock," the organizers of the American Antislavery Society declared at its founding in 1833.[53] From the abolitionist press, from a score of northern black conventions, the same appeal could be heard. When the abolitionists took to politics in the 1840s, they stuffed Jefferson's inalienable rights passage into the Liberty party platform; when William Lloyd Garrison, disgusted with politics, set a match to the Constitution, he chose a July Fourth on which to do it.

So tightly did the abolitionists wed radical antislavery talk to the words of the Declaration of Independence that when abolitionism spilled over into a movement for the rights of woman as well as the rights of man, nineteenth-century feminist leaders took Jefferson's document with them as a matter of course. For the rest of the century, talk of inalienable, "human rights" and flagrant dispossession ran hard through the women's rights movement. Elizabeth Cady Stanton hung the Seneca Falls demands on the Declaration's frame. Others stripped it over and again for usable slogans: the consent of the governed, the equal creation of humankind, the rights of women to the possessions and powers which were "sacredly and inalienably hers."[54]

The rush of Free Soilers into the antislavery ranks in the late 1840s, filling it with men far more agitated by the status of free labor than the lot of black slaves, threatened to swamp the early rhetoric of abolitionism in appeals for a white man's masterless West. In 1860, Jefferson's "certain inalienable rights" passage squeaked through the Republican party convention only on a motion to reconsider and the wings of George W. Curtis's eloquence. But even in its last phase, there were many in the antislavery cause who clung to the rhetoric of inherent, extralegal rights. Lincoln's claim, on the eve of assuming the presidency, that "I have never had a feeling politically that did not spring from the sentiments embodied in the Declaration of Independence," was a pious exaggeration.[55] But George Julian mined the intentions of the creator with a confidence little short of Paine's. Charles Sumner talked of "equal rights" with the repetition of a hiccup. And Lincoln himself brandished Jefferson's Declaration at Stephen Douglas in the debates of 1858 as if it were a broadsword of truth.

Eager for words with which to express their newborn anger and outrage, working-class radicals and antislavery agitators had seized the rights-filled language of the 1770s and injected new life into the formula-ridden words. They had joined the phrases to a fusillade of new grievances, let imaginations loose once more on the terms of original creation. It was in the nature of the abstract, open language of the Revolution that it remained bendable to new employments: that it could cover even so radical a pair of crusades as the wholesale destruction of wage labor and slave property with a veneer of respectability. British Chartists, struggling for shreds of legitimacy, had no resource like it.

And yet it would be a mistake to think that by the middle of the century talk of Natural Rights had finally been domesticated. Lincoln, out of office in 1858, spoke for those still on the edges of power. His abstractions remained the language of outsiders, not of inside maneuverers as smooth and practiced as Douglas. Rights, to be sure, were a dime a dozen in the common lawyer's jargon. But talk of *natural rights*—rights older than political society but so deeply violated by it that one had to think one's way out of the existing frame of law and customs, back to the conditions of creation before the loss became self-evident—this was a tool designed to cover the agitator's legal and practical nakedness, the novelty of his claims, and their nullity before the courts of ordinary law. "All honor to Jefferson," Lincoln declared in 1859, "to the man who in the concrete pressure of a struggle for national independence by a single people, had the coolness, forecast, and capacity to introduce into a merely revolutionary document, an abstract truth."[56] Abstraction was, indeed, the heart of the technique: the elevation of practical claims into the higher stuff of rights, longing into a palpably imaginable state of nature, mere pain into dispossession. The trick hinged on a capacity for imaginative retrospection and a certain confidence in the Creator. Granted that, it was as powerful a tool for the articulation of grievances as the political culture afforded.

Little wonder that those on the inside of Revolutionary politics had hoped so dearly to lock the words up. Little wonder that in the nineteenth century—with the grievances of outsiders sharp once more, with the Liberty party insisting that it was no upstart movement but "the party of 1776," with workingmen's agitators likening the rapacities of their employers to the rapacities of eighteenth-century excise men, with the words of the first Revolution at hand, glitteringly abstract, as common stock for anyone with a second revolution in mind—conservative Americans would be eager to do so once more.

"The doctrine of natural rights was . . . the hard core of Revolutionary political theory," Clinton Rossiter wrote years ago.[57] There is a measure of truth to that, though not the one Rossiter intended. Invented, taken up, formalized, then reinvented once more, the language of Natural Rights had been the central subversive strain in American political life. But from the first, its history was played out against a still stronger, countervailing impulse to organize political society, divide and balance its pieces, tinker with its constitutional machinery. Yoked as it was to a vision of a prepolitical fund of rights, Natural Rights talk had done little to clarify what the uses of that artificial thing called government might be; how it should be organized; who should rule the government of a republic; whose government, indeed, it was. In the first century after independence, Americans argued those questions out with another, equally massive abstraction, pulled out of the arguments of the Revolution, called the People. This time the conflict roiled political talk, not at its edges, but at its center.

3

The People

Mechanics and Majorities

We, *the people.* The edge of the words is duller now than that of rights. It buoys for the moment no crusades. No very advanced course in skepticism is required to see that in modern democracies the people do not rule—not in any straightforward way—except through courtesy of a massive figure of speech. Indeed the words were a figure of speech when the framers of the Constitution set them down: vague and deliberately laconic. But of all things political metaphors do, one of the most serious is to pin down in a word or a slogan the ownership of politics. Does the state belong to the king? Or to a caste or ruling party? To the propertied or to everyone? Given the indefiniteness of the word "belong," the point amounts, at one level, to a verbal riddle—an intensely charged question without (as Bentham might have complained) any conceivably definite answer. But as words employed in a battle for admission to politics, for control over its offices, or for power over its policies, the notion of the ownership of the state is a fiction of a deadly earnest sort.

Post-Revolutionary America belonged to the people; the terms entered the constitutional lexicon at independence. Through the carefully balanced machinery of their constitutions the people ruled. But acquiescence in that covered over massive disagreements. The moments in which the term the People has swelled with power are those in which Americans have chafed hardest at their constitutions. Its moments of currency have been our sporadic moments of democratization—Andrew Jackson's era, the Populists', Franklin Roosevelt's, or Tom Hayden's—when the many with a foot in the gates of politics have tried to sweep out the complicated, power-distributing, constitutional machinery they found in their way in favor of simpler, more straightforward engines of the popular will. Even more than Natural Rights, the People has been a term of power —and hence of conflict.

The survivors of the first era of constitution making knew as much when they heard it in the 1820s. John Adams and James Madison were the grand old men of constitutional politics then. In an age of political deference, deference was still their due. John Adams was eighty-five years old when his Quincy neighbors sent him by acclamation as their delegate to the Massachusetts constitutional convention of 1820. When he entered the convention hall in Boston, the delegates swept off their hats and would have named him their presiding officer had Adams felt strong enough to accept the responsibility. Failing that, they voted to seat him at the chairman's right hand, the better to watch over and legitimate their work, as they took their state constitution—the one Adams himself had drafted, virtually single-handedly in 1779—and prepared to overhaul it for another generation's service. Madison slipped into the Virginia convention of 1829–30 with much less conspicuous homage. His coat threadbare with age, his dress and powdered hair markedly out of fashion, he seemed to the younger delegates something of an antique. He spoke little in the open convention, but the chairmanship of the convention's most important committee fell to him as his due. And when he did rise in the general sessions, the delegates rushed forward in a ring around the old man, not only to hear his whispered words but to honor the man and the political generation he represented.[1]

Adams and Madison were no mere relics in the 1820s, akin to the bent veterans of the Revolutionary armies, pushed forward at Independence Day celebrations for a moment's fleeting homage. Statesmen, presidents, political theorists of no mean ambition and experience, they had done more between them to invent the science of constitutional mechanics than any other two men of the Revolutionary generation. They had not, like that quintessential outsider, Thomas Paine, pinned the science of politics to rights—though both men cared passionately about the rights of property and Madison about the rights of conscience. They represented the mainstreams of post-independence talk: an obsession with the machinery of government, with the efficient division of power into a complicated set of semi-antagonistic agencies. Government, Adams would go home to Quincy to write once again, was "a complicated piece of machinery, the nice and exact adjustment of whose springs, wheels, and weights" held the secret of public liberty.[2] Power was to be checked and balanced by countervailing powers so that no small faction of men, no fleeting majority, not even the people as a whole could ever seize full hold of their governments and bend them, unchecked, to their will.

What Adams and Madison witnessed, rising out of the back rows in Boston and Richmond, however, were men speaking a radically different, majoritarian language. In Massachusetts "the lovers of the people," as their opponents caustically described them, gave none of the celebrated orations of the convention. If the record is to be believed, they found it easier to vote their convictions than to elaborate them against the opposing ranks of lawyers and college graduates or against John Adams's own reminder of what an unchecked majority had accomplished in revolutionary Paris. But the popular party had members enough to come within a hairsbreadth of wiping out the complicated property qualifications which had constrained popular political influence in Massachusetts since independence.[3]

Nine years later in Virginia the popular party had found its tongue. Westerners from the Shenandoah Valley and beyond, bitterly resentful of the political hegemony of the tidewater planters and the inequitable apportionment scheme on which their hegemony rested, they arrived equipped with an eloquent, articulate majoritarianism. "A *majority of the community* possesses, by the law of nature and necessity, a right to control its concerns," John Cooke insisted for them. This was "a great political truth, a self-evident proposition; the primary postulate of the science of Government." The eastern planters decried this appeal to abstractions; they pleaded the necessity for "poising and balancing all [the] interests" of the state; they demanded the provenance of this new "principle of numbers." In the moment so charged with symbolic drama that the delegates afterward could not shake it from their memories, John Randolph—wraithlike in physical frame, possessor of a tempestuous temper and massive plantation holdings, the very caricature of Virginia's slaveholding oligarchy—rose in a torrent of words to defy the pretensions of the new "King Numbers."[4] In Virginia, as in Massachusetts, the men of property and influence beat back the challenges of those who spoke for sheer numbers. But the term of the moment, swelling with new power, was the People: the "dear, dear people," the sovereign people, the unfiltered, unbalanced, unchecked will of the greatest number.

The words have not commonly sat well with political historians. Thoroughgoing majoritarianism, it is still often said, has been alien to the mainstreams of American politics. Home-grown Rousseaus, talking of the unfettered collective will, we are alleged to have been too commonsensical and practical a nation to have produced. Such is the talk of other revolutionary nations, not of ours. But here, for the moment, rising fast enough to rattle the axioms of Madison's and Adams's political science, were the slogans of the general will in full force.

That moment, measured with the approximateness that "moments" of political talk demand, endured another forty years. The cry of the people's sovereignty was the rhetorical tool with which the partisans of mid-nineteenth-century democracy broke apart the deference politics and much of the political machinery of Madison's and Adams's day and inaugurated a new era of popular politics. With it, men democratized government, pried open its offices, ventilated its constitutional machinery, and mobilized fiercely partisan masses of white, male voters. The words moved from the back benches, where they had burst upon Adams and Madison, into the rhetoric of Andrew Jackson's Democratic party, which built its fortunes on their claims. They flooded the floor of every state constitutional convention from the 1820s through the end of Reconstruction, transforming that moribund institution, leaving behind a sea of words spilled in conflict over the people's power and identity. By the 1840s, when the Democratic party's opponents, sensing the dangers and the possibilities in the slogan, tried to co-opt and nationalize it, talk of the people's sovereign will had risen to earsplitting volume.

But to pin the democratization of politics to the sovereignty of the people was to pin it to a verbal contrivance which proved unstable and difficult to contain. To follow the career of the term the People is to watch men invest a word with extraordinary meaning and then, losing hold of it to other claimants, scuttle from the consequences. By the midpoint of the century, with new holders of the slogan (women, free blacks, and slaves) demanding to be counted among the people, with men talking more and more seriously of a house divided into two sectionally rival peoples, the words had begun to turn double-edged and dangerous. Stephen Douglas, struggling to make the dictum of popular sovereignty resolve the accelerating crisis over slavery and section, could not escape the consequences of the battering the words had taken. By the time the Populists, much later, tried to seize the words for new purposes, they had long since given out as the driving force in politics—a casualty of the slavery crisis, war, and a determined counterattack on the fiction of the people's rule. No political term with as powerful a history as the People disappears; their moment past, such words remain lodged in the patterns of speech, open (with luck) for new tasks and occasions. But in mid-nineteenth-century America, swelling with new claims of popular democracy, talk of the People runs an arc, as spectacular in its ascent as in its crippled fall.

Popular Sovereignty

The terms themselves were old; it was the radicalness of their employment that made them new. *Vox populi, vox Dei* had done heroic service in the religious wars of Reformation Europe long before the young George Bancroft—elated at the "radical, democratic, levelling, unrighteous oration" he had just written—hurled the words at the Massachusetts political establishment in 1826.[5] As for the notion of the people as the basic constituent power, that came with the very definition of a republic. Sweep out a king, stifle the growth of a formal aristocracy, and, given the political categories eighteenth-century Americans had inherited, there was no candidate for their authority other than the people. The constitution drafters in 1776 had worked quickly to nail the point home. "All power is vested in, and consequently derived from, the people," the Virginia Declaration of Rights had proclaimed. Political power was "originally inherent" in the people, the eighteenth-century constitution writers insisted; it "originated from" the people, existed solely for the people's benefit.

The still more precise term "sovereignty" was likewise an inheritance, a legal-political axiom fixed in the vocabulary of the Revolutionary generation well before independence. In every state, as Blackstone had put it, "there must be . . . a supreme, irresistible, absolute, uncontrolled authority in which . . . the rights of sovereignty reside."[6] The leaders of the colonial resistance might have been expected to repudiate so Tory-like a notion. But partly because they had invested so many words in a wrangle over sovereignty's location, partly because the idea of law seemed untenably fragile without the notion of a sovereign lawmaker, the political writers absorbed the term, knocking off its Tory crust by investing what belonged elsewhere to kings and parliaments in the people at large. The king was dead, but his power endured; in republics, sovereignty devolved on the people.

The constitutional point did not, to be sure, quiet the acute, nervous controversies surrounding the term. To most of the Revolutionary elite, fearful of the popular political mobilization set in motion by the anti-imperial resistance, the people were a fickle entity, not fully to be trusted. Among nascent Federalists, like John Trumbull, ran an undisguised anguish at the prospect that "the bar and bench and steeple [should] submit t' our Sovereign Lord, The People." So self-evident was the logic of antimonarchialism, however, that even patriots who shuddered at the term "democracy" absorbed a formal obeisance to the people into their language without a trace of embarrassment. James Wilson, as distrusted by the crowd as any man in Revolutionary America, staked his reputation as a legal writer to a demonstration that in every society the "supreme sovereign power" resided in the people. John Adams, in a crescendo of adjectives which echoed the way New Englanders had liked to speak of God, wrote that "all intelligence, all power, all force, all authority, originally, inherently, necessarily, inseparably, and inalienably resides in the people." The Massachusetts constitutional convention of 1779 distilled the point into the phrase, "We, the people," from which it was lifted by the drafters of the federal Constitution—meeting in as effectively contrived seclusion from the people as any deliberative body in America has achieved—to tack onto their handiwork.[7]

The people reigned, but in post-Revolutionary America the political elites made sure they did not rule. Virtually everywhere the powers of majorities were carefully broken up. The legislatures were divided in two, so that the many and the few could more effectively check the vicious designs of each other. The offices of government, closed to all but a fraction of the citizens by special property requirements, were buffered still further by mechanisms of appointment and indirect election designed to refine the people's will and elevate their raw judgment. Even in the election of their representatives, a part of the people spoke for the people as a whole. In the influential words of the Virginia Declaration of Rights, the vote belonged to "all men, having sufficient evidence of permanent common interest with, and attachment to, the community." In practice, that encompassed those Americans, male and white, with enough property that they could not wield the most dangerous weapon of the state, the power of taxation, without nicking their own purses in the process. Even they were federalized, dismembered into rival political bodies, so that no one could pretend to speak for the general will of the whole. "The men who first promoted popular government" in late eighteenth-century America, Edmund Morgan writes, "did not think they were striving for a government by the many over the many." The men of property and status had vested sovereignty in the people, but "they intended to speak for a sovereign but silent people" just as divine right kings had pretended to speak "for a sovereign but silent God."[8]

Only in one extraordinary political act—the popular ratification of their constitutions—was the slogan of the people's sovereignty joined to a deed reflecting the grandeur of the words. Forced into practice from below by the pressures of local town meetings in Massachusetts in 1778 and New Hampshire in 1779 simmering in resentment at their legislatures and reiterated in the specially elected conventions called to serve judgment on the federal Constitution of 1787, the ratification election marked a devolution of authority downward—if not to the people, at least to the electorate. In a world unaccustomed to plebiscites, it was a bold and original invention. Here, it is often said, the popular, democratic forces set in motion by the Revolution found at last their culmination.[9]

What is not nearly as often pointed out, however, is that after the first, hazardous experience with constitutional plebiscites, the framers of American politics abandoned the gesture in ill-disguised haste. In New Hampshire, four different constitutions had to be sent to the people between 1779 and 1783 before the voters finally found one to their liking. The federal Constitution did not suffer so rude a fate, but its ratification in 1788 was a near thing, close enough to dissuade eighteenth-century politicians from trying such a scheme again. Not for another quarter of a century, in 1812, did a state outside New England risk sending a constitution to the voters for their approval. And not for a quarter of a century more, in the late 1830s, did the popular ratification of state constitutions finally become the unspoken rule. In the first half-century after independence, thirty-four state constitutions were put into effect, only six of them through a vote of the people; outside New England, only two had been popularly ratified.[10]

Unwillingness to hazard a ratification election did not mean that the constitution-writing bodies were indifferent to the people's will. Most of them, after 1789, consisted of men directly and especially elected to their tasks, presumably with some notion of what their constituents wanted. To make doubly sure, many states invented some sort of machinery to test their work against the currents of popular opinion. Georgia in 1788–89 created three separate conventions: an initial, appointed body to draft the constitution, a second, elected body to revise the first convention's work, and yet another elected convention to ratify the final document. The Pennsylvania constitutional convention of 1789–90, more simply, took a long recess to test the public waters before reconvening to adjust its work and proclaim it fundamental law.[11] Here then, not in the risky gesture of 1787–88 but in the assumption that the people's power was best exercised indirectly—that public opinion spoke most truly when it was filtered and refined through the complex machinery of representation—here was the mainstream of American politics, the world in which Adams and Madison were still at home.

When the slogan of the people's sovereignty was broken out of these constraints in the 1820s, it was by radically different sorts of men than had drafted the terse, eighteenth-century constitutional acknowledgments of the people's sovereignty. The words rose to power in the hands of those whom Andrew Jackson styled the "real people": men of little property, shut out of the early political arrangements of power, farmers and petty planters in the malapportioned back counties, debtors far from the seats of legal justice, urban mechanics grown restless with the politics of deference and the injuries of merchant capitalism. Most of them had already wedged their way into the electorate by the mid-1820s, when the friends of the people first got their tongues around their most effective rallying cry. By then most of the early barriers to the suffrage had been dismantled, down to the last, crucial stile of white manhood suffrage.[12] The cry of the People—"the real, actual, living sovereignty of the people"—was launched by men already enfranchised, in an effort to clear away the remaining constitutional restrictions on popular influence, to seize government for themselves and grasp a power commensurate with their numbers. In 1821, from the popular faction at the New York constitutional convention, one could already hear complaints that the doctrine of checks and balances, suited as it might be for constitutional monarchies, was out of place where the people ruled. Their successors in 1846, now coalesced into the Democratic party, sneered at the notion of "checks and guards" on the people's will as thoroughly exploded political doctrine.[13] The offices of government were to be thrown open to all comers, without restrictions of property; the apportionment schemes, by which the wealthy preserved their hold on the legislatures, were to be torn down; the early cumbersome machinery of appointment was to be dismantled, and governors, sheriffs, coroners, court clerks, and—in the very eye of antebellum party controversy—state judges made creatures of direct elections and straightforward majorities. "The first principle of our system," Andrew Jackson thundered, still smarting from his experience in 1824 with the verdicts of indirect democracy, is this: *"that the majority is to govern.*"[14] The crucial act of politics was no longer (as political theorists had always imagined it to be) that of governance or legislation but the reading of the popular will, when the people spoke at election.

Turned loose in a constitutional convention, talk of the People served as a powerful instrument of constitutional dismantlement; on the stump the same words formed a powerful language of mobilization. When the languishing business of elections intensified in a surge of voters to the polls in the 1820s and 1830s, spinning off the first modern, tightly organized political parties, national in scope, locked in contest not for the elites but for the electoral masses, the appeal to the majesty, the wisdom, and the will of the people was at the heart of the new-style electioneering. It gave the men massed in party rallies an identity bigger than mere partisanship. Just as importantly, once the marginal victory had been won, it transformed a majority into something more exalted than mere numbers—into a mandate, an utterance of the people's mind. It was no accident that the first president to break decisively from the Inaugural Day custom of attributing his election to some modestly, abstractly stated call of Providence and his fellow citizens and declare that he had been swept into office by "the will of the American people" was Andrew Jackson, back from the bruising partisan battle over his bank policies in 1832.[15] Nor was it an accident that the master of presidential flattery of the people's wisdom was that consummate engineer of partisan coalitions, Martin Van Buren. The rhetoric of a sovereign people, possessed of unitary will, and the practice of partisan political mobilization were two sides of the same phenomenon.

The cry of the people's sovereignty rang most intensely through the antebellum Democratic party. To party orators and journalists the words held protean uses. They hurled them against the old presumptions of deference and the barriers to popular political influence, against the Whig proclivity toward energetic (and expensive) government, against the monstrously bloated power of the banks and moneyed corporations, feeding (so they feared) on the honest labor of the people.[16]

Had Jackson's and Van Buren's opponents been more rigid men, they might have abandoned talk of the People to the sort of men they often scorned as mere "lovers of popularity." Fear of "mobocracy," like mockery of the sort of gentleman who professed himself moved only by affection for the "dear people," never went wholly out of style among Whig orators. But most Whigs quickly learned the advantages of compromise and co-optation. Well before the Whig managers of William Henry Harrison's Log Cabin campaign of 1840 launched national politics into a new world of democratic ballyhoo, local Whig boosters were touting their men as the true candidates of "the people."[17] After 1840, the campaign style of both parties ran openly and unashamedly toward the politics of numbers. Political mobilization meant the assembling of party adherents in a series of mass assemblies, monster parades, songs, marches, torchlight spectacles, crowds of listeners glued together by prodigious quantities of oratory—all of them trial runs at a final, electoral majority.[18]

Thrust to the fore by men who saw in the cry of the people's rule a lever with which to pry apart the complicated constitutional machinery of the eighteenth-century republics, honed to its sharpest in the antebellum Democratic party, taken up in defense by the Democrats' opponents, the rhetoric of the people's sovereignty was wedged into the controversial center of political talk. To catch the words in full flood, one could have done worse than to slip into the public gallery of the constitutional convention which convened in Richmond twenty years after Madison's convention had disbanded. The issues which faced the Virginia convention of 1850–51 were almost identical to those of 1829–30. Once more the delegates faced each other across massive, enduring disproportions in political power between the plantation-dominated east and the farms and settlements west of the Blue Ridge Mountains. Once more the eastern planters insisted on the "absolute necessity" of checks on the majority will, lest the people, in a moment of derangement, begin to tamper with slaves or property. But this time the dynamics of the convention were different. Already in 1841, Abel Upshur, who had helped lead the planters' successful counterassault on majoritarianism in 1829–30, was protesting that the doctrines of his generation had been swept aside as political "heresy." When in the convention itself, planter Samuel Chilton tried to invoke the prestige of John Locke on behalf of "mixed government"—that is to say, government in which both property and persons would be represented—he found himself taunted by his fellow Whig, John M. Botts, to tell the convention if he would dare invoke Locke's name on the hustings. His constituents would demand to know who this man Locke might be, Botts sneered, and what he knew of Virginia, or of popular government:

I did not come here to study the science of government. The science of government—I mean a popular one—is just now beginning to develop itself. . . . I believe we are a different people from any other that ever did live, or ever will live on the face of the earth. I believe that this Anglo Saxon race of people in the United States of America are the only people ever formed by the hand of God, that are capable of self-government. And believing this, I shall endeavor to make a constitution for the people of the present day, and not for the people of the days of John Locke.[19]

This was oratorical bluster of the most transparent sort. But with it Botts, a Whig "radical," pledged "to give power to the people," and Democrat Henry A. Wise (no mere radical, he boasted, but "an infinite radical" on everything concerning "the power of the sovereign people") dominated the opening weeks of the Richmond convention, floating their arguments on a sea of satire, oratorical improvisation, and grandiloquent flattery of the people. One would have been hard pressed to find better, more cartoonlike types of what Madison's generation had meant by the term "demagogue." But the function of demagogues being to squeeze out, with the blare of bagpipes, the faiths and desires suspended in the political air, their words, their style, their dramatic rush onto the political stage are worth taking at least as seriously as the counterscribblings of a John C. Calhoun seeking somehow to still the majoritarian rhetoric all around him.

The words hardened into powerful cadences. In the century's most celebrated, most memorized senatorial oration, Daniel Webster had thrown the slogan of the people's sovereignty at Robert Hayne in 1830: "It is, Sir, the people's Constitution, the people's government, made for the people, made by the people, and answerable to the people." When Webster temporized on the fugitive slave issue in 1850, Theodore Parker hurled the same phrases back at Webster himself, furious at Webster's betrayal of "a government of all the people, by all the people, for all the people." By the time Abraham Lincoln took hold of the phrase, stripping Webster's prose to its simplest, crystalline form, the words were already deeply worn with use. Daniel Hoge from backcountry Virginia had, by his own account, never spoken a word in a deliberative assembly before he got to his feet in Richmond in 1850, but his lines could have been plucked out of the air by a man with a blindfold. If the delegates proposed to set restrictions on their government, Hoge allowed, that lay in government's very nature. But "if you say restrict the people, in whom resides all sovereignty, I must reply, never! never! no, never!"[20]

Revolutionary Assemblies

The doctrine of popular sovereignty, as it emerged full blown in the second quarter of the nineteenth century, was a theory without luminous theorists. No Paine, no Burke, no Bentham emerged to formalize the slogan or to wrest it into an enduring political treatise. Here and there the partisans of popular sovereignty swiped a phrase from the giants of European political theory. The notion of the nation's "will" was lifted, indirectly, from Rousseau to be wrapped around Andrew Jackson's frame.[21] From Bentham, Jackson's partisans borrowed the dictum of the greatest good of the greatest number, accenting the *greatest number* so as to turn the phrase into a straight-out majoritarian slogan. But the eclectically appropriated phrases, the verbal whiffs of London or Geneva, fell a long way short of tangible influence.

Nor did any American theorist fully catch the convictions which fueled the mounting cry of the people's rule. George Bancroft, who of all men was best equipped to put a philosophical foundation under the democratic talk, contented himself with an essay or two and threw his energies into the writing of history. The Democratic editors, though equipped with sharp pens and strong political faiths, had too many urgent questions of policy on their minds to try their hand at a counterballast to the weighty conservative texts of a Tocqueville or Calhoun. The men of letters had, on the whole, too little sympathy, the Democratic editors too little time to play the part of theorists of the people's reign.[22]

But the rhetoric of popular democracy had a more open, accessible forum than books. Where the characteristic text for natural rights was the manifesto, the people's forum was the constitutional convention. Here the claims of the people's sovereignty were concentrated, defined, and fiercely debated. Here the champions of popular democracy and their opponents—insurgents, reactionaries, and would-be co-opters—faced each other in sustained conflict. The nature of the state, the rights of man, the authority of the people—all this, mixed with the crassest of political and economic calculation, came before the delegates, scores of whom seem to have had notes for an unwritten treatise in political theory in their breast pockets. Squint hard enough at these gatherings of lawyers and party retainers crowded into the state house halls, see them through the lens of the words gathering force in the second quarter of the century, and it was possible to imagine them the people themselves, taking up their normally latent authority, creating, amending, destroying with the freedom of true sovereigns. In the constitutional conventions, the language of the people's sovereignty found at once its most expansive forum and its most potent symbol.

The heyday of the constitutional convention and the prestige of the people, in fact, rose and fell together. There had been an initial wave of state constitutional conventions in the first years of independence and a second, smaller flurry of revisory conventions in the 1780s and 1790s. But at the end of the eighteenth century the institution went, relatively speaking, into a state of dormancy, infrequently called other than for the hasty, derivative work of framing a constitution for a new western state. The sharpened political debates of the 1820s, however, ushered in what can only be called an era of permanent constitutional revision. Dissatisfactions, once bottled up in local conflicts, later channeled down narrower courses, erupted everywhere in demands for the assembly of popular conventions. Between 1829 and 1880, it was an unusual political year which did not witness the calling of a revisory state constitutional convention somewhere in the United States. In the space of a single decade, 1844 to 1853, when the convention era was at its apogee, more than half the existing states summoned a constitutional convention into being.[23]

Unlike the conventions of the eighteenth century, closet affairs for the most part, meeting at times behind closed doors, rarely printing more than a perfunctory parliamentary account of their proceedings, the conventions of the mid-nineteenth century did their work under the eye of an intensely interested public.[24] No one recorded the debate over the New York constitution of 1776. The debates in the revisory convention of 1846, in contrast, were scribbled down, more or less verbatim, by two teams of stenographers and set up in close to a thousand pages of double-column type to be hawked as commercial ventures by rival Albany newspapers. The most celebrated speeches of a nineteenth-century convention went immediately to the printers as pamphlets; the chaff was the stuff of newspaper reportage. Extravagantly long, expensive to sustain, lavishly publicized, the convention might reasonably have struck an observer of mid-nineteenth-century America as the fundamental political act of the democracy. In 1860–61 the states of the Southern Confederacy seceded on the authority of their people, gathered in convention; the war over, the struggle for political control of the South continued, Reconstruction convention on rival Reconstruction convention, through precisely the same device. Not in books but in the constitutional conventions, talk of the people's sovereignty found its characteristic form of expression.

Like all political rituals, the antebellum constitutional conventions had a form and, in time, a formula. The basic flow of a constitutional convention's work was straightforward enough. Called into being by the state legislature, often on the basis of a special referendum, a convention was a gathering of popularly elected delegates, a few of them eminent, many obscure, heavily enough stocked with lawyers to keep the proceedings within parliamentary bounds. Their debates began in closed committees, moved to the floor— where the elastic rules governing committees of the whole allowed the tensions and conflicts of the committees to issue into a barely stoppable torrent of words—and then were repeated all over again as the proposals came to their final vote. But often the most extravagant debate occurred not where one might have expected it but at the very outset of a convention's work, when many of the delegates were still sequestered in committee, and sparked by the most trivial of incidents. In Massachusetts in 1853, the delegates spent eight days wrangling over the precise nature of the call they should issue to the town of Berlin, from whom a substitute delegate was needed. In Illinois in 1847 the issue was the convention's authority to appoint, and demand that the legislature pay for, an additional sergeant-at-arms to keep its house in order. In New York in 1846 the subject of the governor's age and residence qualifications tied up the convention for a week; in Virginia in 1850, debate over a governor's ability to succeed himself consumed double that much time and some 150 pages of double-column print.[25]

Debates such as these functioned, in part, as preliminary tests of factional strength among delegates whose political allegiances, even in an age of partisanship, could not always be accurately read from a straight party lineup. In another part, these early debates were signs of underemployment—an opportunity for a handful of oratorically ambitious delegates to test their lungs while the realists worked out the convention's practical compromises behind closed doors. But stuffed with what Richard Henry Dana in 1853 called "the metaphysics of popular government," these debates had their own urgency.[26] For what was at stake—what the popular faction felt it imperative to nail down at the outset—was how far the authority of the people assembled in convention could be said to run.

Trivial as the incidents might be they were far from random. Did the enabling act of the legislature limit the officers a convention could appoint? Could the legislature—it was this issue which twice tore Illinois conventions apart in the 1860s—prescribe the oath the delegates were to take before a legally constituted convention came into being? Could an act of the legislature require that the towns elect their substitute delegates by a voice vote when—as in Massachusetts in 1853—the Democratic majority in the convention insisted on a secret ballot? Could a legislature prorogue a convention or demand that it get its work done within a limited span of time? Could a convention, faced with a recalcitrant legislature, enact its own "ordinances" carrying the force of law or levy taxes for its own support? Was a constitutional convention, in short, an elaborately created constitutional drafting committee, or, once convened, was it loosed from the legislature's authority—no mere servant of normal governance but an extraordinary, temporary reconcentration of the people's sovereignty in its full force and authority?

No one doubted that a convention could write what it dared, reenacting as much of the existing constitution as it pleased, or as little as it pleased. It could expunge offices and reshuffle laws; it could modernize or eliminate the rights so carefully nailed down by its predecessors. Prudence dictated that it be wary of binding the people where popular sentiments were tender. In New York in 1846 and Virginia in 1850 the popular party insisted eloquently that the people could not be blocked, even by their constitutions, from choosing whomever they would as their governors. But nothing limited a convention from disfranchising a part of the people who had called it into existence—as the popular party did in New York in 1821 in disfranchising most of the state's black voters—nor from cutting the ratification electorate to its own notion of who the people ought to be. Nor, as nineteenth-century delegates repeatedly reminded themselves, did anything but prudence require a constitutional convention to submit its work to a vote at all or prohibit the delegates from voiding the existing government and declaring by fiat whatever "republican" alternative they thought the people would stand for.

Given the heritage of the emergency conventions and committees of safety of 1775–76, given the roster of constitutions put in place by the authority of their drafters, none of these were idle claims. With the appeal to the people's will booming out over the crowds massed at election rallies, these claims could not but swell with weight and moment. But the point is not simply that the real, living sovereignty of the people gathered in convention was a hard claim to down; it is that the popular party drove the point home repeatedly, audaciously, insistently. In the constitutional convention, that abstraction called the People found its reification.

The conflation of the people and their conventions went farthest in the slave South. There, where the pressures toward white solidarity clouded some of the difference between the represented and their representatives, where the fear of unmediated political debate made men nervous of referenda, the practice of submitting a constitution to the voters was a late and shallow growth. Until forced to do so under the pressures of Reconstruction, six of the thirteen states of the Confederacy had yet to put a constitution into the hands of the voters.[27] Long after the practice had died out in the North, southern conventions issued ordinances and edicts with the confidence of bodies which knew their supraparliamentary status. The extreme case was South Carolina, whose convention of 1860 did not finally relinquish its authority to the South Carolina legislature until a year and a half into the Civil War. Elsewhere in the South, the tension between state prerogatives and federal power helped keep alive the notion of the convention as a revolutionary committee of the people, ready to spring to life to enact a constitution, to state the people's will, to interpose, nullify, perhaps to secede.[28]

In the North, the friends of the people had to content themselves with words. But these they pushed boldly. "A Convention is the provided machinery of peaceful revolution," George M. Dallas, a prominent Democrat, later vice-president of the United States, wrote in anticipation of the Pennsylvania convention of 1837–38:

When ours shall assemble, it will possess, within the territory of Pennsylvania, every attribute of absolute sovereignty, except such as may have been yielded and are embodied in the Constitution of the United States. What may it not do? It may reorganize our entire system of social existence, terminating and proscribing what is deemed injurious, and establishing what is preferred. It might restore the institution of slavery among us; it might make our penal code as bloody as that of Draco; it might withdraw the charters of the cities; it might supersede a standing judiciary by a scheme of occasional arbitration and umpirage; it might prohibit particular professions or trades; it might permanently suspend the writ of *Habeas Corpus,* and take from us . . . the trial by jury. These are fearful matters, of which intelligent and virtuous freemen can never be guilty, but I mention them merely as illustrations of the inherent and almost boundless power of a Convention.[29]

Fearful as the words were, those at the radical edge of the new popular politics refused to blunt them. The periodic rising of the people, of which Rousseau had merely dreamed, had in America, they insisted, become fact. "I look upon the whole proceeding of calling a convention as a mode of revolution," where "the people take to themselves the supreme control of the whole machinery of government," Benjamin Butler declared in the Massachusetts convention of 1853. "We are the sovereignty of the State," an Illinois delegate maintained with deliberate rhetorical flourish in 1847. "We are what the people of the State would be, if they were congregated here in one mass-meeting. We are what Louis XIV said he was, 'We are the State.' "[30] Granted that only by virtue of a massive political conceit could these lawyers and party hacks, heaping up mountains of words in a noisy and confused hall, be taken for the people. But if the people, or their delegates, were denied the sovereignty of Louis XIV, then what was their sovereignty in comparison to his but an empty fraud?

Cautious Whigs and die-hard Federalists shivered under the words. They pleaded for prudence, sang the virtues of self-restraint, fought hard over every test issue, and complained bitterly of the flight into abstractions. The rise of the democratized, open constitutional convention, however, yanked the notion of the people's sovereignty out of the realm of theory and gave it apparent substance. In these massive contests of words, the heart of the matter was not so much the bounds of a constitutional convention but the prerogatives of that new political entity, the people, reassembled out of the fragments into which the eighteenth-century constitution drafters had splintered it.

How deeply the words had taken hold of some men's imaginations, how far they were willing to push the claims of majoritarian democracy, thrusting aside the counterclaims of reserved rights and balanced constitutional mechanics, came particularly clear in the Kentucky constitutional convention of 1849–50. The battle of words which shook that convention seemed, to many contemporaries, to spring out of the dark. The pressing constitutional issue in Kentucky in 1849 was the organization of the courts. A roadblock in efforts to ease the legal pressures on debtors, often over their heads in the mid-nineteenth century's troubled financial waters, the courts had been in the eye of controversy for a long time. Kentucky Democrats came to the convention determined to replace the state's appointed judiciary with popularly elected and easily impeachable officials, down to the lowliest court clerk. Only after the contest for

delegates began did the far more volatile issue of slavery erupt in
the form of a slate of candidates pledged to a program of gradual,
compensated slave emancipation. Blessed by the patriarch of Kentucky politics, Henry Clay, spurred by the fiery editorial pen of
Cassius Clay and the preaching of Kentucky's Presbyterian clergy,
the issue seared a dark, raw nerve in the state. Emancipationist
candidates and their supporters were mobbed and intimidated; Cassius Clay was stabbed; in one particularly heated courthouse debate,
the contest was sealed when one of the candidates, at the end of his
temper and his arguments, murdered the other.[31]

When the members of the convention met in Frankfort there
was, as a result, not an emancipationist among them; but the convention scrambled quickly nonetheless to try to lock up the slavery issue with still stronger safeguards than the existing constitution afforded. What was wanted was principles. The most fertile
producer of them in the convention was Archibald Dixon, leader
of the Whig minority at the convention, a lawyer turned merchant, and now well on his way toward amassing one of the largest slave holdings in the state. Into the debate Dixon poured a
stream of additions to the Kentucky bill of rights: that property in
slaves was as inviolable as every other form of property; that the
rights of property were prior to and higher than any constitutional
sanction; and finally, "that absolute, arbitrary power over the lives
and property of freemen exists nowhere in a republic, not even in
the largest majority." Ultimately the clauses all passed successfully into the Kentucky constitution of 1850. But the Democratic
leadership refused to swallow the second two—including the con-
demnation of "arbitrary power"—without a concerted fight. The
issue on which the argument turned was not slavery; the participants were unanimous in their professions of regard for that institution. The issue, potent in its abstraction, was the people's sovereignty.

The Democratic spokesmen would not let the point go. Who was
bold enough, they demanded, to think that the people could not
"declare what shall and shall not be property?" Who was foolish
enough to fetter the powers which in an emergency the people
might need to employ? Title to property was "the creature of political association," William Mitchell, the most eloquent of the Demo-

cratic spokesmen argued. "The power which created it . . . is able to destroy it." Nor should anyone blink the fearsome word "arbitrary." "Arbitrary power, in my conception, is an attribute of popular sovereignty," Mitchell insisted. "What contract is there," what constitutional limit (he meant) could there legitimately be, "which cripples popular sovereignty?"[32] Here, skirling out of the democratically transformed politics of antebellum America, cutting across the talk of rights, was a creed of unfettered majoritarianism, revolutionary enough to have stood the hair on end of those who, long before, had announced the transfer of sovereignty from the crown to the people.

Revolutionary words, to be sure, do not always imply revolutionary intentions. The leaders of the Kentucky Democratic party were no Jacobins; no visions of land reform or property redistribution danced in their heads. To the contrary, the most vocal opponents of Dixon's amendments, Mitchell among them, were economic promoters from the bustling towns of the Ohio River, up to their ears in canals, railroads, urban real estate, and bank investments.[33] If entrepreneurs like these could be expected to know the cash value of the power of eminent domain, even they had no very ambitious plans for state power. The majority of their fellow Democrats elsewhere, pushing the claims of the people to the limit, had still less. "As little government as possible; that little emanating from, and controlled by, the people; and uniform in its application to all," the *Democratic Review* summed up the party creed in 1838. At the core of antebellum radical democracy, John Ashworth writes, was a drive for "equal" but "atomized power."[34]

There was no paradox in this. Talk though they did of the people's "will" and arbitrary prerogatives, the partisans of democracy were far more fearful of power than their opponents, hymning the sacredness of Governments. What mattered, and mattered deeply, was the metaphor of ownership. At root, the popular party's notion of the people's sovereignty was not active but possessive. Its spokesmen meant not to elaborate the authority of the state but to make clear whose state it was: that it belonged to the many, not the few.

But the words carried their own momentum; no one could ride them hard without consequences. Having hitched the claims of democracy not to rights or the public weal but to the people's sovereignty, the partisans of the people could hardly afford to qualify the awesome term to which they had bolted their arguments. To hedge the definition of sovereignty vis-à-vis the Blackstone in their pockets, now that sovereignty had fallen into the people's hands, would have been to let the most potent words in their arsenal crumple in front of them. "Sir, the people are here themselves," Peter Livingston had declared, putting the prerogatives of popular governments at their boldest in the New York constitutional convention of 1821. "No restriction limits our proceedings. . . . Sir, we are standing upon the foundations of society."[35]

The Identity of the People

In the 1840s the sovereign people seemed everywhere on the march. When news of the French revolution of 1848 reached the United States, the Democratic party greeted it in an outburst of self-congratulatory pride as a sister movement to its own. England, a decade after the first halfway measures of parliamentary reform, seemed to confirm the same trend of events. Burke's dictum, that "the sovereignty of the people was the most false, wicked, and mischievous doctrine that ever could be preached to them," lay under siege by men talking in ways unknown since the 1790s of the rights of the people. Working-class champions of a new "People's Charter," who in the 1830s had toasted the fortunes of Andrew Jackson, pressed their case for genuine political democratization in a rhetoric which, in many respects, matched slogan for slogan that of the post-Jackson Democratic party. With Chartists, whose volcanic fires still ran hot in the 1840s, talking of assembling a grand convention of the people to meet under the nose of an unresponsive Parliament, with knots of men gathering in constitutional conventions throughout the Continent, boldly proclaiming an end to the era of kingly absolutism, the partisans of the people in America had reason to think that a new political world was in the making.[36]

But the language of the People was no more stable than the

language of Natural Rights. Shift the occasion, open the words to new users other than the white, male farmers and mechanics who had pushed them so hard against the older concentrations of power, and the terms refused to remain fixed. By the end of the 1840s, even as the Democrats were proclaiming to a revolutionary world "the grand political truth of the sovereignty of the people," the slogan was beginning to twist and buckle in their grasp.

The dangerous term, as it turned out, was not sovereignty; it was the People. The identity of the people had not bothered those who had picked up the phrase to force their own kind—a democracy of white adult males—into the statehouses. But once that occasion had passed, how was the word to be contained? What if Americans still farther outside than they—penniless men or aliens or women or free blacks or (at the heart of mid-nineteenth-century democracy's nightmare) slaves—were to claim membership in the people? What if, in the name of the people as a national whole, the vital interests of the people of a state should be invaded? Eighteen-forty was the year in which the Whigs converted to the politics of mass democracy. By the end of the 1840s, Democrats and Whigs alike were already scrambling back from big, loose talk of the people's will.

The issues on which the words turned sharp and double-edged were most dramatically rehearsed in Rhode Island in the early 1840s. The Rhode Island contest, known by historical convention as the Dorr War, was not really a war at all. In a military sense, it was a comic opera affair, acted out in something of a comic opera of a state, too tiny and politically archaic to be fully believable in mid-nineteenth-century America. After the Connecticut voters finally replaced their colonial charter with a constitution in 1818, Rhode Island stood all alone in having no written constitution. Its legislature possessed in theory a virtually unlimited sphere of action, and in practice a disinterest in doing anything to lower the property barriers to the suffrage, which in 1840 were more tightly restrictive than virtually anywhere else in America. Only holders of land (and their eldest sons) could vote in Rhode Island elections. As entrepreneurs with an eye to accessible water power began to crowd the state's river courses with mills and millworkers, as Providence's artisan population expanded, a disfranchised state swelled within the legal, closed corporation of Rhode Island's freehold farmers.[37]

Suffrage expansion societies, vigorously promoted by working-men's associations and seconded by manufacturers and professional men, rose and disintegrated in the 1830s, only to splinter on the legislature's refusal to call a constitutional convention or to take one seriously when called. Finally in 1841, a year after the tumultuous Log Cabin campaign, the radical leaders determined to organize a constitutional convention—whether the legislature approved or not. The idea of calling a convention directly from the people, without intermediaries, was not new. It had been tried before, and in the politically charged atmosphere of the 1840s, it was not surprising that someone should try it again. Elsewhere, however, the legislatures had eventually blinked and compromised. In Rhode Island neither side gave way. When the legislature refused to call a convention into being, the proponents of suffrage expansion submitted the question to a carefully organized extralegal election, open to every white adult male in the state. Whatever the Rhode Island radicals originally had had in mind, the success of this initial referendum set them moving, at ever-quickening speed, toward the construction of a new, people's government in the bowels of the old state. Within six months a People's Convention had met, drafted a new constitution, and submitted it for ratification to a second, heavily subscribed, extralegal election. Ratification in place, the radical party proceeded with a third election to choose the People's legislature and a slate of state officials. Thus by the spring of 1842 Rhode Island possessed what revolutionary Chartists in Britain only dreamed of: two governments, two fundamental laws, the land-owners' frame of government and the People's constitution, a constituted state and a revolutionary one built on the people's sovereignty, moving closer and closer toward collision.

Only at the last minute did the deadly earnest contest collapse into something close to comic opera madness. The new people's governor, Thomas Dorr, who had helped marshal this still unfulfilled display of symbolic politics, now determined to seize the stuff of power itself: the state seal and the guns in the state armory. With a pair of cannon, which failed to go off, and some two hundred militiamen, Dorr tried to lay siege to the Providence arsenal. Routed, he fled the state, his militiamen were chased out of their encampment, military law was imposed, and the Dorr cause spent the rest of the 1840s working its way through the courts. By the time the United States Supreme Court decided against it, yet another constitutional convention, this one sanctioned by a shaken legislature, had reformed Rhode Island's suffrage and granted it, at last, a written constitution.

But not before the Rhode Island events had sent their shock waves across the country. Radical northern Democrats eagerly took up Dorr's cause; Calhoun and Henry Clay scribbled out angry rejoinders. The events in Rhode Island forced all that was problematic and troublesome in the term the People to the surface. Which of the rival electorates in Rhode Island was—and by what right—the people? What limits bound the people—whoever they were—from taking their sovereignty into their own hands, in whatever way they might choose? The questions split talk of popular sovereignty not simply in two but in three.

The Whigs, shocked by the events in Rhode Island, were the quickest to state their case. Let the principles of Thomas Dorr prevail, Horace Greeley retorted, and "all Courts, all laws, all Constitutions, become the merest frostwork, which the next breath may dissipate, or which a bushel of votes, collected by a peddler on his rounds may utterly set aside." It was typical of Whigs, when caught in a hard place, to contrast a mere bushel of votes to the sublimities of courts and constitutions. When it was Daniel Webster's turn to rebut Dorr's lawyers before the Supreme Court in 1848, he took the same course. No one, Webster supposed, would doubt that in America the people were sovereign. But as his argument unrolled it became clear that Webster was intent on whittling the words down to their smallest compass. "The aggregate community is sovereign," Webster admitted, but it was not sovereign in the sense that it could act in mere "public meetings" or "tumultuous assemblies," outside the laws and constitutional framework it had made or to which (in the Rhode Island case) it had long acquiesced. The people were *constitutional* sovereigns. Back of their constitutions or outside them, even under the most adverse of circumstances, they could not go.[38]

But in what sense was Rhode Island's closed corporation of farmers truly a government of the people at all? The Whigs' response was that in popular governments the people as a whole were politically represented through an especially delegated fraction of their members. The people, the Whigs insisted, comprehended everyone: women, children, slaves, Indians, lunatics, paupers, criminals. Over and again they skewered every narrower definition of the people as mean and self-contradictory. Every one of Dorr's partisans, they acknowledged, belonged to the people. But membership in the people, the Whigs quickly added, did not imply equal political competence. Even the original social contract, John Quincy Adams declared when the Dorr controversy was at its height, was necessarily made "by a portion of the people for the whole." To vote, the Whigs insisted, was to hold a distinct "office" of government, which nowhere, by Adams's calculations—not even in democracies—had been very widely distributed.[39]

If Whig debaters sometimes betrayed a mite of nervousness about this aspect of their argument, they had their reason. For it looked suspiciously like the argument the British had thrown back at the patriot demands for self-government: that however far from the colonies or rottenly apportioned Parliament might be, the entire realm was "virtually" represented there in its deliberations. Despite its checkered past, however, the Whigs dusted off the argument for virtual representation and shoved it into the breach. No mere count of eligible voters, they insisted, could prove or disprove the existence of republican government. A popular government was one in which the people's will filtered freely upward: from the people to the voters, from the voters to the holders of legislative office, finally into the structures of law. "No man makes a question that the people are the source of all political power," Webster insisted. "There is no other doctrine of government here."[40] But in a cloud of qualifiers the Whigs were backpedaling hard from talk of the people's sovereignty.

The northern, radical wing of the Democratic party, in contrast, used the events in Rhode Island to push the people's claims to their farthest limit. Their briefs swelled with the stock eighteenth-century acknowledgments of the people's sovereignty. They leaned on James Wilson's incautious claim of 1790, that the citizens retained the right to alter or abolish their constitutions "at whatever time, and in whatever manner, they shall deem it expedient," as a pillar of literal truth. " 'We, the people,' the paramount power of a free elective government, have but to speak, and their voice must be obeyed, for their will is the fountain of government and laws," Dorr's partisans declared. Benjamin Hallett, who knew the hardness of the case on his hands before the Supreme Court, reminded the justices that in the special circumstances of Rhode Island, where there was no formal constitution, there could hardly be a legal, constitutional mode of amendment. But Dorr and his allies preferred not to stress the peculiarities of Rhode Island. The higher principle at stake was "THE INHERENT SOVEREIGNTY RIGHT OF THE PEOPLE TO CHANGE AND REFORM THEIR EXISTING GOVERNMENTS AT PLEASURE."[41] "We contend for [the people's] absolute sovereignty over all Constitutions," Dorr wrote in 1848, in a letter that pushed the doctrine simmering under the surface of a generation's constitutional conventions to the surface: "Constitutions [are] . . . but forms of expressing, protecting and securing the Rights of the People, intended to remain in use until the People shall otherwise indicate and direct." And no longer.[42] Against the will of the people a constitution was, just as Horace Greeley guessed, mere "frostwork."

Still, with what legitimacy could Dorr's voteless partisans claim to be—and act as if they were—the people? Their answer, seized from the language of rights, running so hard through working-class radicalism, was bold enough to rattle political nerves for the next third of a century: that the suffrage was theirs by "natural right." The House Select Committee on the Rhode Island affair, stacked with radical Democrats, put the point at its sharpest:

The right of suffrage is a *natural,* not a *conventional* right, which attaches to the *man,* independent of the accidents of birth or fortune; of which right he cannot be divested, except by usurpation or force. It exists antecedent to the formation of the social union and the political compact, and inseparably belongs to him as certain qualities inseparably belong to things.

Logically the argument was rickety at best. What kind of natural right of voting could men have possessed "antecedent" to the social agreements which made such an act as voting even conceivable? The People's Convention, not yet having thrown political realism to the winds, had cautiously limited the suffrage to white males and (when it came to important fiscal matters) to property holders. For the rest—those whose interests were so closely "blended" with the voters that their votes would be redundant—the radical Democrats fell lamely back on their own version of virtual representation.[43] But the admission did not much diminish the audacity of what they had done in welding the soaring talk of the people's sovereignty to the open-ended language of Natural Rights. Suffrage belonged to the "whole people," by inalienable, inextinguishable right.

The people the Rhode Islanders had tacitly left out, however, were no small number. Paupers, Indians, women (even John Quincy Adams in 1842 could hear the first stirrings of the woman suffrage arguments which crystallized at Seneca Falls in 1848), or (still closer to the most exposed nerve of the Democratic party in the 1840s) blacks: could they not, on the wings of the radical Democrats' argument, claim their own natural right to vote? And if not, why not? The question roiled American constitutional conventions for the next thirty years—Whigs and Whig-Republicans talking of the suffrage as a special office requiring special qualifications, radicals countering that suffrage was an inherent, inalienable right.

The southern and prosouthern wing of the Democratic party, caught in a particularly hard squeeze between its popular sover-eignty slogans and its dismay at the anarchy-tinged events in Rhode Island, was the slowest to come to words. The answer it found, however, was brutally simple: the "people" were those who—in the race to form the basic civil compact—had gotten there first. The right to vote belonged to those white males who had put the first American constitutions in place, together with those whom their constitutions had enfranchised. None of the rest were members of the political body. The "non-voting classes" possessed no claims against the people; they were not represented either actually or virtually. They were the "subjects" of the people.

This was the argument which poured out of the New York consti-tutional convention of 1846 from Democrats bent on holding the line against any expansion of the state's tiny black vote. But even so raw an act of power and racism demanded a principle for its justification. "He was disposed to be radical in rooting out an-tiquated evils and principles intended to create or to perpetuate inequalities and disqualifications—whatever might tend to the erec-tion of one class above another," Charles O'Connor, the convention's leading proslavery Democrat insisted. "He would have a pure, perfect representative democracy, where all men who had any share in the government would stand equal." But the people were a closed corporation of equals: an omnicompetent, self-selected fraternity, over which outsiders—from within or outside a state—had no claims at all.[44]

The Democrats had come to the convention of 1846 determined to engraft a statement of the people's underlying power onto their constitution. The effort dissipated on the convention floor, not (as some delegates said approvingly to themselves) because such clauses were a mere "abstraction" but because, as the term the People came apart under the pressure of new claimants, any choice of words touched nerves too exposed for the delegates to accept.

Had the slavery issue not come loose from its moorings, the divisions brought into relief by the events in Rhode Island might in time have healed. But events were not kind to the terms on which Jackson's party had staked so much of its fortune. The proponents of a people's empire had one victory left. In the late 1840s, in as close a thing to a popular war as the nation had yet experienced, the Americans turned upon the rival republic of Mexico and hurled the people's domain out to the Pacific. But the consequence was to wedge the slavery issue into the very eye of politics, where it remained, unbudgeable and dangerous. Out of the Mexican War and the constitutional compromises in its wake, out of the new fugitive slave act, out of the bitter clashes over the status of slavery in the new territories and the burgeoning antislavery movement these issues fed spilled so sharp a set of political and sectional tensions as to decompose the people into angry fragments.

In this new political climate, the Democratic party watched its cry of the people's sovereignty grow treacherous and complex. For those terrified of antislavery talk, the sectional crisis added a new nightmare: that a national majority, intoxicated with some compound of Dorrite principles and abolitionism, sweeping across the boundaries of state immunities with tyrannical power, might crush the constitutional safeguards to slavery like pasteboard. As both parties fractured under the pressures of the slavery issue, the politicians scuttled from majoritarian arguments toward a rhetoric of minority rights, local immunities, and constitutional limits. But the men Jackson had helped propel into power had put too much faith in the notion of the people's sovereignty to desert the claim in a crisis. To read the debates of the late 1840s and 1850s over the identity of the people is to watch men struggle with words they knew to be treacherously unstable and yet too vitally needed simply to abandon like wrecked and shattered hulks.

The uses of the People were clearly far from exhausted. Chief Justice Roger Taney, backed into a hard legal corner in the Dred Scott case, seized on the argument rehearsed in the New York constitutional convention of 1846 to cut off legal redress to the federal courts from every slave descendent (no matter how free by subsequent manumission or state law) on the grounds that the immunities of federal citizenship belonged to those who had constituted the "people" in 1789 and their posterity, but to no one else. When Lincoln's election set a match to the long-standing southern talk of governments as ready to be dismantled whenever they ceased to guarantee the security of the constituent people and their property, the southern secessionists ripped apart the constitutional threads binding them to the North in conventions of the sovereign people. "We the people of the Confederate States" set in place the revolutionary southern government. When the constitutional crisis escalated into a violent clash of armies, Lincoln rallied the northern troops by insisting theirs was the "people's" cause and a "people's" war.[45]

It was Stephen Douglas, however, who labored hardest to make the slogan of the people's sovereignty do one more major piece of work. By converting the controversy over slavery in the western territories into a question of popular sovereignty—by putting slavery (where it was not yet established) to a local vote of the people and accepting it (where it did exist) as unalterable—he hoped to pull the teeth of the sectional crisis and reunite his badly splintered party. Scarcely another political figure ever tied his fortunes as tightly as Douglas in the 1850s to a single pair of words. He hammered away with tremendous energy at the principle of "popular sovereignty." In his exalted moments, he called it "the sacred right of self-government"; in his coarser ones, the cause of governments "made by white men, on the white basis, for the benefit of white men and their posterity forever."[46]

Once more the theme of possession was uppermost. "If there is any one principle dearer and more sacred than all others in free governments," Douglas insisted, "it is that which asserts the exclusive right of a free people to form and adopt their own fundamental law, and to manage and regulate their own internal affairs and domestic institutions."[47] But one could hardly miss the fact that in Douglas's hands the notion of a people, gathered in revolutionary conventions, wielding (for a moment) a power as fearful as any European monarch had ever grasped, had turned defensive and localistic. From the first it had been one of the ironies of political argument that those who talked so much of popular sovereignty had had so weak a notion of what the people's extraordinary power was good for. Jackson's revolution had been in many ways a preemptive revolution, a seizure of the state by the many to insure that its uses not be stretched too far by the few. Still, as Douglas threw the words into the sectional crisis, hunting for the language of compromise, there was no disguising the newly conservative turn of the possessive theme. Douglas's people was a patchwork of local peoples, each clutching its vested rights, its fraternal exclusions, its peculiar notions of human property and human freedom. The principle of popular sovereignty and the principle of noninterference from all outside peoples, Douglas insisted, were one and the same. In Douglas's majority faction of the Democratic party, the voice of the people no longer reverberated with truth or revolutionary zeal but with dozens of locally convenient compromises.

Even Douglas's skillful trimming and formidable oratorical talents, however, could not make the words work. The southern firebrands, certain that slavery belonged by right in the territories, whether the territorial voters approved of it or not, wanted nothing of Douglas's electoral gimmicks. Lincoln, whose understanding of the people was national not local, sneered at Douglas's slogan as a shabby "squatter sovereignty."[48] Douglas, his party rent in two, pounded home the words, but colliding with race and slavery, talk of the people's sovereignty was no longer the sharp, single-edged tool it had once been.

As words go, this one began with no mean career. With it men had lodged the claims of the majority will in American politics as never before. The slogan had helped the architects of party organization create the instruments of a new style, mass democracy. It had helped turn men's imaginations from the mechanics of governance to the drama of elections. With it the offices of government had been simplified, democratized, torn away from the old, deference-commanding elites.

Like all powerful political terms, however, the career of this one, too, had been inextricable from conflict. Since independence, it had been fiercely resisted. If Douglas could not make the words stem the disintegrative forces all around him, it was partly because the words themselves were under new siege. For the democratic revolution of the early nineteenth century had barely gotten under way before a movement gathered strength—not merely to co-opt or compromise the rhetoric of the people's sovereignty—but to inter it altogether. Spilling out of the great revivals of the nineteenth century, full of counterrevolutionary confidence, men of these convictions burst into mid-nineteenth-century political argument talking not of the people's sovereignty nor of rights but of the claims, the powers, even the divinity of governments. Natural Rights, the People's sovereignty, God's government—even before secession made it impossible to say with certainty any longer who the people were or what they willed, a new, rival set of abstractions challenged the others for primacy.

4

Government

The Rhetoric of Counterrevolution

Most governments, most of the time, contrive to wear an air of inevitability. Not many persons, after all, have ever witnessed the birth of the political state, and their governors, as a rule, have little interest in their prying into such things too closely. The sources of the political arrangements of the moment fade off into a misty past: into the eye of God, the forces of history, the caprices of fate. Such is the usual state of things. The American Revolution, however, had turned political argument down different channels and set men talking seriously, heatedly about origins. That governments were *made;* that human beings (and their most basic rights) predated the political forms they had constructed; that having made their governments once, they could tear them up, dissolve political society into its individual, constituent atoms, if they chose, and make their governments anew—all this lay deeply embedded in the post-independence language of American politics. It was this that gave the talk of Natural Rights and the People's sovereignty their radical edge. Every Independence Day homage to the nation's Founders, every passing reference to the social compact, the seating of every new constitutional convention conspired to reemphasize the point that governments were a late, artificial, amendable construct in human history.

On this, since the Revolution, Americans of deeply divided political loyalties had agreed. One might contend that the framing of governments was a complicated science, demanding special skill and deliberation. One might imagine the formation of a government as a momentary fracture in time, in which the original rights of human beings lay open for repossession. One might, raising one's voice to be heard over a milling crowd of voters, insist that governments were brought to life by the breath and will of the people. But sharply fought as these disputes had been, the contestants had rarely denied that nations and governments were made in an act of conscious will. When individuals abandoned their prepolitical state and contracted to make a government, they crossed a line so clearly marked that only fools could miss it. The natural rights of human beings were older than their political obligations; they possessed their rights by titles more ancient than any state could claim. Collectively they possessed the state itself by virtue of having made it.

In certain quarters of post-Revolutionary America, to be sure, one could hear a much older way of talking of governments: as inescapable, aboriginal with man and creation. Since New England's beginnings, its preachers had insisted that the necessity of living in obedience to some sort of government was a primordial edict of God. The occasion of making governments belonged to men, but the authority of those they chose to preside over their dim and imperfect imitations of God's grander government came not from themselves but from God. New England Federalists, terrified at the specter of an unholy, Jefferson-led leap into anarchy, had wrung what use they could out of such transcendent talk of Government. Even the commonplace Enlightenment obeisances to the "Governor" of nations, "the great Legislator of the universe," sustained a vestigial reminder of the connections men had labored so long to prove between the governments of men and the cosmic administration of God himself. Convictions of this sort never fully melted away, even in the caldron of the colonial resistance; the partisan quarrels of the 1790s revived a good deal of it. But in post-Revolutionary America, Edmund Burke's talk of the state as a partnership between the living and the dead, which went back time out of mind—as "but a clause in the great primeval contract of eternal society"—was largely confined to the margins of political life.[1]

Then in the middle third of the nineteenth century, just as Jefferson's Declaration was being inflated with new importance, just as talk of the majority will was rising to a pitch, Burke's counterrevolutionary talk found a new constituency. Out of the great nineteenth-century religious revival, out of the Whig party, out of the new, rapidly proliferating colleges, out of a thousand fears sparked by Jackson and Dorr, the workingmen's movement and abolitionism rolled a sweeping counterattack on the Revolutionary language of Natural Rights and the People's sovereignty. There was no way back, even in the mind's eye, conservative orators insisted, to the original rights of man. The notion of a state of nature, it was said, was a fairy tale. Men were born into political societies, subject to law; that was their "natural" state. They did not *possess* rights, as men might possess a horse or a chest of clothes. They did not possess their governments; nor in truth did they make them, except as the agents of God and history. We have "learned from Rousseau and Locke, and our own revolutionary age," Rufus Choate, the silver-tongued Whig orator declared in 1845, " . . . that the State is nothing but a contract, rests in contract, springs from contract; that government is [simply] a contrivance of human wisdom for human wants." But the revolutionary metaphors, Choate retorted, were all wrong. The state was no mere "encampment of tents on the great prairie, pitched at sun-down, and struck to the sharp crack of the rifle next morning." The state was "a structure, stately and eternal," "unchangeable," "indestructible," "immortal," "framed for a duration without end,—without end—till the earth and the heavens be no more."[2] This was not merely Burke, embellished with nineteenth-century oratorical devices. This was the language of a counterrevolution, more tardy and pious, but not a whit less deliberate than Burke's own.

Perhaps because the counterrevolutionaries proposed no king, no abject retreat from democracy, perhaps because they were members of the bourgeoisie, not glitteringly titled aristocrats, our history books have yet to take their measure. Louis Hartz, hunting for American counterparts to the counterrevolutionary publicists of nineteenth-century Europe, abandoned the count with Fisher Ames and George Fitzhugh.[3] But Fitzhugh, tilting at Jefferson's windmill, was far from an isolated figure. By the middle of the century his likes (if not his wit and exaggeration) were legion—full of anti-

Revolutionary animus, fervent talk of government and obligation, and sweeping political ambitions.

The counterrevolutionaries did not win the clear-cut victory they longed for. For a moment during the Civil War, with northern ministers thundering of the divine origins and prerogatives of government, with Lincoln talking of political destinies and obligations over which men had no sovereignty, conservative Americans had reason to hope they were about to bury for good the anarchic language of inalienable rights and popular sovereignty. That illusion evaporated with the war's end. Reconstruction forced political talk back onto rights and sovereignty, tangling them with the strident Civil War talk of obligations in all sorts of strange compromises and combinations. But though the counterrevolution in political talk was incomplete, its effects were far more powerful and lasting than our histories have acknowledged. A powerful hunger for obligations shunted arguments over rights onto unfamiliar tracks, wrenched the word "rights" from retrospective fantasies and fused it with duty. It dealt a massive blow to loose talk of revolution. In the place of the People it squeezed into political language the still higher, person-eclipsing abstractions—Nation, State, and Society—on which political science was to lay its foundations for the rest of the century.

"The whole theory [of the social compact] is wrong," a foot soldier of the counterrevolution pleaded in the Ohio constitutional convention of 1850–51. "It came from the infidel philosophy of Hobbes and his successors. It assumes that man is an *independent being,* at liberty to choose his own course of life, the law by which he will be governed; or that he may deny to be governed by any law at all. . . . No, sir, Government is founded on no such weak and miserable device as a *social compact.* It is of divine origin; not the invention of man—but the appointment of God."[4] The patriot writers of the Revolution, sensing how dangerous this sort of talk was for the project of resistance, had tried to put it to rout. Now in the middle third of the century, in dress altered for the changed occasion, it came back into its own.

A Christian Party in Politics

Like all counterrevolutions, that of the mid-nineteenth century flowed from an untidy coalition of forces. Die-hard Federalists, traumatized by the French Revolution into certainty that an incipient Robespierre lurked behind every appeal to the rights of man; ministers, for whom the word Government remained the central metaphor for God's relationship to his subjects; southern slaveholders, Whig pamphleteers, men of property and affairs, and sequestered college professors, all took a hand in shaping the attack on the axioms of late eighteenth-century politics. But whereas the driving force behind counterrevolutionary politics in Europe had been the political crisis in France, in America it was the shifting fortunes of Protestantism. The reconstruction of political talk and the resurgent ambitions of Protestantism were, to a great extent, part and parcel of the same phenomenon.

Protestant piety, to be sure, had run deep for a long while in America. Jefferson in 1800 escaped being fatally tarred with the stigma of infidelity only by soft-pedaling his religious opinions. Paine, who soft-pedaled nothing, caught the smear of atheism in full force, and by his death in 1809 it had reduced his reputation in America to a pittance. A Protestant-born literalism had sharpened the edge of the Revolutionary abstractions; Protestant millennialism had buoyed the colonial resistance; Protestant quietism had nurtured acquiescence to the status quo. Malleable and multiform as religion is, neither its force nor its political thrust has been constant in American life.

In the second quarter of the nineteenth century, however, a popular, morally charged Protestantism gathered force with a speed that set its partisans talking of miracles. Waves of Protestant revivalism rolled out of the South, out of western New York (set aflame so often that contemporaries call it the "Burned-Over District"), into the seaboard cities, until by the 1850s every section of the country had felt its effects. Rival denominations vied hard with each other to produce recruits, preachers, schools, and colleges. Even Jefferson's pet University of Virginia, by the mid-1840s, had fallen in line with the appointment of a clergyman to its professorship of moral philosophy. But what distinguished the early nineteenth-century revival from its predecessors was not merely its scale but its immense moral fervor. In the wake of the preachers erupted a vision of a morally purged land, cleansed of profanity and drunkenness, its children gathered into Sunday schools, its family life purified, its sabbaths undesecrated by railroads and the delivery of mails, its frontiers civilized, its cities reformed, its laws observed. Out of moral anarchy, the nation was to be brought into obedience: into conformity to the laws and government of God.[5]

Government. The word thundered through the preaching of a Charles Finney, a Lyman Beecher, and scores of others. It stood for government of the self, the harnessing of the temper and appetites to the sober discipline of the will. It stood for familial order: for children reared in the close and careful "government" of parents. It stood for God's moral administration itself, as the preachers explained the consequences of sin not in terms of God's arbitrary will but his law and justice. The antonym of the word was "anarchy": the specter of human beings left to their isolated, ungoverned passions in a terrifying Babylon of disorder. With the word Government, the preachers conjured up not simply the institutions over which the men of politics presided (that meaning of "government" came fifth in Noah Webster's definition of the term) but a way of life saturated with moral obligations, mutual bonds, and law.[6]

The characteristic devices of Protestant moralism were the personal pledge and the voluntary association; but a movement as steeped as this with political metaphors was bound to have political consequences. When in a Fourth of July sermon of 1827 Ezra Stiles Ely called for a "Christian party in politics," pledged to the moral uses of governmental power, he dipped his finger into a tide already running hard in that direction. In the North, in particular, Protestant moralists were quick to see the possibilities of alliance between the coercive powers of the state and a morally disciplined electorate. By the 1840s northern state constitutional conventions were scrambling to placate the growing evangelical sentiment by tacking brand-new statements of gratitude to Almighty God onto their handiwork. Yet if the constitution drafters hoped by such pious gestures to keep religion out of politics, they failed badly. Politically minded evangelicals, drawn to the Whig platform of an economically and morally active state, eager for schools and temperance legislation, flooded the Whig (and later Republican) ranks in extraordinary numbers, large enough to shape party loyalties—and political argument—for the rest of the century.[7]

The new political pieties of revivified Protestantism had no such obvious, public forum as the declarations of rights or the constitutional conventions. The ministers bore down hard on the theme of moral government; but overt attack on the everyday talk of politics was more risky pulpit material. Anticlerical sentiments, fanned to a heat by openly partisan preaching, ran hard in Jackson's party and throughout the South. Many fervent Protestants, in addition, were themselves fearful of tarring their project with the mire of politics. Baptists, who harbored their sect's particularly vivid memories of the persecutory powers of government, hard-shell Calvinists, skeptical of politics altogether, southern evangelicals, who combined an eagerness for discipline with prickly notions of rights, generally preferred to make their separate peace with the state than to try to capture it. Even in New England, where the old pre-Revolutionary dream of a righteous state died hard, the mid-nineteenth-century clergy gradually sensed the advantages of caution. Badly burned by their openly partisan alliance with the Federalist reaction, the ministers trimmed their words and steered for the shelter of apolitical topics.[8]

The piety-saturated colleges, however, were another matter. Here the construction of some sort of political theory was inescapable. Here, at a slight remove from the public eye, before a captive and (for the most part) nonresistant audience, the political visions of a resurgent, morally ambitious Protestantism burgeoned into a distinctive political language, saturated with talk of obligations. Here talk of Government found its texts and forum.

Those who constructed the new language of the Protestant counterrevolution lived in what can only be called an acutely fractured world—a compound of high intellectual ambitions, raw denominational politics, piety, and the murderously dull routine of adolescent discipline and cramming. The job of the mid-nineteenth-century college professor was to make such splintered obligations whole, to bind the cosmos itself to a coherent frame of law, and put the hunger for order and discipline sweeping through antebellum Prot-

estantism into systematic form. The college's vehicle was the oblig-
atory, capstone course in moral philosophy. Taught (as a rule) out
of some unrecoverable combination of Paley's text, counter-Paley
rebuttals, and the pet political convictions of the college presidents
who taught them, the moral philosophy courses had by the middle
of the century begun to attract the systematizing efforts of textbook
writers. On a market fueled by the continued proliferation of colleges, a new set of authoritative political texts worked its way onto
shelves which had once borne the works of Locke and Montesquieu,
the pamphlets of the radical Whigs, and the great natural law compendia.[9] The result, despite the occasional thread of continuity, was
no mere modernization of eighteenth-century political talk. Set in
the context of the Natural Rights and popular sovereignty talk
swelling from below, the moral philosophers' political science
amounted to a counterattack on every anarchy-tinged survival from
the vocabulary of the Revolution.

The first piece of Revolutionary talk to be tossed overboard was
the state of nature. The notion that human beings had pulled themselves out of a state of original independence through a mutual
political contract had been live enough at the opening of the century
to be taught in even as Calvinist a college as Princeton. Thirty years
later, a Baptist like Brown's Francis Wayland still found it hard to
let social contract reasoning go.[10] But by the middle of the century,
most of the moral philosophers wanted no part of the idea. To
reason retrospectively from some imagined state of natural independence, they warned their students, was to build politics on a
chimera, a "mere figment." What rankled the moral philosophers
was not merely the historical flimsiness of the idea; it was the claim
that human beings could, even for a moment, ever have been independent of society and each other. Wayland might write that "every
human being is, by his constitution, a separate and distinct and
complete system, . . . responsible, separately, to God for the manner
in which his powers are employed." But the far more powerful
emphasis in the colleges was on the inescapability of dependence.
Human beings had been social beings from the moment of creation,
the moral philosophers insisted, framed and fitted by God for social
bonds, family discipline, and civil obligations. They realized their
nature not "in holes and caverns" (as Harvard's Francis Bowen put

it) but in society, in "a condition of responsibility, submission, and trust."[11] The line of argument was not entirely novel. Paine himself had acknowledged that human beings were not hermits, that though they were born equal and independent, a thousand wants and desires impelled them toward society "as naturally as gravitation acts to a center."[12] But the professors were determined to cut off every attempt (like Paine's) to pry apart the moment of creation from the moment in which society began. There was no state of nature: no recoverable nick of time before relations and obligations were born.

The term Natural Rights, on the other hand, touched a more complicated tangle of nerves. None of the moral philosophers proposed to throw it, like the social contract, overboard. But here, too, there was no mistaking their eagerness for means to tame the vocabulary of the Revolution. Some chose to hang the whole edifice of ethics on one's "duties"—in a grand descending staircase from one's duties to God, to the nation, to family, to one's self—so that one's rights emerged rebaptized as the "duties of reciprocity."[13] Others, bitten by Kant, wrote of the ethical realm as saturated with right and natural rights. But rights of this sort were worlds away from the hard, tangible rights of the artisan radicals. All rights, the moral philosophers hastened to show, had their limits. None could be divorced from duties or relations. "Political science dwells upon this most important elementary truth," Francis Lieber announced in his inaugural lecture at Columbia College in 1858, "that the idea of right cannot be philosophically stated without the idea of obligation." At Williams College, Mark Hopkins put the point more succinctly: "A man has rights in order that he may do right."[14]

For higher than rights were law and government. Here—in the sleight of hand with which the moral administration of God was silently conflated with the governments of men—was the heart of the moral philosophers' counterrevolutionary talk. Men might imagine that they created governments or that the transition from natural freedom to political society represented a momentous break in time. But history, the moral philosophers replied, brooked no such fractures. "God created man subject to law, and that is his natural state," Joseph Burleigh wrote in a textbook aimed at grammar school scholars. From the original government of God to the governments of men ran a historically unbroken chain; the coercive powers of the law had their source in the still more terrible coercive powers of God. Government was natural, the moral philosophers insisted, not a late, makeshift arrangement, not a thing of men but "an ordinance of God in the very process of nature's ongoing." Francis Lieber in 1838, in language which hovered halfway between that of his native Germany and the new pieties of the Protestant revival, gave the point its most elaborate expression:

The state is aboriginal with man;—it is no voluntary association, no contrivance of art, or invention of suffering, no company of shareholders; no machine, no work of contract by individuals who lived previously out of it; no necessary evil, no ill of humanity which will be cured in time and by civilization; no accidental thing, no institution above and separate from society, no instrument for one or a few—the state is a form and faculty of mankind to lead the species toward perfection—it is the glory of man.

Government was moral; it was inescapable. By the 1840s the old claim had risen to the surface once more: it was "divine."[15]

No moment of original independence. No rights without duties. No state of being before the inception of the state. With each of these counterassertions, the mid-nineteenth-century moral philosophers labored to chink in the potentially unstable dualisms of Revolutionary political talk, to construct an edifice of obligations against which there were no simple claims or easy revolt. Theirs were words more pious than Burke's, more orderly than Thomas Carlyle's thundering denunciations of the "huge anarchic roar" he feared rising all around him. But there was no mistaking their common counterrevolutionary design. The hunger for unity and discipline sweeping so strongly through resurgent Protestantism, the lust for multiplication of obligations, the longing to see the hand of God at work in every compartment of human affairs were shaped into a political language at odds at a dozen crucial points to the erupting claims of popular power and rights.

Books have no impact on a culture without assenting readers. Possession of a captive adolescent audience did not give the moral philosophers the ear of the nation itself. But set loose in the unstable political circumstances of the 1840s and 1850s, their words had consequences. The Whig journals and Whiggish literary reviews threw their pages open to the moral philosophers. They in turn leaped eagerly into the fray of controversy, grasped hard for public influence, filled reams of printed pages with their distinctive political talk. By the middle of the century, the echoes of their words outside the lecture hall could no longer be mistaken. At the Massachusetts constitutional convention of 1853, Richard Henry Dana, who had learned his politics at Harvard and at Joseph Story's law office, took upon himself the task of sweeping John Adams's musty references to the social compact out of the Massachusetts constitution on the grounds that it was all "a mere fiction, which served its turn against tyranny, but cannot stand examination." Elsewhere men routed such talk out of their constitutions as infidel and heathenish. Whig orators like Choate translated the moral philosophers' apotheosis of government into rolling periods. Francis Bowen, plunging into the Rhode Island affair, insisted that the precise form of the landowners' regime was beside the point. "Call it a republic, a democracy, or anything else; *it is still a government.*"[16]

When at the outbreak of the Civil War, against every southern calculation, a tide of strident, righteous nationalism rolled over the North, the professors, the preachers, and their discipline-hungry congregations could claim a share of the credit. The new forms of political talk had gathered their force quickly. In the 1830s Francis Lieber's Kantian vocabulary had left reviewers confused and dissatisfied. Twenty years later the rhetoric of the eternal state and inescapable obligations was no longer strange. "I love your books," New York's Chancellor James Kent wrote Lieber in gratitude. "I love you, you are so sound, so conservative, you are so very safe."[17]

Property Reconsidered

Safe. The adjective was carefully chosen. If piety fueled the new hunger for obligations, sending many of those it touched in search of alternatives to the contractual language of the Revolution; if

piety, joined to a new, swelling faith in collective moral regeneration, brought back to the word Government a measure of its old
transcendent authority; the mid-nineteenth-century counterrevolution in political talk was not the work of piety alone. The second,
tightly intertwined ingredient was fear.

The terror did not lie in the Revolutionary vocabulary itself. As
always it was the use of the words—and the social identity of their
users—that gave them their edge. The eighteenth-century commonplaces, from which many Americans were now backpedaling
with such furious energy in a cloud of homages to Government, had
not always done badly by men of property and standing. But as new
persons seized the Revolutionary vocabulary for new ends, turning
the commonplaces volatile and unpredictable, it was hardly surprising that some mid-nineteenth-century Americans untouched by the
fires of moral evangelicism should have joined the skittering movement away from the language of rights and political contract.

The defense of property is a case in point. However subversive the
idea of a state of nature had been, it had had its advantages for men
of property. The point of Locke's excursion into so "chimerical" a
notion, after all, had been to pin down the rights of private property
by titles so strong that no sovereign authority could lightly invade
them. He had tried to show, he wrote, "how Men might have come
to have a *property* in several parts of that which God gave to Mankind
in common, and that without any express Compact of all the Com-
moners."[18] The trick was to insist that labor, and the property to
which it naturally gave title, preceded the compacts which brought
governments into being. Men had owned, exchanged, and bar-
gained, Locke contended, long before they had obeyed. He fashioned the state of nature into an ingenious argumentative ploy to
demonstrate that private property rights were natural rights, older
than the state, with a precedence over all the laws and claims that
came later.

The patriot writers, hesitant as they had been to move away from
simpler constitutional arguments, fearful as they often were of state
of nature talk when it slipped out of their hands, had not been slow
to see Locke's point. Life, liberty, and property—virtually every
Revolutionary list of original, natural rights began with these.
Granted that Jefferson deliberately left the term "property" out of

the long, pregnant second sentence of the Declaration; in time he, like Paine, would try to worry through the point where the natural rights of property ceased and the artificial, social rights of property began. But none of the drafters of the bills of rights seconded Jefferson's choice or his subsequent qualifications. For seventy years after independence no constitutional statement of man's general, natural rights failed to include the rights of acquiring and possessing property among them. Lawyers and judges, squeezing the words for their advantages, fashioned the notion of the prepolitical origins of property into a buttress for all sorts of vested rights. The revolution in France, to be sure, so powerful in stampeding the English bourgeoisie away from the rhetoric of the rights of man, had sent sympathetic shivers up the spines of many propertied Americans. Still, the lesson of the American experience was that the doctrine of natural rights could, with a few twists and modifications, be turned into a wonderful engine for the conservation of property.[19]

And yet here by 1838 was Francis Bowen arguing that property was not a natural but a "social" institution, "the creature of law" and "subject to those limitations and instructions, which increase its tendency to the . . . general welfare." Here was as deeply hued a conservative as Justice Joseph Story writing that property "is a creature of civil government." Here was Daniel Webster admitting that property rights were merely "conventional" rights. Here, to the outrage of the workingmen on the radical flanks of Jackson's party, was Henry Clay declaring flatly: "That is property which the law declares to be property." Here, in short, was the propertied Whig establishment in headlong flight from John Locke.[20]

The phenomenon, so puzzling at first glance, was not without its utilitarian side. In the expanding, capital-dominated economy of the second quarter of the nineteenth century, men of wealth were not necessarily interested in preserving all vested rights heedless of their economic consequences. There were railroads to be cut through the lands of resistant farmers, water power sites to be developed, bankruptcies to be survived, even if that meant shaving off a bit of other men's property to make the enterprise solvent again. There were property rights to be destroyed, as Willard Hurst and his students have shown, in order to make the new, economy-propelling, dynamic forms of property flourish.[21]

But joined with these advantages was certainly the fact that, in the face of an aggressive natural rights radicalism from below, the old defenses of property were no longer stable, and the men of property knew it. The trouble, as always, lay in the retrospective employment of the term "natural." It was "an unalterable law in nature, that a man should have the free use and sole disposal of the fruit of his honest industry, subject to no control," the Massachusetts House of Representatives had put the cry running so hard through the tax revolt of the 1760s.[22] But suppose that what a man owned was not, in any clear moral sense, the fruit of his own industry at all but the work of slaves? Or a system of wage labor or some skillful pyramiding of stocks and bank notes or seizure of what God had reserved as the common property of mankind? Let men pry hard into the origins of property, let them measure the economic institutions of mid-nineteenth-century America against the state of nature in their mind's eye, and the results were not necessarily to property's advantage. By 1813 Jefferson thought it "a moot question whether the origin of any kind of property is derived from nature at all"; land ownership, he was certain, was not. His fellow Virginian John Taylor was already writing savagely about the distinction between "natural" property and the fictitious, artificial, property-destroying stuff of stock and paper.[23] Still sharper was the abolitionist cry, which had sent Henry Clay reeling away from the natural rights defense of property: that no one could claim a natural property right of any sort in another human being. By the 1830s, with arguments like these exploding out of radical workingmen's and abolitionist circles, it was not hard for men of property to see the advantage of drawing a veil over the origins of what they possessed. As long as any shred of credence in the state of nature persisted, the Paines, the Skidmores, and the Garrisons had far the more compelling argument than the men with bank notes or slaves or rail stock on their hands. The revival of natural rights radicalism, in its working-class and abolitionist forms, did what piety alone could not and sent propertied Americans scurrying to set what they owned on less treacherous verbal foundations.

The southern slaveholders' struggle in this regard is the more familiar story. Intellectually more conservative than their social counterparts in the North, more skeptical of the new political pieties swirling through the northern colleges and northern Whiggery, bound all the tighter to the rhetorical legacy of the Revolution by every felt blow to their sectional rights, slavery's nineteenth-century apologists labored harder than the spokesmen for northern commercial property to make the old coil of words do. "The doctrine of inalienable rights, if properly handled, will not touch the institution of slavery," A. T. Bledsoe wrote in 1856. But the effort to find a proper way of handling the matter propelled southern writers into all manner of strained rhetorical inventions.[24]

Bledsoe's course was to re-identify the inalienable rights—not as life, liberty, and property but as "conscience, truth, and honor," which, being states of mind not of body, no mere physical enslavement could touch or tarnish. Another tack was to insist that southern slaves were not really dispossessed of liberty at all. The masters, it was said, owned merely the labor power of their slaves, a share in a tacit reciprocal contract, a trusteeship in the rights of their black "warrantees." Round and round the words went, in grimly ludicrous syllogisms, as slavery's apologists attempted to convince themselves that the "powder-cask abstractions" of the Revolution could still be made safely to cohere with their peculiar form of property.[25]

There were other alternatives: racism, biblical exegesis, the paternal case for slavery's educative functions, the economic case for slavery's advantages. Some southerners sensed that the safest course lay in a retreat from political abstractions altogether. In the first years of the century William and Mary's law professor, St. George Tucker, had labored to Americanize Blackstone's *Commentaries* by balancing that suavely practical text with long elaborations of republican political theory. His son in the same chair in the 1840s worked almost as hard to demonstrate that the American frames of government were not in any sense the creatures of theory whatsoever. *"There are no original principles of Government at all,"* Abel Upshur insisted at the Virginia convention of 1829–30. "Novel and strange as the idea may appear, it is nevertheless, strictly true, in the sense in which I announce it. There are no original principles, existing in the nature of things and independent of [human] agreement, to which Government must of necessity conform, in order to be either legitimate or philosophical." But even Upshur had plunged quickly on to declare that the sanctity of property was a principle of precisely that sort. It was not easy to do without principles in the conflicted political terrain of antebellum America.[26]

The more tempting course was to cut rights talk loose from the frame of discourse which invited men to pry backward into origins. By the late 1840s, Calhoun had managed the feat, or nearly so. In 1843, Calhoun was still writing that "although the human race cannot exist without society, nor society without government, yet, in the order of things, man must have existed before society, and society before government"—precisely Locke's point. By the end of the decade, however, with the mounting attack on slavery ringing in his ears, he had concluded that Locke's state of original freedom "never did nor can exist." The point of political inquiry was not some "purely hypothetical" state of nature but *'the law of our nature.'*[27] Attend to that, and the difficulties in the way of slavery's defense disappeared. Ask what manner of relations human beings actually sustained with one another, and it was clear (*contra* Mason, *contra* Jefferson) that nowhere were they born free or equal.

In Europe the counterrevolutionary writers were at work on precisely that demonstration, welding the term "natural" to whatever history had produced. The naturalness of slavery, the naturalness of inequality were written in present-day social fact. Turn the inquiry from the origins of human rights to the laws of human nature, and the apologists for slavery were free to sweep the edicts of history, the iron laws of race, the dicta of Henry Hughes's and George Fitzhugh's sociology, into a massive defense of the naturalness of their peculiar form of property. To transform the rhetoric of revolution into the shibboleths of reaction, as Carl Becker pointed out years ago, all one needed was "a slight twist in the definition of nature."[28]

Not many of slavery's defenders were willing to cut themselves this boldly from the moorings of accustomed political talk. As long as the rights of white southerners needed simple, unambiguous defense, as long as the idea of dismantling the federal contract remained alive, as long as southerners imagined that the slogans of the Revolution might come in handy again, the language of inalienable rights and original contracts retained a utility too great to dispense with altogether. Better to trim one's words to the moment, letting logic fall where it might.

It was not in the South, despite its Calhouns and Fitzhughs, but in the North that the recoil against Locke went farthest. Well before Calhoun emerged from his books and manuscripts to announce that the social contract was a fiction, northern conservatives had contrived to create their own firmer arguments for property than the double-edged language of Natural Rights. The trick was to make men think *prospectively* about property—not about origins or history but property's service in propelling mankind forward. This was the argument conservatives mounted in Massachusetts in 1820, when pressed to defend the special privileges of the propertied in the state's constitution. Locke's talk of the formation of property rights, like the Revolutionary generation's commonplace case for the special virtues of the propertied, they bypassed altogether. What mattered was the propulsive force of the institution itself. Property should be fostered and represented, men said, because it formed the "universal stimulus," the prod to action and moral growth, the basis of charity, the foundation of human kindness, the "living principle, which keeps the great machine of society in motion." Love of property, Yale's Timothy Dwight wrote in the same vein, cultivated sound morals, "reconciles a man . . . to the restraints of government," stoked his ambition, "compels him to lead a life of sobriety, and decency." As Francis Lieber put the argument in a crescendo of claims in 1841:

Private property and the unshackled right of acquiring it is . . . the nourisher of man and the cement of society; the incentive of individual industry, and broad foundation of general prosperity; it is the basis of social advancement, the support of knowledge, and a mirror in which man beholds his rights; it is the promoter of manly consciousness and individual independence, and a firm foundation-stone of the fabric of national liberty.[29]

Rhetoric of this sort, ubiquitous in the antebellum North, pushed property beyond the status of inherited right, beyond the reach of working-class complaint, beyond the iron laws of southern sociology and hitched it to the wagons of democratic destiny, individual ambition, progress, and economic growth. To call this a utilitarian defense of property is to employ too spare a name. Private property was no mere useful contrivance; it was God's engine for the advancement of civilization itself.

Were property rights thereby natural rights? Lieber, whose Kantian allegiances ran deep, insisted that they were. But northerners
closer to the economic revolution we call market capitalism sensed
that the more defensible ground lay elsewhere. Property rights, one
heard with ascending conviction, were conventional rights, a product of law and social agreement. Property could be traded in all
manner of artificial forms; it could be held (as Joseph Story forcefully insisted) by all manner of unnatural corporate persons. It could
not escape the framework of laws and contracts which sustained it,
any more than a legislature could revoke a land grant it had lawfully
given or than a slave, by slipping across the Ohio River, could hope
to escape the fabric of contract and obligations which held a stable
society together. Whether or not the rights of property belonged
among the inalienable rights of man, Timothy Walker advised, in
one of the most widely used elementary lawbooks of the first half
of the century, "is a matter of speculation, upon which I shall not
waste time." It was enough that property's protection was "a leading object" of the law.[30]

Away from the vocabulary of Natural Rights the men of property
skittered. Let the Skidmores talk about man's natural right to property. Let the artisan radicals worry how what God had given to all
men in common had become the private property of a few. Let an
abolitionist like Theodore Parker fume that men could not simply
brand as property whatever they chose to call property. The higher
ground for property's defense was not Locke's quaint exercise in
speculative history but property's inextricable part in the fabric of
governance, relations, and obligations which moved society forward. By the 1820s, the lawyers were already shifting from natural
rights defenses of property to enshrinement of contracts. Property
rights were social rights; they reached their full development late in
God's unrolling scheme of things; that was all the more reason why,
like the law itself, they needed to be so vigorously protected.

Perhaps it is the zeal with which we have so often tried to throw
a single label over the language of our politics—to claim the whole
contested terrain for Lockeanism, republicanism, utilitarianism, or
whatever—that has caused us to miss the event. Here were men of
property, North and South, beating a retreat from the patron saint
of property rights in the face of an aggressive natural rights radicalism from below. As Natural Rights talk escaped its formulas, how-

ever, propertied Americans found it easier to wrap what they owned in the ample skirts of custom, law, and destiny. Fitzhugh excepted, they did not talk of obligations with the thunderous intensity of the preachers. They found their note, rather, in the theme of inter-dependence. Property was no mere private right but a social bond, a sociological law, a historically destined institution, a thread in an ever-thickening web of relations. In pieties such as these, in their nervous recoil from the troubling language of retrospective justice, the defenders of property added their bit to the counterrevolution-ary talk rising all around them.

Human Rights and Sacred Obligations

In the middle years of the century the outcome of these assaults on the vocabulary of the Revolution remained open and unpredictable. In the constitutional conventions of the 1850s the delegates could still debate in deadly seriousness whether men were by nature de-pendent or independent creatures, whether the social contract was fact or fiction, whether property rights preceded the creation of political society or vice versa. Though Richard Henry Dana claimed that not a man he met at the Massachusetts convention of 1853 believed in the old fairy tale of a social contract, he could not get the drafting committee, fearful of the public's response, to abandon it. In workingmen's circles, the cry of equal rights had not lost its momentum. In California, Henry George would soon begin to wres-tle with the riddles of land and poverty in ways that would breathe new life into Thomas Skidmore's doctrine of man's natural right to property. The movement for women's rights, springing out of aboli-tionism, continued to grow apace into the 1860s. And, not the least, there was abolitionism itself.

And yet the closer the ties between the advocates of rights and the Protestant revival, the clearer it was that the counterrevolution in political talk had had effects far beyond the ranks of conservative Americans. It was the antislavery cause, stocked as its radical flanks were with preachers, that showed most clearly the power of the new terms to transform political talk into all sorts of strange combinations. The language of radical opposition to slavery was the language of rights. But for those fired with visions of God's unrolling Providence, the commonplace Revolutionary talk of rights as possessions—some exchangeable, some not—sounded often like mere shopkeepers' jargon. Paine's heirs in the antebellum workingmen's organizations and the Democratic party, with their notion of government as a limited, joint-stock venture, and their piecemeal lists of rights as items of property brought down, as it were, from the attic of mankind, had never sprung wholly free of the assumptions C. B. Macpherson has styled "possessive individualism."[31] To square human rights with the new piety-fueled evocation of obligations and destiny meant somehow overhauling the notion of natural rights without losing hold of it in the process.

Of those who tried it, the most open and generous reformulator was William Ellery Channing. For a certain kind of earnest, educated New Englander in the second quarter of the century, Channing's status came very close to sainthood. He inspired scores of young men to reform without ever holding the office he so radically disliked of "reformer." As the nation's foremost Unitarian preacher, with an audience far larger than the boundaries of that sect, he was what that other Unitarian preacher, Ralph Waldo Emerson, hoped to be, a moral conscience—not to the nation, of course, nor even for the North but for his class and region. The abolitionist campaign, rising so quickly in Channing's New England, turned him to the subject of slavery. The widely circulated essays he wrote on the subject between 1835 and his death in 1842 were in an important sense, however, less about slavery than about freedom. What Channing attempted was to haul the natural rights out of the past: to make the language of inalienable rights prospective.

Growth was for Channing the beginning and the end of the matter. "It is hard to weigh human rights against each other," he wrote. "But there is not one which nature, instinct, makes so dear to us as the right of action, of free motion; the right of exerting, and by exertion enlarging, our faculties of body and mind; the right of forming plans, of directing our powers according to our own convictions of interest and duty; the right of putting forth our energies from a spring within our own breasts." These were Channing's inalienable rights, the liberties imperative to human development. "The only freedom worth possessing is that which gives enlargement to a people's energy, intellect and virtues," which sets "man's powers at large, exciting, quickening them."[32] Property rights, reason of state, economic calculation were meager claims, Channing insisted, in comparison with this. Thus the real crime of slavery, in Channing's view, was not that it dispossessed human beings of some past freedom; down that line of argument lay a thousand quibbles over Old Testament slavery and the sins and color of Ham. Slavery violated what was still more precious, the natural rights of "improvement," "self-culture," "self-motion," and self-development.

It should not reflect badly on Channing that the originality of the argument lay in the volatile political context into which he was bold enough to press his borrowed words. The philosophical work of redefining freedom as a realization of one's potential self rather than the cashing in of primordial claims, as process rather than property, had been done in Germany by Kant and his followers. Samuel Coleridge, whom Channing, like Emerson and John Stuart Mill, had sought out for inspiration, had been sounding the theme for over a decade. By Channing's death the moral philosophers were already drinking heavily of the same well.

Nor should it reflect badly on Channing that this new way of talking about rights was—like the old—a rhetoric of a myriad, contradictory uses. Channing and Emerson deeply distrusted the state; Coleridge came out of the upheavals of the 1790s a Tory paternalist of the most thoroughgoing sort. Francis Lieber turned Kant into a Whig of Daniel Webster's stripe; John Stuart Mill used his Kantian borrowings to defend an inglorious retreat from Bentham's simple, arithmetical defense of democracy (every man to count for one and none for more than one) to his own complicated, nervous suggestions for plural voting (for if voting was a sort of school, Mill argued, whose highest goal was to promote the moral energies of men, then it stood to reason that the better pupils should get an extra influence). Channing, who distrusted the meddling of the reform societies, preached self-culture; the Kantian moral philosophers lectured on the identity of rights and obligations.

"Rights, Rights lie at the foundation of a popular government," not as the gift of society but of God, Channing insisted. Men groped in the dark until that idea "towers above expediency or wealth."[33] It was Channing's hope not to muddy the language of rights but to unlimber it, to graft it to a more fluid, generous notion of human nature, to spring the word "rights" itself open to unfettered growth. Still, when it came to the practice of politics, Channing himself was full of ambivalences. He was a powerful recruit to the antislavery cause but not (though they worked hard for his allegiance) an outright abolitionist; a man broadly sympathetic to the claims of workers ("Let not the sacredness of Individual Man be forgotten in the feverish pursuit of property") but never so far as to lose his doubts about universal suffrage. "There is a law of humanity more primitive and divine than the law of the land," Channing wrote in anger at slavery. But he doubted that emancipation would do the slaves much good unless it came in the free, uncoerced action of their masters.[34] Perhaps it was Channing's gentleness, rather than the indistinctness of the words with which he talked of rights, that let his theoretical and his practical politics drift so far apart. Channing's prospective notion of rights was bigger and more inspiring than the workingmen's brittle, straightforward talk of dispossession. But it was harder to grasp. Out of it came no revolutions.

To Channing's left among the abolitionists, where talk of a revolution in human affairs was intense, the juncture of piety and rights produced a very different outcome. In the evangelical wing of the antislavery movement, that is to say, where its agitational edge was sharpest and least compromising, the radical potentials latent in Protestantism erupted in full force. But even there the language of rights and revolution was mixed—this time not with metaphors of growth but obedience.

Rights—inalienable and uncompromisable—were at the very eye of abolitionist rhetoric. Not since the Revolution had any group of Americans followed that call as boldly as they into outright civil disobedience. The anarchist, "no government" label the majority of Americans hung on the antislavery radicals, with their rescues of fugitive slaves, their contempt for all slavery-upholding governments, and their burnings of the Constitution, had its undeniable foundations in fact. Man-made governments and majority-made laws the abolitionists distrusted deeply. Wendell Phillips might write of government as a "voluntary association," contracted in precisely the manner of a bank partnership or a temperance society. But many abolitionists wanted nothing of the verbal formulas which seemed to allow men to declare as law whatever moral crimes they might agree upon. Social contract reasoning, Theodore Parker declared from his Boston pulpit, stank with "atheism." William Goodell, a pilgrim (like Parker) through a long series of radical moral and religious causes, called Locke's notion of government by contract "a pit of ashes."[35] As for the pretended sovereignty of the people, that was built on sand and falsehoods. A human being had no sovereign lawgiver, no moral commander, but his conscience.

Yet this extraordinary clear-cutting of the legitimating props of governments was, for the abolitionists, only a preface to the invocation of a purer, stricter, less compromising government. "MAN WAS MADE TO BE GOVERNED," Henry C. Wright declaimed. But the governor from whom there was no escape was God. Freedom meant no escape from obligations but, rather, a radical transfer of authority. "When will men see that they can only *discover* and *obey*, not *construct*, the laws of the world!" Goodell wrote. Parker seconded the point: "The law of God has eminent domain everywhere. . . . You may resign your office, and escape its obligations, forsake your country, and owe it no allegiance, but you cannot move out of the dominions of God." Even Garrison insisted that "ours is no anarchical movement, but one of order and obedience." For abolitionists of this sort, as Lewis Perry aptly writes, God had "preemptive sovereignty" everywhere. Set against this cosmic royalism, it was no wonder that talk of men making governments for their own purposes, contracting with each other in any way they chose, seemed blasphemous and Machiavellian. The holding of slaves was not merely a denial of rights, not merely a stunting of desires and potential, but, in the phrase the abolitionists chose, both for its shock value and its literal truth: a *crime* against the laws of God.[36]

Rhetoric of this sort escalated sharply in the 1850s, as a tightened fugitive slave law moved the contest between conscience and manmade law into the eye of politics. But the rhetoric of "higher law" had run hard in abolitionist talk long before William Seward dropped the phrase onto the Senate floor in 1850, and it persisted well after Seward's inglorious retreat in a fog of evasions and partial retractions. It deserves more than its current footnote status in the history of antislavery thought. Nothing more clearly showed the hard place in which the abolitionists found themselves: with the Constitution, the courts, precedent, expediency, prejudice, and the vast majority of the voters, all arrayed against them. They had no choice but to find a line of argument which, somehow, transcended them all. When you break the slaveholders' law, Charles Beecher urged, "tell the court that you obey Christ, not Belial." Tell them that obedience to them was treason to "the very government of God."[37]

The Choates, the Websters, the Calhouns could not but recoil in uncomprehending fury. The angry reaction to Beecher's "Duty of Disobedience" cost him his pulpit. The abolitionists yearned to do nothing less than smash to pieces the great fictitious chain with which the counterrevolutionary spokesmen had bound together the government of God and the governments of men. And yet between radical abolitionism and Choate's hymns to the enduring state, between Beecher and his furious parishioners, there was an unmistakable line of connection. Out of the moral fires of the revival, out of the ubiquitous talk of God's government swirling through antebellum Protestantism, the abolitionists siphoned off the divine law strain and focused it sharply, uncompromisingly on slavery.

Abolitionism is not the first instance in which human beings, crying obedience, have mounted a rebellion or pried open a new domain of freedom. The extraordinary moral stamina of the abolitionists flowed, in great part, from their conviction that they were mere soldiers arrayed under the generalship of God. Still we should not slight the transmutation of terms at work in abolitionism. Wave Jefferson's Declaration aloft as they would, there was no disguising their departure from the rhetoric of a Jefferson or a Paine into a language more urgent, stocked with starker choices of loyalty. In the rhetoric of radical abolitionism, liberation slid into duty, conscience into command, human rights into the edicts of divine law. What was natural to man was not a list of rights, hard and tangible, carried over from a state of nature. What came naturally to human beings were not compacts, nor Channing's principle of growth. What was inalienable—if human beings would only clear the clutter of expedients and compromises dimming their consciences to see it—was allegiance.

The People Deposed

In constitutional law, not God but the people still ruled. It was their compact, their deliberate contrivance, that came apart in 1860–61 as the nation separated into rival peoples, uncompromisable distrust, and, finally, war. Secession forced Americans back on every scrap of political argument they possessed as they tried to bring the careening events under control and lay siege to legitimacy. What did the people's inalienable right to make and abolish governments mean if, in a pinch, they could not do it? What, on the other hand, did the people's sovereignty amount to, if it could be nullified in a moment by the whims of a few? Never before had the orators loaded their verbal canons with so clear a knowledge that words were weapons.

Southerners took their stand with the Revolutionary cries of rights and social compacts. The anticontractual talk of the Fitzhughs and Calhouns, brought in to defend slavery against its assailants, was sloughed off like a spent cartridge. The states of the South seceded in the name of their peoples gathered in extraordinary conventions, just as they had gathered in 1776 to exercise the same ultimate right of revolution. Jefferson Davis never tired of stressing the identity of the Confederacy's cause with that of the patriots' revolt against England. In Georgia, which had long resisted a formal declaration of rights, the secession convention drummed home the parallel by finally nailing a bill of rights onto the state's constitution. Talk as the southerners would of a new southern nation, the nationalists among them were unable to stem the contractual talk so deep in the South or the war-crippling effects of state and local particularism.[38]

In the North, in contrast, the war loosed a whirlwind of patriotism. From the pulpits the pent-up, abstract talk of loyalty and law poured in a great torrent into the northern cause. Where the secessionist manifestoes talked of the rights of the people and the security of property, northern sermons reverberated with the higher imperatives of divine Providence. "God has not conceded to man the right to rule himself," an Indiana preacher urged in the midst of the war. Men did not make (nor could they break) their governments, Horace Bushnell told his Hartford congregation. "When we assume to make a government or constitution, we only draw out one that was providentially in us before." Let southerners talk about compacts. Northern war propaganda rang with talk of loyalty and union. And, on a plane still higher than that, with the word "nation." "This American people is not a set of [mere] civilized squatters upon a common territory," New York's Henry W. Bellows declared three months before the war began in earnest, "[not] a school of wriggling fish accidentally caught in the federal net—an aggregation of petty communities, confined to some political kaleidoscope, to which, any strong hand at every election may give a shake that alters its whole aspect and identity; but instead of this, it is *a Nation.*" Toward that end, the torrents of blood must flow, the Providence of God must unroll, until (in Bushnell's words), "we shall no more be a compact, or a confederation, or a composition made up by the temporary surrender of powers, but a nation— God's own nation."[39]

Farther from the pulpits, northern unionists showed more reluctance to let the South escape with the entire verbal heritage of the Revolution. The cadences of the Declaration of Independence continued to flow through Lincoln's speeches. He admitted in his first inaugural that whenever "the people" (the whole people, not a mere faction) "shall grow weary of the existing government, they can exercise their constitutional right of amending it, or their revolutionary right to dismember or overthrow it."[40] Well into the war he continued to think that yet another piece of constitutional tinkering would finally put the slavery crisis to rest. And yet as the war ground on and as Lincoln's broodings over the hard course of God's Providence grew, the mystic term "nation" rose even in his vocabulary. It recurs five times in the extraordinarily compressed compass of the Gettysburg Address. Nationalism, prefigured in the prewar talk of Government so strongly that the desire for it lay deep in the Whig-Republican-evangelical alliance, held the North together against the war reversals, the weariness, the angry war resistance.

Victory, when it finally came, brought no end to the furious outburst of political theory making. In and out of the Reconstruction Congresses, men struggled to decide how the federal system was to be reconstituted, whether the rebel states retained their political competence or had died of willful suicide, what the war had done to the right of revolution, what rights it had brought the slaves. Stripped of its occasion, a good deal of the theocratic war talk evaporated, and Republican circles filled once more with the language of rights. During Reconstruction's culminating, radical phase, northerners bore down on the South, constitutional drafts in their hands, to stuff Jefferson's and Adams's general declarations of rights for the first time into the southern constitutions—together with new, northern-style professions of piety. The stock cry of the artisan radicals, that human beings had an inalienable right to the "enjoyment of the fruits of their own labor," was, in a few instances, shoved into southern bills of rights in an effort to preclude slavery from rising up, phoenixlike, under a new name. On the federal level, too, constitutional law was alive for the moment, as it had not been since the late eighteenth century, with novel natural rights claims. And in the South, among the former slaves, freedom loosed a flood of urgent rights talk: the rights of full citizenship, of subsistence, or (most potent of them all) to property in the land on which their sweat and toil had been expended so long.[41]

In the end the postwar settlement hinged not on the new declarations of rights, however, but on the way the victors would reconstitute the people. At the war's close, some four million former slaves stood in a murky legal twilight, somewhere short of political citizenship. At the other extreme of the South's pyramidal social structure, the leaders of the Confederacy were poised to pick up as many of their old political privileges as the North would tolerate. To the Republican party, now clearly in the saddle, was given the task of cutting the South's people to a new cloth: enfranchising those on whose votes it could rely, disfranchising those it distrusted, all with a facade of logical consistency.

As the party moved at a stumbling gait toward black enfranchisement in the first years after the war, pushed by the former abolitionists in its own ranks, by southern intransigence, and the search for loyal voters, the argument closest at hand was that of the Rhode Island radicals of the 1840s: that suffrage was a "natural right." On the radical flanks of the Republican party, men seized the line of argument with alacrity. The right to vote—to defend one's liberty and property in the fray of politics—belonged not to political society (though political society might justly confiscate it for so bald a crime as treason) but to free persons as a natural, original right. That was the way the radicals in the party pressed their case for black suffrage in the District of Columbia early in 1866. George Boutwell, hedging a bit, called the suffrage a "natural social right." Either way, George Julian was sure that the notion of the suffrage as an inherent right "greatly simplified the whole subject"; the right to vote was "as natural, as inborn, as any one of those [rights] enumerated by our fathers."[42] Here was a way of reconstructing politics in terms that would bind the new order by threads of verbal legitimacy to the Revolutionary past.

The tests of the words, however, were not long in coming. One of the most revealing took place in Virginia in 1867–68 where, in a Reconstruction convention jammed with radical Republicans, one of the radical leaders proposed to declare the suffrage an "inherent" right. Thomas Bayne, slave, fugitive, Boston dentist, now the most courageous of the black delegates in Richmond, spoke eloquently in the motion's defense, against a storm of ridicule and racist abuse from the conservative rump in the convention. But more telling was the wholesale desertion of the white Republican radicals from the principle Bayne hoped to nail down. The right to vote, they countered, was a "political," not an inherent, right. It belonged not to anyone—not to paupers nor nomadic Indians nor (let there be no mistake) secessionists—but to those who would use it well. Virginia Republicans swept through the enfranchisement of the state's former slaves on the grounds of their exemplary character, their industry, their readiness to advance themselves, and their loyalty. But they would not run the metaphysical risk of calling it, as Bayne did, a "God-given" right, unalterable by circumstance. Six of the twenty-one black delegates present cast their vote in favor of Bayne's amendment; only two white Republicans joined them.[43]

The question posed (and quickly stifled) at Richmond was

debated the same year at much greater length at Albany. No constitutional convention of the Reconstruction years boasted a more
illustrious membership. Horace Greeley was there, a lifetime of
mercurial but always advanced political opinions behind him, as
chairman of the committee on the suffrage. So was Theodore
Dwight, head of the law school at Columbia. Francis Lieber,
Dwight's Columbia colleague, was not present in the flesh, but his
friends printed up his suggestions in pamphlet form and laid a copy
on every desk in the hall. Among the veterans of the Republican
party's antislavery past was Martin Townsend, a self-professed
Jeffersonian, who had followed the doctrine of the rights of man out
of the Democratic ranks into the Free Soil and Republican causes—
outspokenly enough to find his Troy mansion mobbed by antidraft
rioters in the middle years of the war. Another was George W.
Curtis, editor and orator of no mean talents. These mixed with the
usual collection of party figures, lawyers, businessmen, and a badly
outnumbered minority of Democrats.[44]

Staring them all in the face was the suffrage issue. Greeley, obsessed with voting fraud, arrived in Albany with a bundle of registration and literacy tests designed to curb the fleeting, fraudulent
voters on whom, as he saw it, New York City's Democratic machine
had built its fortunes. Lieber championed a literacy test and, in New
York City elections, a special status for property holders. The Republican party establishment, even before the convention began,
had hitched its political fortunes to the cause of black enfranchisement. Curtis, as everyone knew, was waiting to throw all his per-
suasive powers into the cause of woman suffrage. As for the Democrats, it was certain that they would resist all these innovations with
every tactic at their command.

For three weeks the convention hall roiled in high-minded debate
over the nature of the suffrage, paeans to womanhood, vicious
racism, and constant political maneuvering. Townsend, in the interest of black suffrage, and Curtis, in the interest of the enfranchisement of women, tried hard to appropriate for their separate causes
what remained of the language of the Revolution. Curtis's opening
speech reverberated with the rhetoric of 1776. Townsend insisted
that suffrage was a "natural right," etched where no one could
mistake it in the "consent of the governed" clause of Jefferson's

Declaration. The Democrats, returning to the ground they had occupied in 1846, countered that the suffrage issue was not a matter of rights at all but a question of "taste and association," of "expediency and national prosperity," which could be settled only by those white, male New Yorkers who had inherited the original compact.[45]

An ordinarily astute observer could easily have predicted as much. The more surprising phenomenon was the speed with which the vast majority of Republicans fled the ground of rights. Some, like Greeley, simply retreated to their erstwhile Whig proclivities, protesting that the suffrage did not belong "to persons of any class, whose vote will not contribute to the general intelligence and capacity which go to make up the popular verdict." Theodore Dwight, with the precision due a college professor, ticked off the categories of persons in whose hands the vote would work public injury: subversives (that is to say, secessionists), lunatics and children, criminals, bettors on elections, persons not sufficiently incorporated into the state to use the vote wisely (that is, the Irish crowding into New York City) and those dependent on the will of others (paupers and—as Dwight soon made clear—women). The old arguments for virtual representation, mingled with extravagant praise of the family as the nucleus of every other social bond, were pushed to the fore to block the passage of Curtis's amendment. It was said that "no respectable writer upon the science of civil government" could be found who believed that voting was a natural right. Francis Lieber, lest the delegates mistake the meaning of his expansive notion of rights, had taken pains to make clear that the right to vote was a "noble" right, "natural" in the sense that the course of history bent its way toward its realization, but not "natural" in the sense that anyone who chose could lay claim to it. The status of voter was an office, a privilege, men declared, which "society" bestowed as it thought fit. B. Platt Carpenter, about to slip into the sort of patronage post that only party loyalists received, summed up the sober second thoughts of the Republican majority: "Every page of the world's history prove[s] the elective franchise to be a privilege and not a right."[46]

Under the onslaught, Curtis concentrated all his force on the question of woman's sphere and talents, before going down to abject defeat. The radical Republicans pushed their black suffrage proposal through, not on Townsend's grounds but on those of expediency—only to see it, together with the rest of their labors, rejected by the voters. As one of the delegates noted, the Republicans had come to the convention prepared to defend Negro suffrage as a matter of right until Curtis, threatening the convention with "the nameless horrors of female suffrage," had stampeded them onto the Democratic ground of raw expediency.[47] Under the pressures of race and sex, the delegates fled from talk of rights.

The result was no mere strategic retreat but a rout of startling dimensions. None of the slogans of the Revolution, Carpenter had declared, were strictly true—certainly not the musty old abstraction "No taxation without representation," with which the advocates of woman suffrage, inside and outside the hall, were so strongly pressing their case. "There is no right, not even to life itself, that is perfectly absolute"—that was not subject to regulation by the state, "having reference to its own safety and perpetuity." Stephen D. Hand, like Carpenter a Republican, put the line of argument still more strongly: "There is no such thing as an inalienable right. There is no such thing as a manhood right of any kind or name whatever, but that man may be called upon to yield in society." "You can see the uses that will be made of this doctrine of natural rights," he warned the delegates. "It meets us at every turn. I wish to dispose of it upon the threshold. . . . It is not the right of man to do anything except the interests of society permit it." "Away then, sir, with any such theory as the doctrine of natural right!" Abraham Conger echoed the sentiment from the Democratic side of the hall, in a speech reeking of the pieties of divinely ordained government. "What a monstrous fallacy; what abominable heresy this is, in this age of the world."[48]

These were the arguments of beleaguered men, determined to crush every last ember of legitimacy which might survive from the southern misadventure, terrified by the specter of woman's suffrage. But in them the counterrevolution in political talk—the fuzzing of lines between rights and duties, the pieties, the terrors, the denigration of the government-making capacities of the people, the apotheosis of obligations and government—all came home. Natural Rights talk had been a tool to crack the bonds chaining politics to history and custom. With talk of the People, mid-nineteenth-century Americans had made high drama out of the government-creating, will-asserting powers of the citizenry. But against the counterclaims of governments higher and far older than mere contrivance, of law's inescapability, of sociological bonds and historical destinies which unrolled beneath human beings without bothering to consult their will, the retrospective, contractual language gave way. Under Townsend's and Curtis's eyes, an arsenal of arguments was broken in pieces.

The need for principles remained; in this matter, nineteenth-century politics permitted no vacuums. Even as they harried the idea of natural rights off the convention floor, the Republicans proceeded to erect a new abstraction in its place. It was "society," Hand insisted, which bestowed the right of suffrage on some and withheld it from others. It was "society's" interests that were paramount. "Society," not the people, made governments. "My theory and position is this," Horace E. Smith interrupted the debate to define the words swirling through the convention hall, "that society is an institution of God, a divine institution; that government is a necessity of it, and presupposes the existence of society, and that society uses government as a power or instrument by which to regulate the civil conduct of its members, and secure their rights and their liberty."[49]

Townsend and his cluster of supporters backed off in alarm from this new despot, "society," being slipped in between the people and the governments they made. "We are a government making people," he protested. "There is no divine society."[50] But the people, the kind of people who could make and unmake governments at will, indifferent to Providence and history had—at least at Albany —been deposed. They had reigned, they had locked themselves in war, and now the victors, their backs set against the remnant language of the Revolution, had slipped other abstractions in their place. For the moment, no one knew exactly what they meant or what they would be good for in the emerging postwar world of rawer economic competition and mounting economic conflict. That task was to fall, not to the politicians or the moral philosophers with their talk of Government but to those who called themselves political scientists.

5

The State

Professional Political Science

In mid-nineteenth-century America, the science of politics remained an arena of amateurs, its keywords close to everyday speech. Should one be inclined to doubt the fact, there is no surer cure than to spend an hour with the records of any mid-nineteenth-century state constitutional convention. Do so, and one puts to sea in an eclectic, democratic flood of talk. Out onto the floors of those conventions rolled an astonishingly variegated tide of words: graceful periods and vicious satire, spontaneous insult and laboriously memorized quotation, close legal reasoning and the worst of doggerel poetry, self-indulgent reminiscences and inspired perorations. Granted that men of the law, a legal axiom from Blackstone at their lips and a copy of some other state's constitution in their waistcoat pocket, were vastly overrepresented in these gatherings. Granted, too, that in a state's early years, when time was urgent and the public's willingness to pay the daily maintenance of their delegates was still tender, such men often pushed the proceedings through with dispatch. But throughout most of the century the hedge of arcane jargon fencing off the law from the discourse of ordinary citizens was not yet very high. Words like Government or "rights" slid easily from political to religious, moral, or economic meanings. Nor was the willingness of the delegates to confine their oratorical freedoms at all great. On and on they talked—72 days in the Massachusetts convention of 1853, 139 days in the New York convention of 1867–68, 188 days in the Ohio convention of 1873—against the sporadic efforts of convention chairmen to stem the flow of words or, at the least, confine them reasonably closely to the mundane subjects at hand. The rhetoric of political science was a permeable language, open to the people, graspable by virtually any political contender.

Those at the forefront of the counterrevolution in political rhetoric had often worried about the undisciplined and amateurish state of political argument in the United States. From the 1830s on—from the moment it became clear, that is, that property-based restrictions on the suffrage and political office had been swept clean away and were not to be restored—many an earnest writer and printer had combined to publish a political "grammar" for the instruction of the newly empowered demos: small, cheap volumes, as a rule, consisting of the text of the federal Constitution, glossed with controversy-skirting commentary, and prefaced with dire warning of the dangers of political illiteracy.[1] But neither they nor the moral philosophers nor the formidable law compendia of a Kent or a Story succeeded in wedging the keywords of politics very far away from the vernacular of common talk.

Only in the wake of the Civil War did a new coterie of professionals boldly and systematically undertake the task of formalizing the amateur talk of politics. Against a background of still rawer class conflict than the nation had yet experienced, constitutional lawyers and professional political scientists poured a heady new set of abstractions into political talk. Their words carried few of the explicitly pious overtones of the mid-nineteenth-century counterrevolutionary talk of Government. They formed a vocabulary not of religious but of professional authority. But the intent, transposed into novel terms and sharpened with new anxieties, was the same: to wrest the language of political legitimacy away from the people.

In this effort, the first off the mark were the lawyers. Alarmed at the pretensions of the constitutional conventions, made doubly nervous by the willingness of state legislatures to meddle more and more actively with economic legislation, they rushed to devise a new set of constitutional limits around the powers of the people. By the mid-1880s, having found their voice, they had started the courts on a career of judicial interventionism which was to litter the law books with unconstitutionality decisions through the midpoint of the New Deal, leaving behind a formidable jargon of legal constraints on popular rule.

Somewhat slower to organize were the professional political scientists; but in the end the biggest of the new words, the State, was to be their construct. University political science departments were unknown before the 1880s. Most of the massive, creedal volumes of the discipline came off the presses in the 1890s, a decade of wrenching economic depression, Populist radicalism, and the first serious stirrings of socialism. Twenty years later the axioms of late nineteenth-century political science were just beginning to be filtered down through the medium of the college textbook. Those texts, dead and dust covered now, have long been an embarrassment to the historians of modern political science. Bernard Crick, in his magisterial history of the discipline, hurried past them with a barely disguised grimace.[2] The sovereign omnipotence of the State—the notion the professional political scientists placed at their discipline's core—disappeared long ago from the lexicon of their trade. The central formulas of their science now grate on the ear like misplaced phrases from a strange political tongue.

But in the contest over political language in America the theorists of the State played a role too big, too revealing of the tangled skein of vast words and crass ambitions to overlook. Like the lawyers, but still more boldly, the pioneer generation of political scientists tried to pull the vocabulary of politics away from day-to-day speech into an empyrean of higher and higher abstractions, farther and farther from the people's grasp. The moral philosophers' devotion to government, the New Yorkers' talk of "society" in 1867 were but premonitions of the audacity with which the professional political scientists set about to raise the stakes of legitimate political talk: to seize politics itself (if they could) from the grubby hands of the amateurs. The State was the antonym of the People; it was a formidable barrier to popular claims of rights. No matter that in late nineteenth-century America, the state—as a structure of public officials, rules, and rule-making bodies—was, in comparison to the other industrial nations, barely discernible. The political scientists taught a social class and generation to imagine something else, an abstract holder of sovereignty called the State, shimmering behind the conflict-ridden screen of everyday life. Not until that was done did their glistening edifice of words suddenly collapse and leave Americans talking nakedly, for the first time, about interests.

Constitutional Law

In a democracy, the counterpoise to the people is the law. So Alexis de Tocqueville was told by his informants in the American bar in 1831–32; so he, like they, had hoped.[3] It was a point Whiggish lawyers were fond of repeating in antebellum America, whistling against the dark of Jacksonian democracy. But it was not until long after Tocqueville's conversations, not until the last years of the century, that the lawyers coalesced into a separate, powerful force in politics, talking a political jargon peculiarly their own. Only then, in a frightened, aggressive rush, did the courts and lawyers try to elbow out the people, the men of elections and legislatures, and plant at the very apex of politics the special edicts—and the language—of constitutional law.

Like many revolutions, the lawyers' revolution of the last quarter of the nineteenth century had precedents enough to disguise some of the audacity of the event. Since independence, lawyer-politicians, one foot in the legislatures, the other in their private law practices, had played a central role in shaping the contours of political argument in America. John Marshall and his brethren on the early Supreme Court had been political players of no mean weight; in New England the Federalist legal fraternity had put up a massive front to the forces of popular politics. But the democratization of law practice in the second third of the nineteenth century, as the restrictions to entry into the bar were broken down, had crippled the consolidation of a professional legal interest distinct from party and politics. And the courts, where the lawyers brought their weight most directly to bear, had been on the whole relatively timid players in antebellum politics. As arbiters of everyday conflicts over property and persons, as shapers of the new forms of contracts, conveyances, and immunities indispensable to an expansive market capitalism, there was no mistaking the social importance of the courts. But democratized themselves, as more and more judgeships were pried open to popular election in the 1840s and 1850s, they had hardly formed a sizeable counterforce to the flow of public, political power into the hands of the voters.

The sharpest authority the courts possessed was the power of constitutional review. That they had appropriated quickly and forcefully in the first years of the republic. But the prerogative of inserting the higher will of the judges over that of the people and their legislators, awesome as it was in theory, was in practice mistrusted, controversial, and hesitantly used. The point, too often lost in a flourish of precedents, is worth making carefully. After John Marshall's pathbreaking *Marbury* v. *Madison* decision in 1803, over half a century went by before the United States Supreme Court found another federal statute (in the ill-fated *Dred Scott* decision) to declare invalid. State statutes were more vulnerable. Once a year on the average between 1789 and 1860, the Supreme Court intervened to strike down a piece of state legislation, but that was all. Far more controversial legislation passed through the state court systems, to be sure, than reached the bench of John Marshall or Roger Taney; and at the state level there had been a wave of judicial activism in the politically volatile 1830s, 1840s, and 1850s. But the results remained modest. Between independence and the Civil War, the Virginia state supreme court voided only two pieces of legislation, the Massachusetts supreme court, ten. A more generously designed count of cases of judicial review in the New York court system yielded sixty-two instances in the first sixty years of the century, almost precisely the number New York's vastly more aggressive courts handed down in the four-year span from 1898 through 1901. The essential domain of the antebellum courts was private law. Constitutional law they left, by and large, to the politicians.[4]

The first signs of a markedly new era of legal activism appeared with Reconstruction. The constitutional tangles of Reconstruction were ripe for lawyers. Even more so was the raft of new statutes which the state legislatures began to produce in the 1860s and 1870s, buoyed by the wartime experience with the active, broadly competent state and by new demands, many of them from below.

Working-class radicals, sensing the possibilities of a radical Republican–labor alliance, dropped their long-standing fear of state power to agitate for shorter-hours legislation, bureaus of labor statistics, conditions of employment statutes, and state regulation of the new, power-engrossing railroad corporations. In Ohio in 1873 and in California in 1878, state constitutional conventions were invaded by workingmen's party spokesmen, talking of Bentham's "general happiness" and of ambitious programs of state power. In the South, radical Republicans often played the same role. Elsewhere subsidy-hungry entrepreneurs took the lead.[5]

That this resurgence of popular sovereignty in radically new guise should have provoked a counterattack by those whose interests it threatened should hardly be surprising. Through the end of the century and beyond, a continuous, ragged battle raged along these lines—workers, economic promoters, and Protestant moralists, all by turns sounding the call for state activism and scuttling for rebuttals as the issues turned and shifted. What was not quite so predictable at the outset was the extraordinarily prominent role the lawyers would play. But by the end of the Civil War the lawyers were already hard at work on a shelf of new law books and legal briefs, designed to preempt the postwar political order not only for their clients but for their peculiar habits of talk—and themselves.

The books (being the easier to produce) came first. Of the post–Civil War law volumes that looked backward to the antebellum controversies over the people's power and sovereignty, the most important was John A. Jameson's *The Constitutional Convention* of 1867. A Chicago lawyer, Republican, and sometime judge, Jameson was not by nature a writer. *The Constitutional Convention* was a book wrenched out of him in anger at the havoc wrought by the southern secession conventions and (closer to home) by a rebellious, Democratic-dominated constitutional convention in Jameson's own Illinois in 1862. Fueled by the old, expansive claims of the people's sovereignty, the convention had set itself up virtually as a rival government to the Republican-dominated legislature: promulgating ordinances, striking off bond issues, sending instructions to the governor, acting (as men had so often claimed) as a quasi-revolutionary council, possessed of sovereignty itself. Frightened by the precedent, Jameson set out to bring the extraordinary powers of the people's conventions under the heel of ordinary law.

The result was dull work for the most part, a lawyer's handbook for other lawyers, specifying how a constitutional convention was to be organized, its committees appointed, the rules of debate established, votes counted, its conclusions framed. But as Jameson clamped form and precedent over the least regularized of the people's institutions, there was no mistaking his bigger point: to hook this Leviathan so tightly by the nose that it would never break loose again. Jameson was an honest enough historian to admit the precedent of "revolutionary conventions" in the American past. Heroically in 1776 and foolhardily in 1860–61, he wrote, men had stepped "outside the circle of the law" and trusted their destiny to war and Providence. But a *constitutional* convention, he protested, was a gathering of an utterly different sort. It possessed no sovereignty, Jameson insisted: no imagined right of revolution. Its delegates were not the people, and they spoke with no special authority. The constitutional convention, Jameson countered, was nothing more than a consultative body, a mere drafting committee, an intermittently convened branch of the government answerable to the courts and "subaltern" to the legislature which called it into being.[6]

In the post–Civil War North, terrorized by secession, Jameson's assault on the autonomy of the people's conventions found a quickly responsive audience. No sooner had the book come out than the Michigan constitutional convention ordered up a copy for each of its members. Convention managers shaped procedure to Jameson's prescriptions. For decades it sustained a major presence in the footnotes of constitutional lawyers, who used it to clip the antebellum claims for a convention's power to mere stumps. On occasion in post–Civil War America, but then only in the South, a constitutional convention succeeded in gaining back a measure of its forfeited autonomy in the passage of an ordinance or two or in sporadic defiance of its legislative instructions. During the disfranchisement movement of the 1890s, when southern constitutional conventions swept the last of the Reconstruction-enfranchised black voters out of the polls, most of them did so on their own authority, even when otherwise instructed by the legislature, rather than hazard the results of a ratification election. But these were exceptions. In New

York state, where constitutional convention debate had once sprawled over all of political theory with every clause of the constitution up for grabs, the delegates to the 1894 convention found their discussion limited to a list of specific amendments, filtered through a complex system of committees.[7] Born out of revolutionary necessity, nurtured in talk of the people's will, the constitutional convention was finally chained to forms the lawyers would prescribe.

The more threatening Leviathan of the moment, however, was the legislatures, and the bigger book, accordingly, was Thomas M. Cooley's *Constitutional Limitations* of 1868. Men quoted it with alacrity in the constitutional debates of the late nineteenth century, bestowed on Cooley a stature unmatched by any other law writer of his generation, and paired his name with Blackstone, Kent, and Story. In truth Cooley's lawbook was like none of theirs. Blackstone and Kent had tried to wrestle the law into a semblance of order; Story had devoted himself to working out the tenets of federalism. All of them had written impassionedly of the sublimity of law. But the point of Cooley's project was different: to stake out the domain beyond which legislation could not go, no matter how alluring the public benefits. *Constitutional Limitations* was a handbook unabashedly designed to facilitate constitutional challenge to the legislature's will. Its technical legalism could not disguise Cooley's larger, political aim: to thrust the courts as never before into the eye of day-to-day politics as arbiters of what the people's representatives could and could not do.[8]

Cooley's work did not manufacture on its own the rising tide of judicial activism. *Constitutional Limitations* entered a profession in the process of tightening its entry requirements, bolstering its status, and hitching its fortunes, more clearly than ever before, to the ascendent course of railroad and business corporations. At Albany in 1867, the partisans of a "beneficent" government, actively committed to promotion of the public welfare, had locked horns with men talking more shrilly than ever before of self-governing economic laws and the legitimate "sphere" of legislative meddling. That keenness on the part of those with vulnerable property rights to define the precise boundary of legislation's legitimate "sphere" grew apace in hard times. As each of late nineteenth-century capitalism's recurrent crises brought a stronger whiff of class conflict into politics, as the angry victims of economic collapse turned to the legislatures for acts of relief or regulation, for subsidies or reform, as the expansive Whig-Republican rhetoric of Government faded into nervous talk of a socialist rising from below, the judges' temptation to substitute court-made law for the hazardous verdicts of electoral politics mounted. But desires alone do not make a politically effective language. What remained to be seen were the words on which the courts would launch their experiment.

At first it appeared that the lawyers might run their arguments through the big, still unexhausted terms of Jefferson's Declaration. The old inalienable rights of property might be dusted off, wiped clean of their radical connotations, joined to the antislavery talk of free contracts and free labor, and fashioned into a defense of the social arrangements of barely regulated capitalism. On the United States Supreme Court, Justice Stephen Field pressed this line of argument with all the resources at his command. From his dissent in the Slaughterhouse cases in 1873 until old age overtook Field's faculties in the mid-1890s, he and a faction of like-minded justices shot off new natural rights like Roman candles. Most of them derived, in one fashion or another, from the rights of "free labor": the right to enter into whatever calling or pursuit a person should pick out; the right to make cigars in one's tenement, if one chose, or set up a butchering business in one's back yard (though the legislature should call both a menace to public health); the right to manufacture colored margarine (though the legislature called it fraud on honest dairy farmers); the right to set up a laundry where one chose (though the California legislature swelled with talk of driving the Chinese, their laundries, and their economic competition from the state altogether). All these economic rights, Field and his fellow dissenters insisted, were grounded on the bedrock rights of life, liberty, property, and—where those were not expansive enough for the purposes—happiness.[9]

Yoked to the Fourteenth Amendment, the notion of a vast new domain of imprescriptible economic rights burst as a powerful argument into constitutional law. Not merely property but property's competitive uses were baptized with natural right. Jefferson—who in the flesh had distrusted economic ambition no less deeply than ambitious government—was recast as the champion of something very close to laissez-faire. But Natural Rights talk, volatile as always, was not easily confined to the service of entrepreneurial aggressiveness and maximal labor mobility. Out of the rights of man and the principles of natural justice the judges and corporation lawyers made their public speeches.[10] Out of the same words Stephen Field produced a career of judicial dissents, vigorous enough to set men talking of his presidential capacities. But most judges, speaking from the bench, preferred more cautious language.

In the centennial year of 1876, as the orators picked their way through the words of the Declaration more nervously than usual, it was clear that co-optation was not an easy course. After 1876, the antislavery uses of Jefferson's words now exhausted, the Republican party dropped the last of them from its platform pieties, leaving platform quotations from the Declaration for the rest of the century to outsiders once more: the partisans of woman suffrage, Henry George's coalition, and the legitimacy-hungry Socialist Labor party.[11] Thomas Cooley, for one, had already made it clear that he thought appeals to natural or inalienable rights void of any standing in the courts. Rights—property rights included—were creatures of the law. Beyond the formal language of statute, precedent, and constitutions, Cooley insisted, the judges could not go. The courts "cannot run a race of opinions upon points of right, reason, and expediency with the law-making powers," Cooley warned; down that path lay no clear-cut alternative to the amateur political talk of the legislatures.[12]

For all these reasons, when the courts finally moved into the business of aggressive judicial review, it was not (by and large) on Field's terms that they proceeded, but Cooley's. The movement began in earnest in the mid-1880s, against a background of bitter labor disputes, renewed struggle to tame the railroad corporations, and a rash of new placating labor legislation. The judges' engine was what legal historians call formalism, a whole series of judge-made principles, designed piece by piece, cemented in precedent, until they took on constitutional status themselves. The rights of "due process" are the most famous, but there were others: "liberty of contract" (by which the courts excluded the terms of a wage earner's employment from most forms of legislative regulation), the doctrine that tax moneys could only be spent for a "public purpose" (still live

enough in the early years of the New Deal to bedevil public programs of housing construction), the right of property owners to a
"reasonable" return on their investments (by which the courts,
having already yanked the setting of railroad rates into the realm
of judicial prerogative, emasculated most of what was left of railroad regulation), or the right of the courts to enjoin any act (strikes
in practice) which the judges themselves deemed an overt threat to
the public safety.[13]

On these grounds the judges—and the lawyers who fed them
their arguments—seized a vital chunk of power from the amateurs
and spiraled it upward into the hands of higher, state arbiters. In the
New York courts, where cases of judicial review in the 1870s and
1880s had numbered between four and five a year, the rate had
tripled by the end of the century. In Illinois in the 1880s, the courts
locked themselves in a battle with the legislature which ended in a
bushelful of invalidated labor protection statutes. In the crisis years
of the 1890s, the United States Supreme Court added its weight to
the movement toward judicial activism in a series of decisions
which were to leave their mark on the law until the midpoint of the
New Deal.[14]

The courts, it must be said, voided only a tiny fraction of the
statutes which came before them. But they chose their cases carefully—income tax, railroad rate legislation, labor regulation, anti-
trust legislation—right in the eye of the sharpest economic conflicts
in fin-de-siècle America; and they did so with the full burden of
consciousness. Judicial review "is the loftiest function and most
sacred duty of the judiciary," the president of the American Bar
Association declared in 1892, when the new judicial activism was
rising to its height. "This is the only breakwater against the haste
and the passions of the people—against the tumultuous ocean of
democracy."[15] Sovereignty, law books like Cooley's piously insisted, belonged where the Founders had placed it, in the hands of
the people; the courts acted the part of mere regents. But by the
century's close the people's will had been channeled down a gaunt-
let of judicial reconsideration at which Tocqueville's friends would
have stood agape.

The words with which this revolution in power was accomplished
formed no tidy whole. At once powerfully resonant and profoundly
arcane, the vocabulary of legal formalism enveloped the expansive

amateur talk of rights and liberties in a jargon which was exclusively the lawyers' own. If outsiders mistrusted their talk as a veil over rawer considerations, drawn with more haste than logical forethought, they had their reasons. From doctrine to doctrine, precedent to precedent, courts and lawyers tacked as the case and their propensities demanded. They never came close to creating anything as consistent as the laissez-faire with which they were later charged. Hesitant as they were to allow the legislatures to set limits on the bargains employers struck with their workers, they had no such doubts about the power of legislation to intervene between a saloon keeper and his liquid property or between a prostitute and her customers or in scores of other ways to buttress with state power what they took to be the moral feelings of their countrymen. Tender when it came to property rights, they let the civil rights of the former slaves be steamrollered to a shadow. They had at their fingertips both a doctrine of legislative inhibition and a doctrine of the general "police" powers of the state which, when they chose to use it, was as broad as anything Jeremy Bentham had imagined. As they oscillated between loose and tight construction, intervention and acquiescence, the swing votes on the courts moving back and forth like shuttlecocks, it was hard to avoid thinking (as Oliver Wendell Holmes was bold enough to say outright) that their legal doctrines were simply a cover for the ordinary political prejudices of the judges.[16]

The function of their talk, however, had not been to clamp a logical coherence on the law. It had been, rather, to spiral political talk upward out of the popular forums into a code no amateurs could manipulate with the skill of the lawyers themselves. In the law schools, where insularity had always run deep, the professors were now admitting that their aim was not to teach the principles of justice but to make their students think like lawyers—as if that were to think and argue differently from other political persons.[17] Self-conscious as never before, a profession now, not merely an agglomeration of self-trained pleaders, the lawyers had shown how a profession could gather authority not by tapping a vocabulary deep in the vernacular of everyday speech but by inventing one of its own. Down those same tracks toward power a good many other professions would follow in modern America.

But the judicial revolution did not so much answer the old, central questions of politics as, quite deliberately, draw a veil of mystification across them. How were the people to comprehend this recession of authority from their grasp? With what metaphors were they now to imagine political legitimacy? With the people in eclipse and the courts playing the role of the people's regents, who now held the vaunted powers of sovereignty? The clearer and more startling answers, spinning off the word State, came not from the lawyers but from the nascent profession of political science.

The Grammar of a Profession

The discipline of political science, like the rising fortunes of constitutional law, was a product of the post–Civil War years. Forged by a generation profoundly affected by the war and Reconstruction controversies, consolidated in an era of sharpening social and economic tensions, political science carried its birthmarks deeply. Instruction in the fundamentals of politics had had a place in the collegiate curriculum, to be sure, for a long time. Most of the antebellum moral philosophers had held the field of "natural and political law" or "civil polity" somewhere in their omnibus list of responsibilities. But it was not until the 1880s, as the old subject of moral philosophy began to splinter into smaller disciplinary pieces, that the first academic departments of political science took shape. Columbia inaugurated what was to be the largest and most influential of the new departments when its School of Political Science opened its doors in 1880. The University of Michigan followed suit in 1881. Johns Hopkins, which was to become Columbia's nearest rival, launched its *Studies in Historical and Political Science* in 1882. By 1890 the number of colleges and universities which claimed to teach something called "political science" was 10; by 1912, that number had grown to 141.[18]

Born in the economically troubled and strike-ridden 1880s, political science, like the law, swelled from the first with immense coherence-making ambitions. The first generation of political scientists did not imagine simply another, narrowly circumscribed academic discipline. They hoped, rather, to sweep the public, social sciences together into a common front. The first results of those efforts were far from even. At hide-bound William and Mary College in the 1880s, students got their political theory from Calhoun and Abel Upshur; at the University of Michigan one could read Hegel; at Yale those who elected political science got a heavy diet of social Darwinism from William Graham Sumner. But where the leading architects of the field got their way, the domain of their subject reached out with a sprawling grasp. The University of Michigan's short-lived School of Political Science offered courses in economics, law, the treatment of crime and destitution, forestry, and the science of sanitation. At Columbia, John W. Burgess gathered the teaching of history, economics, statistical science, and constitutional law all under the School of Political Science's domain.[19] Through the sub-discipline of history the political scientists proposed to study the evolution of the body politic; through constitutional and public law, its anatomy; through economics and sociology, its respiration and diseases. They would comb the globe for examples of political societies, compare them, working upward, finally, to the general laws of the body politic. Political science in its formative years was shot through with imperial ambitions.

Before the century was out, it was clear that this institutional effort to stem the onward fracturing of the social sciences had failed of result. The professors of law resisted the political scientists' embrace; the professors of economics, history, and sociology hived off to establish their own disciplinary shops. By the time the professional students of politics finally banded together in 1903 in a professional organization of their own, they knew themselves engaged in yet another splintered academic discipline. Their ordering ambitions flowed instead into a professional language, with the State at its core, saturated with immense abstractions.

To talk of a professional language is a shorthand for a whole series of formative experiences, the upshot of which made one a conversant member of the league of fellow political scientists: a college degree, graduate work at Johns Hopkins or Columbia, a year perhaps in Berlin, a modest doctoral dissertation, and a willingness to teach a brace of courses in government, history, jurisprudence, or constitutional law. By 1886 one had a professional journal to which to subscribe and by the mid-1890s, a collection of books, the foundation stones of the discipline, to place on one's seminar shelves: Theodore Dwight Woolsey's *Political Science* (1877), Woodrow Wilson's *The State* (1889), W. W. Willoughby's *An Examination of the Nature of the State* (1896), and, weightiest of them all, John W. Burgess's *Political Science and Comparative Constitutional Law* (1890). But to catch the grammar of the trade and its rules of initiation, the most revealing texts are the classroom handbooks the professional students of politics put together in a spasm of disciplinary consolidation in the first decade of the twentieth century.

Open any one of those textbooks, and it is clear that initiation into the political science fraternity entailed a massive repudiation of most of the political convictions still in the air in late nineteenth-century America. To claim any serious knowledge of politics, the textbooks asserted, was to know that political societies never began through contract. The idea that sovereignty rested in the people, though still at hand in the formulas of virtually every law text, was dismissed as a solecism, a "contradiction in terms." As for the notion of inalienable rights, however current it might still be in corners of the law or among the people at large, to the political scientists it was an "abandoned" theory, "no longer believed in by any scholar of note." A student who arrived in graduate school naive enough to harbor any of these notions learned that the entry rule of the profession was to recognize that the hard light of science had "exploded" them all.[20]

Some of these repudiations of the keywords of antebellum politics, given the Protestant, Whiggish backgrounds of the discipline's recruits, were relatively easily made. The startling element in these initiation rituals had to do with rights. For unhappy as the moral philosophers had been with the idea of rights unless pinioned firmly to duties, they had never really imagined throwing the idea out altogether. When Theodore Woolsey's massively learned monument to that generation's writings on government appeared in 1877, it left hardly a doubt in that regard. President of Yale College, editor and preserver of Francis Lieber's works, and as erudite a champion of the notion of moral government as the century could boast, Woolsey was a man whose every political instinct went out to the active, morally benevolent state. "The sphere of the state, then, may reach as far as the nature and needs of the man and of men reach,"

Woolsey wrote. The state was necessary, natural, and in consequence "divine."[21] But of the three books into which Woolsey's *Political Science* was divided—Rights, State, and Practical Politics—the first in priority was Rights: Kantian rights, to be sure, claims of self-realization rather than birthright possession but rights no less firmly engraved in human nature for that. Let the state clash directly with conscience, and Woolsey's first allegiance (like that of most of the antebellum moral philosophers) could not but go to the higher government of God.

Woolsey's *Political Science* had been thirty years in the making by 1877. A half-dozen years later, had one opened the new basic source book for an up-to-date political scientist's library, John Lalor's *Cyclopaedia of Political Science, Political Economy, and the Political History of the United States, by the Best American and European Writers,* and tried to turn to the term "rights," one could only conclude that the word had dropped clean out of the discipline altogether. Nor would that impression have been wholly wrong. For the next thirty years, no serious textbook in the discipline ever again introduced the business at hand as the science of rights. To a man, the new professional political scientists shuttled talk of rights—both natural and conventional—off into their back pages, compressed it drastically, or simply dropped it out as irrelevant to the central concern of their science.[22]

What the amateurs called rights, the political scientists countered, were simply grants of custom and law. The point was made in any number of ways. At Princeton in the 1890s, Woodrow Wilson told his students that all rights rested on "the broad ground of *convenience";* they were set by "the state of opinion and the stage of social convention." To think otherwise was to fall for the brittle, ahistorical abstractions which gave Jefferson's writings their "false and artificial" and (as Wilson patiently explained) "un-American" note.[23] At Columbia, John W. Burgess was still less compromising. The dream of rights independent of the state was "unscientific, erroneous, and harmful." "Liberty," he wrote, is "a creation of the state. . . . The so-called laws of God, of nature, of reason . . . are legally, and for the subject, what the state declares them to be." Two decades later the force of the axiom was not a whit diminished. "It is not wise in political discussion to speak of natural rights," New York University's professor of government maintained in 1907.

Each one may do things, ought to do things, that will be of benefit to the community, but he has not the right to demand anything of the community. . . . The citizen may and must do what the community determines it is best for him to do; he must stand in the forefront of battle if so ordered. He must not do what the state forbids. . . .[24]

The phenomenon was not a little startling. In precisely the same decades in which the lawyers were shoveling new constitutional rights into the law, the political scientists seemed to be doing their best to sweep talk of rights, of conscience, indeed of every island of immunity from the coercive powers of the state, clean out of politics altogether.

As rights dropped out of political science, the term which swelled to fill their place was the State. Even the rankest beginner knew that the State was the fundamental subject matter of the profession. Political science was the science not of rights or governmental institutions or the still larger number of activities one might call political but of an abstraction which stood above and "back of" them all. For the next quarter of a century, virtually until the eve of the First World War, the term State was the password by which one gained admission to the fraternity of professional political scientists.

Forcing that talismanic word into clear definition was no easy task. The political scientists' State was not simply the moral philosophers' Government in new guise, though there were continuities. The work of a generation grown uneasy with religious metaphors, the State formed no part of a great chain of governments soaring to the heavens. The State was deliberately made by no one: neither by contract nor by God. It came about through the quiet forces of history, the textbook writers explained, when a people somehow found itself acting as a coherent "whole." It was "the outward organized manifestation of a conscious spirit of political unity"; it was the creation of a successfully realized "general will."[25] Whatever figurative words the political scientists chose, the State captured a straining for wholeness so sharp one could virtually taste it in the word itself. The State by definition was a unity, a moral "person," whose will radiated outward into what men called law. The State stood back of all the outward institutions of politics, bound them together in an entity, a word, which somehow comprehended them all.

At this level, the notion of the State was hard to hold in focus against the fuzz of the professors' language. When it came to the powers of the State, however, the political scientists minced no words. The State was "omnipotent." It held in itself the full powers of sovereignty: "original, absolute, unlimited, universal power over the individual subject and over all associations of subjects." It held "absolute authority" over all its citizens, the textbook writers asserted: a "virtual ownership of the services, property and land of its subjects." These were "hard" sayings, the political scientists occasionally admitted. But "really," John Burgess advised, "the state cannot be conceived without sovereignty, i.e. without unlimited power over its subjects. That is its very essence."[26] If claims of this sort sounded for the moment like the language of state socialism, so be it. The political scientists' State was the logical consequence of their antirights talk. The State was the entity which held all rights and powers, which in an extraordinary act of aggrandizement had swallowed them whole.

Though the political scientists chose their words to shock the uninitiated, to set the people with their chaff about fundamental rights and democratic sovereignty back on their heels, the assertions they pressed into the theoretical core of their discipline were not wholly their own invention. Blackstone long before had insisted on sovereignty's boundlessness. So had Bentham's friend and disciple, John Austin, and a distinguished line of "analytical" jurists who had followed him, talking of the law as a system of commands from sovereign to subject. But in America theoretical sovereignty had been packed off onto the people, and practical sovereignty had been divided among a maze of contending authorities which had routinely given British observers (reared to the straightforward sovereignty of Parliament) no end of trouble to comprehend. Austin himself, committed to sovereignty's inherent indivisibility, had found the location of sovereignty in the American federal system a particularly knotty case to solve. Austin's English critics, by the same token, routinely trotted out the American example to prove that laws did not necessarily derive their force from a discernible sovereign at all but took their rise in more complicated ways from custom, habit, or the workings of public opinion.[27] This in the 1880s was Woodrow Wilson's line. Though he sensed the tendencies of his discipline well enough to title his book *The State*, what interested him was "society": that entity "compounded of the common habit, an evolution of experience, an interlaced growth of tenacious relationships, a compact, living, organic whole."[28] But by the turn of the century virtually all Wilson's colleagues had abandoned his concern with society. Slipping past the mounting English criticism of Austinian jurisprudence, they placed sovereignty—undivided, awesome in its new glittering literalness—in the State.

Not all those who caught the drift of the new orthodoxy were pleased at the recession of political authority to an entity so abstract, so tautologically framed as the State.[29] But even the most democratic of the textbook writers were firm in dismissing the old pretensions of the people. "The relations of [the] people to the state are obvious," James Dealey, one of the discipline's most democratic figures, wrote in 1909; "they are its subjects." Not "mere subjects," to be sure, but subjects nonetheless, recipients of the State's commands.[30]

Higher and higher the locus of sovereignty had spiraled since the fractious people had locked themselves in civil war. The People had hardly been a word of precision; but in comparison with those which threatened to supplant it, it had a powerful simplicity. Above the people, so scores of northern Civil War publicists had insisted, was the Union. Back of the Union was the "nation" —"such a unity of blood, of interest, and of feelings" (as Judge Jameson had put it in 1867) that its parts must "fly together by a force of attraction that is practically irresistible." Back of the nation, men were saying in New York that same year, lay society. But back of them all, in Platonic remove from the cave of day-to-day politics, stood the State. The State was not simply a juristic fiction, a crutch to bring the law into a semblance of order, though some of its partisans later preferred to remember it that way. The State was a legal person; its will was the general will; being all but invisible to the eye, it could not be possessed or resisted or laid claim to even by the most wild-eyed of Populists gathered under the banner of the people.[31]

Sovereign by definition, the State could do anything. But it could not avoid channeling its commands through ordinary governments: through the party-ridden, corruptible, mismanaged agencies of everyday politics. But with that thought the political scientists suddenly turned on the magnificent verbal edifice they called the State and cut its practically employable powers down, relatively speaking, to a sliver. Never as bitten by antistatist animus as late nineteenth-century economists or many of the constitutional lawyers, the political scientists tended to work their way evenhandedly through the rival dogmas of socialists and individualists, hunting for those practical compromises on which prudent persons could agree. They preferred to talk in terms of the "functions" of the State, rather than the harder lawyers' language of limits or spheres. But they had no doubt that most of what the State might do, its agencies were pretty sure to bungle. State and government, the political scientists insistently reminded their students, were utterly different things. The State was sublime, the practical agencies of state power were frail and enormously fallible. On that distinction they rested a crucial part of their analytical science. But for those who did not have the hang of the political scientists' way of talking, it was hard to resist the suspicion that the all-sovereign State, whose theoretical omnipotence produced so niggardly a practical outcome, was nothing but a gigantic verbal riddle.

The nation's first generation of professional political scientists were, without a doubt, eminently practical men. They had no sympathy for the ahistorical abstractions of eighteenth-century political argument. Like Wilson, what they "went in for" was the *life* of the State, and they followed that hunger for action into an extraordinary range of public activities. One could find them at the end of the century overseeing the administration of the Philippines, preaching at Chautauquas, pressing for the overhaul of urban government, or promulgating laws for Puerto Rico.[32] Only a few of them contributed to high political theory. But whether the tip-off came in their evocation of the social "whole" or more mechanically in the inviolable subject order of the textbooks (State, Sovereignty, Government) or merely in offhand reference to that force they called "State will," the peculiar axioms of their discipline were never far from view.

The lawyers' revolution was crystalline and elementary in comparison to the extravagant abstractions and strained tautologies the political scientists had heaped into a science. How could it have come about?

Webs of Contradiction

The puzzle is a deep one and not easily cleared away. Take, for example, the career of John W. Burgess. If any man stamped the discipline with his personal impress, surely it was he. The School of Political Science, which he singlehandedly put together at Columbia in 1880, was the biggest of the new departments of political science and by every measure the most influential. Burgess staffed it with a talented faculty, most of whom had once been his own students. Together they controlled what remained until 1906 the discipline's central outlet for published work, *The Political Science Quarterly.* Burgess's own *Political Science,* when it came out in 1890, saturated with the new doctrines of State and sovereignty, did more to formalize the axioms of late nineteenth-century academic political science than any rival book by any American author. For a boy who had run away from home a jump ahead of a Confederate impressment gang and let chance launch him on his life's work, it was an extraordinary record.[33]

And yet considered as an intellectual career, Burgess's was a jumble of contradictions. As a scholar he was deeply and incurably Germanic. He filled his footnotes with German references and dispatched his graduate students to recapitulate his own academic *Wanderjahre* in Germany. And yet he defended the Columbia School of Political Science as the center of a distinctly American discipline. In a racist age, he was a racist of the very first order; he was convinced that the Aryan race was appointed to civilize the politically inferior peoples of the world. Yet he thought the American adventure in the Philippines a catastrophic mistake. He was an ardent and stubborn admirer of imperial Germany, enough so to make him an acute embarrassment to the discipline during the First World War. And yet he hated in any other context the institutions of concentrated state power at the core of Wilhelmine Germany. No one wrote more forcefully than Burgess that rights and liberties were nothing but grants of the State; and yet he spent a large fraction of his career rummaging through the world's constitutions to prove that the American system of a "well-defined sphere of Individual Immunity against all governmental power" was the goal of universal history.[34]

The problem of state power, indeed, lay at the heart of Burgess's exfoliating contradictions. He was an architect of the idea of the absolute, unlimited State, who found himself appalled at the idea that the State might take its powers seriously. He felt betrayed by McKinley's imperialist adventure, betrayed by the statism of Theodore Roosevelt (who, to make matters worse, had once sat in his Columbia classroom), betrayed by the administration of Woodrow Wilson. He wrote his last books in the 1920s "with great effort and no joy," deeply out of sorts with the legacy of the Progressive years. Down to the Spanish–American War, he thought, "the movement of [our] history had been an almost unbroken march in the direction of a more and more perfect individual liberty and immunity against the powers of government." But "from that date to the present the movement has been in the contrary direction, until now there remains hardly an individual immunity against governmental power which may not be set aside by government, at its own will and discretion, with or without reason, as government itself may determine."[35] Bernard Crick, trying to puzzle Burgess out, suggested that his was "the agonizing position of an Hegelian who was of a nation, but a nation which had no sense of the *State.* "[36] But Burgess was no real Hegelian. He was in the agonizing position of a devotee of the idea of the State who found the real thing deeply unnerving.

Burgess himself, wielding the razor of distinction between State and government, would have put it differently. Since liberty was sustained by the plenitude of state power, the most perfect liberty and most perfect sovereignty could never conflict. It was government that made the trouble. But as one of Burgess's reviewers observed, to insist on the State's unlimited though unusable sovereignty was to indulge in a "perilous kind of figurative language."[37] Burgess himself must have known as much as early as the mid-1890s, when the lectures of one of his former students, now teaching at Union College, were published under the title *The Sphere of the State.* For here was Burgess's State yoked to a Christian socialism of the most sweeping sort: a State whose responsibility extended deep into the economy; which had "not only the right but the duty . . . to abolish all private possession and use the moment any other system will better promote the well-being of the people"; whose sphere was limited only by the question, "Will the good of the brotherhood be best subserved thereby?" Burgess dispatched a colleague to make the obvious rebuke that such an argument completely ignored the distinction between omnicompetent State and fallible government.[38] But Burgess could hardly dodge a share of responsibility for the confusions and misunderstandings he felt had so badly dogged his work.

Few of Burgess's colleagues were as extraordinarily out of sorts with the active, tangible state as he. Younger men who arrived at Columbia early in the twentieth century slipped from Burgess's seminar into the agencies of Progressive reform with little of Burgess's private agony. And yet none of them were what contemporary Europeans would have called thoroughgoing statists. Many of them were later to wake up with a startled suspicion that the keywords of their science had no more substance than the emperor's splendidly invisible clothes. By 1917 Charles Beard had concluded that Burgess had left political science desiccated and lifeless, "hanging in the vacuum of closed legal speculation." Yet as late as 1908, Burgess's terms had still seemed to Beard of "great scientific value."[39] What could the abstract and convoluted language of the State have meant to men such as he?

Nationalism is a place to start. Burgess's own flight from a southern impressment gang across the Tennessee River into the arms—and the service—of Grant's army camped at Shiloh had been no picnic outing. Burgess's father was a southern Whig and nationalist, and so from childhood on was Burgess. Younger men in the profession had been born too late to play so dramatic a wartime part, but the atmosphere of retrospective heroics in which they grew up left them, too, with little doubt that the Civil War was the fundamental historical event of the modern age. Political science—the science of the State—was from its inception unabashedly nationalistic: a science for northerners or southerners (like Burgess and Wilson) of Union principles.

Under these circumstances, it is not surprising that the founders of the discipline should have recoiled from the secession-tainted notion of popular sovereignty. That they tried so hard to scotch the idea that citizens had claims against the state which might permit them to tear out its very foundation stones, should not, under these circumstances, be surprising. In placing the state's own autonomous, indivisible sovereignty at the axiomatic, unchallengeable center of their science, they sought to resolve for good the indestructibility of the nation, to trample underfoot every lingering ember of secessionism. And yet, ample as their nationalism was, it cannot be made to hold all their obsessions with State and sovereignty. The victors themselves had done well enough, after all, with mere celebration of the "nation." As for sovereignty, would not a simple assertion of its indivisibility have done the trick? Why had the founders of political science muddied the discipline with their talk of state omnipotence?

Another set of answers leads toward Germany. For there in the late nineteenth century, one could find persons talking about State authority with an expansiveness as grand as the American political scientists' own. Off to Germany they had indeed gone, bypassing England, where the study of politics seemed to them crude and barely developed, to hear Johann Bluntschli lecture on the State at Heidelberg or to sit in Rudolf von Gneist's public law seminar in Berlin, at the feet of one of the drafters of the new imperial law code, or to listen to the heated arguments over state socialism that flew back and forth in the lecture halls everywhere in late nineteenth-century Germany. Here, in fact, they had acquired the term State; learned to think of their discipline as crowned by the "science of the State" above the rough-and-tumble study of politics or administration; learned to call the State a legal and constitutional "person" possessed of autonomous will. Burgess himself had arrived in Berlin in 1871, just in time to see the Prussian army make its victorious return from the Franco–Prussian War, just in time to witness the promulgation of the new German imperial constitution, just in time to conflate forever in his mind the cause of the German Empire with the cause of the American Union. If none of Burgess's fellow professional scientists were as deeply smitten by Germany as he, the stamp of German learning on their professional talk was deep and unmistakable.

And yet it must also be said that the Americans brought back only a small and selective fraction of German *Staatslehre*. They skipped over Rudolf von Jhering, writing (Bentham-like) of the ends and purposes of law, just as they bypassed the figures in the *Verein für Sozialpolitik* who so inspired the young American economists in Germany and fastened on the now-forgotten Bluntschli as the master of their fledgling science, filling their footnotes with references to his *Theory of the State* and preserving his papers in a special case in the Johns Hopkins seminar room.[40] Still closer were their affinities to the constitutional jurists. In codifiers like von Gneist, Paul Laband, and Georg Jellinek, hard at work sorting out the tangled jurisdictional order of the new empire in the 1870s and 1880s, trying to make juridical sense out of the brute impositions of Bismarckian federalism, the Americans sensed a project and a temperament close to their own. From these jurists and imperial apologists they learned the utility of an abstraction like the State as a way of forcing conceptual unity over federalism's confusions. Here, too, they found the claim that may well have struck them as the birthright of the truly realized, war-tempered nation state: that the State was limited by no other restraints than those it willingly chose to place on itself.[41]

Still it would be a mistake to think they simply brought home the terms of their trade in a rucksack. Their concept of sovereignty was John Austin's, clamped onto the German *Staat* in ways few of their German teachers were prepared to stomach. The Germans preferred to talk of state competence and state power, terms vast enough, to be sure, but potentially more porous than the hard, American talk of sovereignty. Nor did the German political scientists try with half the intensity of their American counterparts to sweep away the older rhetoric of natural law, which hung like a mist over late nineteenth-century Germany.[42] The Americans' assault on the language of the Revolution, like the radical disjunction between their praise of the State and their fears of government, was their own. Their sovereignty-armed State was not the *Staat* but an instrument of their own invention.

As a tool it had its advantages. It gave their science a logical frame. It enabled them to come to terms with the Civil War. It let them borrow a mite of the intellectual luster of imperial Germany. Did it matter that it had lured a man like Burgess into a web of contradictions?

The Uses of an Abstraction

In truth the advantages of the splendid abstraction the political scientists called the State touched still deeper nerves than these. Over the terrifying class and ethnic divisions of late nineteenth-century America, it spread a wonderful coherence. Against the angry talk of rights, dispossession, and potential power seeping out of that conflict-strewn terrain, it maintained a wall of no mean thickness. What sustained the word State, like the big words before it, were big and urgent uses.

Coherence, to begin with, was not easily purchased at the end of the nineteenth century in industrial capitalism's rawest, most aggressive phase. By war the nation had been preserved. But as the wartime victory over the forces of disintegration was obscured by economic conflicts, whose pain and explosive angers at Haymarket, Homestead, Pullman, and elsewhere were brought to the surface, by reports which showed the poorest sections of the American cities as impoverished as the worst of London's East End, by a mounting ethnic cacophony and intensifying racial violence, it was no easy task to find the unitary nation for which so much blood had flowed.

It was the middle-class heirs to the old Whig-Protestant longings for unity who felt the pain of fragmentation most acutely. Elbowed out, so they feared, by a swelling tide of immigrants, their local power challenged by new sorts of machine politicians, they had their own particular nightmares to add to the general sense (strong everywhere in the West at the end of the nineteenth century) of a world moving too fast for real comfort. An earlier generation had answered similar anxieties with cries of discipline and moral government. Unable to believe as literally in religion as their parents or grandparents, incapable of seeing the hand of God as firmly at rest on the tiller of state as the antebellum moral philosophers, many of the late nineteenth-century Protestant middle class's most influential talkers took refuge not in orthodox faith but in abstract words.

In the last years of the century, every corner of university life, in particular, resounded with abstractions—Society, the Law, the self-balancing laws of Economics, the destiny of History—more real, loaded with a far heavier burden of logical necessity, than the mere

surface phenomena they held in order. In the philosophy departments, that impulse was known as Idealism. Idealism's intellectual
pedigree stretched back through Hegel, Emerson, and Kant, ultimately to Plato's insistence that the real lay behind and on a plane
higher than mere facts. Politically that assertion was capable of a
myriad uses, both radical and conservative. But Idealism's vogue at
the end of the century derived from its ability to salve middle-class
terrors of social conflict by pasting over the wound a conviction
that, at some higher, Ideal level, the apparent chaos cohered. Behind
the cries and countercries of the newspaper headlines lay the silent,
unswervable forces of History. Behind the polyglot admixture of
peoples in America, elbowing each other for space and opportunities, lay the Nation. Behind the statehouse gangs, the unscrupulous
party bosses, the push and pull of contending interest groups lay the
State. The trick required, in Alan Trachtenberg's words, "a special
kind of denial of social fact."[43] But when one was in this mood,
these Ideal entities needed no proof. To do without them was too
vertiginous to be thinkable.

William James later styled this line of thinking as the flight of
panicked men away from "this colossal universe of concrete facts,
... [with] their awful bewilderments, their surprises and cruelties,"
into "a kind of marble temple shining on a hill." But even James
himself spent a large part of the 1880s and early 1890s under Idealism's spell, trying to work himself free of its logical self-sufficien-
cies. To the extent that the nation had an officially established
philosophy at the end of the century, it was not the pragmatism
toward which James was groping; rather it was Idealism. One could
hear it preached at Harvard by the giant of late nineteenth-century
philosophy, Josiah Royce. One could hear it, as John Dewey and
Woodrow Wilson had, in George S. Morris's lectures at Johns Hopkins or, like Burgess himself, in Julius Seelye's classes at Amherst.
"Idealism is or has been *the* System," Ralph Barton Perry wrote as
late as 1918. "It has largely controlled the means of philosophical
production, such as the vocabulary, the professorships and the public ear. It has furnished all the teachers in the philosophical Sunday
School."[44]

Into philosophy's sister disciplines the coherence-making vocabulary of Idealism rolled. "We should become accustomed to the use

of the word State," the economist Richard T. Ely pleaded in 1896. Not merely the active, interventionist state—though Ely, at the forefront of the insurgent economists' assault on laissez-faire in the 1880s and early 1890s, was eager enough for the expansion of tangible state power—but the State behind the state, built not of human will but of brotherhood and divine necessity. For turn-of-the-century sociologists, the reality beyond the incoherent gauze of appearances was "society." For the modernist theologians, straining (as Robert Woods told Andover Seminary students in the 1890s) for a "philosophy presenting mankind, and indeed the entire universe, as an organic unity," greater than any "mere aggregation of the parts," it was the "brotherhood of man."[45] Through all these conduits, from a common pain within Protestant, middle-class America, came a longing for reassurance that something like a "common mind," a social will, still ruled—or could be made to rule again. One could see that desire, with half an eye for symbolism, in the new vogue for classicism in public architecture, out of which shot a dozen new state capitols, rising out of their surroundings in carefully proportioned wholeness, like the shining granite temples they were designed to be. One could hear it in the hope that some trick of consciousness or words—loyalty, community, or State—would pull the "intolerably confused" character of "mere facts" into unity.[46]

Given these propensities all around them, the peculiar logic of the academic political scientists, the web of contradictions they seem so needlessly to have spun, take on sense. Given their time and place, given the particular sort of well-positioned, modernist Protestants they tended to be, their convoluted intellectualism was not in the least peculiar. The acrobatic leaps toward abstraction which came into vogue in the 1880s and 1890s, the perilously figurative language, were not liabilities; they were precisely what made this form of intellectual reassurance work. If the political scientists' talk of collective imperatives was so much more vigorous than their tangible sense of public goods and public life, the defect was not entirely their fault. Through talk of the State, held together by a sovereignty no discordant social fragment could resist, they found a way of bringing an increasingly pluralistic, fragmenting polity back together, if not in fact, at least in the mind's eye.

The other gain, however, was at least as precious: a fortress against every upstart claim of rights. The language of Idealism had not been peculiar to the Americans. In England, too, a wave of enthusiasm for philosophical Idealism rolled over Oxford in the last quarter of the nineteenth century that was at least as fervent as the corresponding movement in America—made out of the same combination of a doubt-filled Protestantism and the powerfully fragmenting forces of capitalism. But the Oxford political philosophers, drawn as they were to the concept of the State, never wedded it to that brittle abstraction the Americans called sovereignty.[47] Only where revolutionary talk of Natural Rights and popular power persisted did that verbal tool take on not merely logic, but urgency.

In the troubled 1880s and 1890s, talk of precisely that sort ran hard through the kingdom of amateurs. Most unnerving to the middle-class professionals was Populism and its army of angry farmers, marching in the 1890s under the banner of a People's government, responsible to the People's will, dedicated to an expansion of "the power of government—in other words of the people" (as the Populists declared in 1892) until "oppression, injustice and poverty, shall eventually cease in the land." Workers through the end of the century still claimed the Fourth of July as their own, trotting out the phrases of the Declaration as vessels for their grievances. Out of a burgeoning socialist movement, the right to the whole product of one's labor reverberated with new powers. Still closer to the language of antebellum radicalism, woman suffragists pressed home their demand for the vote as an original, natural right. Not until early in the new century, their slogans corroded by the cultural changes around them, did the suffragist platform writers finally abandon the phrases of the Declaration and begin to demand the vote as woman's "duty" or plead (in still more soberly reconstructed language) for "a larger infusion of the mother element" into politics. Into the language of the people's rights, older than the wiles of legislatures and lawyers, poured once more a host of discontents.[48]

Against all these cries, the political scientists' State stood as an extraordinary bulwark, unmoved by claims external to itself. If words are instruments, then one of the clearest uses of the sovereignty-endowed State was to blunt every dissident claim of right outside those rights the State itself chose to bestow: to remove the locus of authority to a sphere where the people, angry and aggrieved, could not get hold of it. Their "general will" was not a thing which rested on the political surface, subject to revision or repudiation by the election returns. The "real will" of the State lay farther from grasp than that: in the silent forces of "custom"; or in some "common mind" beyond the ken of any party boss or Populist demagogue; or, safer yet, in the law, unfolding with its own higher logic.

It was at this juncture, finally, where the jargon of legal formalism joined the political scientists' talk of State omnipotence, that the logic hidden in Burgess's verbal contortions came at last to the surface. The corpus of constitutional law he pressed on his students was no idle concern for Burgess. Imagine constitutional law as the highest expression of State will, imagine at the apex of the State not the people but the Law itself, and the convoluted claims of sovereignty at the heart of Burgess's political science flowed suddenly into a powerful justification for judicial review. Burgess had never envisioned sovereignty as a plaything of convention delegates or legislators. It was in those moments when the Constitution itself spoke with majestic, invincible power through the judgments of its agents on the bench that the sovereignty Burgess so longed to find, and so deeply distrusted, came closest to a tangible home.

The law's apologists were quick to see the advantages of the line of argument. It required that the people learn to look past the flesh-and-blood justices themselves, past their erratic judgments and florid economic prejudices to the higher entities they served; but this was not too much to attempt. The judges did not *make* the law nor decide it, the law writers began to insist with mounting strenuousness in the 1890s. They were the mere "finders" of a higher, unwritten law, etched in history or shimmering somewhere in logical self-sufficiency behind mere precedent and statute. Their rulings (James C. Carter wrote for them in 1905) were not "the dictate of Force but an emanation from Order." The law they served was not "the mere product of the popular will or of a legislative majority of the hour" (John F. Dillon cautioned) but "the beneficence of civil society acting by rule, . . . the absolute justice of the State enlightened by the perfect reason and morality of the State." Mid-nineteenth-century legal pieties fused with the orphic terms of

Idealism to vest the jargon of constitutional formalism with a powerful, borrowed coherence.[49]

Not many of the younger political scientists were as awed as Burgess by constitutional law; but the terms of their trade endowed them with little sympathy for straightforward democracy. Up and down the line on the eve of the twentieth century, with an extraordinary fertility of imagination, the political scientists could be found hunting for new modes of consent to replace what they thought to be the archaic, mechanical practices of democracy. To a man they insisted that suffrage was not a right, but a gift of the State. Most of them acceded without pain to the final disfranchisement of those black Americans to whom the Reconstruction conventions had given the vote. The shreds of political power still in the hands of southern blacks, Stephen Leacock's textbook of 1906 announced, had amounted to "a false and hopelessly abstract view of political rights." In the North, the professional students of politics rallied to the idea of radically shortening the number of elective offices, to schemes of proportional voting so as to weight independent votes more heavily, and to educational tests and tighter registration laws to elevate and purify the suffrage.[50]

The political scientists were not reactionaries. They did not wring their hands, like the turn of the century's more terrified misfits, over the tragic "mistake" of democracy. Even Burgess had no love for the "barbarism" of unbridled individualism.[51] The professional political scientists, moreover, were far too few to have stoked by themselves the antidemocratic tendencies which swirled through the middle class in the last years of the century. The counterattack on the people—whether upon the transient voters whom the new registration boards hoped to bar from urban elections or black voters clinging to the tattered legacy of Reconstruction or the party bosses whom the urban reformers hoped to drive out of business—was too widespread to imagine that a handful of professionals was in any fundamental way responsible. When, on the opening day of the Alabama disfranchisement convention of 1901, the convention's president took the time to explain (on Thomas M. Cooley's authority) that the suffrage the delegates were about to strip from so large a part of the Alabama population was in no way a natural right but "exists where it is allowed only for the good of the State," it is hard to think the words were needed, or mattered.[52] Where desires ran hard, political theory provided little more than the gloss of legitimacy.

Yet in the contest for control of the language of politics, nothing in the end mattered more than the metaphors of legitimacy. From the beginning, that was what the intense struggle over words had been all about. And in that sense, the strained, abstraction-filled jargon of political science, so far from the everyday talk of the people, had its barely hidden elements of power. The political scientists' reification of an entity higher than the people, their axiomatic dismissal of every upstart claim against the State, their search for devices which would discern (more clearly than mere votes) the commonweal and the general will, all served to ease the recession of legitimate power from the people's hands. Of all the uses of that glitteringly inaccessible abstraction the political scientists called the State, the handiest was to lend the assault on the amateurs a vital measure of authority.

The constitutional lawyers entered the new century stronger than ever. The courts moved through the 1920s into their collision with the New Deal with extraordinary confidence, dispatching invalidated statutes right and left. The verbal structure the political scientists built did not fare as well. In 1908, Arthur Bentley looked at their carefully spun definitions of sovereignty and pronounced them "a piteous, threadbare joke." There was no State behind the veil. Politics was a clash of interests, pure and simple; the rest was mere intellectual fancy-work.[53] Bentley's readers (such as he found) did not accept the conclusion easily. Farther and farther from the Benthamite terrain of advantage and utility the abstractions had flown, as Americans unhappy with the unstable rhetoric of inalienable rights and popular power had struggled to hold their fissioning polity in some sort of unity. Into the Progressive years of the new century, the orators brought an intensified yearning for the political whole. But when their edifice of words fell apart, under the radically altered pressures of twentieth-century politics, there was no putting the old terms back together again. When the State finally evaporated as a word of consequence, all Burgess's heirs could find were interests.

6

Interests

Highbrow and Lowbrow

From the beginning, the language of politics in America had never been of a single piece. Its superstructure had harbored a handful of powerful abstractions, their meaning indistinct and deeply contested. Its basement stories resounded, in contrast, with a street language of practical calculation, bargain, shrewd maneuver, and deeply skeptical wit. Since Charles Dickens's complaint of a people capable of veering from grandiloquent expressions of patriotism to huckster's talk of real estate prices without pause for breath or embarrassment, foreign observers had puzzled over the rift between the extravagantly abstract and the exuberantly material tendencies of everyday American speech. But never had that chasm struck observers as sharply as in the opening years of the new century. How was one to comprehend the relationship between the furious material energies of this new industrial giant and the wordiness of its politics? Its high-flown State theory and the everyday stench of its political corruption? Its headlong economic growth and the formal language of its politics, still encased (so H. G. Wells thought in 1906) in wigs and shoe buckles? How else but as a culture of antonyms—or as a set of terms and reassurances at the end of their useful tether.[1]

"Highbrow and lowbrow," Van Wyck Brooks crystallized the sense of an impending crackup in 1915: "What side of American life is not touched by this antithesis?" "Between university ethics and business ethics, between American culture and American humor, between Good Government and Tammany, between academic pedantry and pavement slang, there is no community"; only the "irreconcilable planes" of "stark theory" and "stark business." The failure of mind lay in no paucity of ideals, Brooks was certain. The typical American grows up "in a sort of orgy of lofty examples, moralized poems, national anthems, and baccalaureate sermons; until he is charged with all manner of ideal purities, ideal honorabilities, ideal femininities, flag-wavings and skyscrapings of every sort." But between his transcendent ideals ("unmapped regions to which nobody has the least intention of building roads") and "every untrained, greedy, and aggressive impulse in him" there was no mediation, no language, no common ground.[2]

There was a whiff of extravagance in Brooks's complaint, but truth enough to catch the temper of a large number of his contemporaries—pilgrims like Brooks himself in a world of power, equipped with a heavy load of university-imbibed platitudes. Off in a rush the younger students of politics went to create a behavioral political science. With a sense of relief, they shucked off the verbal baggage of Burgess's generation. State, sovereignty, the general will, the common mind—one by one they all went overboard. The political realists would no longer be moved by the fictions of the law, the ritualistic pieties of the orators, the word-worship of Idealism, or the "soul-stuff" (as Arthur Bentley called it) of *Staatslehre*.[3] They yearned to fill in the rifts and vacancies in the American mind with facts. To the extent that utilitarianism meant an acute ear for political cant, they brought Benthamism to America at last, and with a vengeance.

When they were done, the highbrow words had been swept into the back corners of American political talk. In their place, they constructed a language of political "realism"—hard-boiled, savvy, wise to the mystifying functions of eloquence. *Who Gets What, When, How*—the subtitle of Harold Lasswell's *Politics* of 1936 put the lowbrow realism of the new political science into self-consciously abrasive formula.[4] Look behind the screen of words, and there was nothing to be seen but a crowd of interest groups jockeying for power. Where the People had once ruled, where the State had reigned, where men had grasped for symbols of unity, the inventors of political realism substituted a buzzing, bewildering plurality of groups, associations, factions, and parties, maneuvering for a primacy none successfully achieved. "Interest group pluralism" we now style the results of that radical deflation of the metaphysical element in politics. Well before the encounter with the terrifyingly grandiloquent rhetoric of fascism in the late 1930s, the language of interest group pluralism was waiting in place.

The terms remain with us still, too familiar for their origins to provoke more than fleeting thought. To those who put them into currency, the result seemed a triumph of simple realism. But what Clifford Geertz has called, in a powerfully illuminating phrase, "the struggle for the real"—the struggle to wrest the label of rock-solid certainty from one set of phenomena to another—is never simple.[5] And in this instance there was no disguising the audacity of the outcome. In the opening years of the century, the word Interests had been a smear of no mean force. To the Progressive generation it stood for the predatory corporation, the unscrupulous party boss, for every selfish design on the public treasury and the public weal. "The business of government is to organize the common interest against the special interests," Woodrow Wilson had declared in 1912. The task of the hour was to "lay aside special interests," Franklin Roosevelt charged in the first year of the New Deal, to think and act for the good of "the great whole." Within another twenty years, the political scientists were debating whether so patently oratorical a term as "public interest" had any reality whatsoever.[6]

Vague and malleable as the old words had been, they had served as a reminder that politics was not quite a marketplace like any other: that it was a realm not only of power but of things common and public. When talk of "the great whole"—overextended and ripe for puncture—gave way to an unabashedly economic word like Interests, politics itself could not but shrink and diminish. The story of the word Interests is not merely the story of the political scientists' belated revolt against highbrow abstractions. It is the story of how, in a world transformed by admen, propagandists, and public opinion shapers, among men shaken by these hucksters into a deeply skeptical attitude toward words of every sort, a mud-stained term of opprobrium swallowed up the whole of politics.

The Common Good

The collapse of the turn-of-the-century State into a jostle of interests was an event still hidden in the future during the opening years of the twentieth century. Crosscurrents of all sorts cut through the Progressive era. The strident moralism of a Theodore Roosevelt, the gruff complaisance of a congressional boss like Joseph Cannon, a swiftly rising anger at economic concentration and hymns of confidence in corporate efficiency, all swirled together at the moment of politics' decisive collision with the world which large-scale industrial capitalism had made.[7] But no one looking back on the years before the First World War has failed to be struck by the vigor, the massive confidence of the era's appeal to ideals. The big, highbrow words which had fueled political argument so long went out not with a whimper but, unexpectedly, in full career.

The language of the commonweal, bottled up in the nervous tautologies and convoluted reassurances of the pulpit and the lecture hall, burst into politics in the first years of the new century with powerful effect. From the settlement houses, from the social gospel preachers, from scores of crusading politicians girded for Armageddon, the dream (so deep in middle-class Protestantism) of reknitting the social body into wholeness blossomed in new, inventive forms. Into angry crusades against the greed and malfeasance of the swollen corporate giants, into assaults on the party bosses and the political machines, into dreams of civic regeneration and efficiency, the old integrative abstractions rolled: the nation, the common good, the "social will," the public weal. In England in the early years of the century, the Liberal party, jolted into consciousness of the exploitative underside of industrial capitalism, moved against many of the same evils—often with more powerful and lasting effect. But the rhetoric of the New Liberalism, ethically saturated as it was, was never half as charged with appeal to the common will as the rhetoric of the American progressives. The "big noise" of the early twentieth century, as H. G. Wells remembered it, was neither Asquith nor Lloyd George but Theodore Roosevelt, all teeth, energy, and talk of national righteousness.[8] Whatever the inner dynamics of Progressive politics, its dominant public rhetoric—as Richard Hofstadter remarked long ago—was that of morally ambitious Protestantism, revitalized and confident.[9]

No one caught the moral tenor of Progressive political rhetoric better, or did more to shape it, than the muckrakers. The language of exposure and shame was not new when the muckrakers took it up in their explosive moment, 1902–10. But the muckrakers used it with telling effect, thrust it upon an audience already uneasy at the new scale of the cities, the trusts, and the financial giants, rising around them like colossi from dragons' teeth, and fashioned out of it a powerfully new political drama. The muckrakers' revelations came with head-spinning speed and no particularly tidy order. Bigness is often said to have been their central theme, though in truth the muckrakers—like the Progressives as a whole—made their peace relatively easily with bigness and the efficiencies of scale. The shame they decried, far more powerfully and consistently, was the purchase of public power for private ends, the degeneration of politics into a mere auction house for interested bidders. Before the eyes of the startled readers of the slick, new, middle-class magazines, the muckrakers unveiled the mechanisms of a commodified politics. The world they revealed was one in which graft ruled at the expense of the social will, where statehouse "rings" did a profitable business in special favors, where streetcar franchises were traded under the table, votes bought and sold, meat inspectors bribed, legislatures hired, laws ignored or purchased at a discount—where the State itself had been put up for sale, transformed into a thriving, open market for private interests.[10]

This sense of betrayal by their own economic institutions, so keen in the muckrakers and their readers, preceded the solidification of a word to hold their anger. Lincoln Steffens, flaying the enemies of "good" government in 1903, did his best to make "boodler" and "grafter" into general terms of contempt. By 1906, however, the new word was everywhere. It was "the Interests," David Graham Phillips wrote in that year, which had the United States Senate so tightly in their grip that a quarter of the members bore on their foreheads the brand of the trusts and corporations which owned them. It was the Interests which now marched through the muckraking magazines, shameless and powerful. By the summer of 1910 Theodore Roosevelt had absorbed the word—pushed by muckraking, outrage, ambition, and a keen sense of the political moment. By the end of the year, so had Woodrow Wilson.[11]

The force of the word Interests flowed at once from its sharp ethical claims and its powerful indistinctness. It bundled together a hodgepodge of interests—from those of the petty grafter to the giant corporation—in a label which spoke more eloquently of the muckrakers' moralism than of their prided economic realism. Nor, indeed, was there much in the muckrakers' outcry against the politics of trade and barter that was radically new. For at least half a century, the primary function of government had been the distribution of economic favors. Railroad subsidies, paving contracts, veterans' benefits, jobs, tariff protection. The most common task of legislators, as a generation of political historians has now made clear, had been to barter them away—in the interests of one's party, one's friends, the promotion of economic growth, or the promotion of oneself.[12] At the national level the ripest plum of all was tariff protection. Into the hearing rooms at the Capitol, thick with an atmosphere of smoke and barter, the businessmen had flocked with every fiercely contested revision of the tariff: men with interests in steel, tobacco, buttons, or pocket knives to plead their cases in as bald an example of interest politics as one could find. Let the forces of economic consolidation, running hard and barely opposed through late nineteenth-century America, collide with so weak a set of state and national governments, and only a political naif could fail to predict the results. "Young man, tariffs are the whole of politics," a fledgling senator in turn-of-the-century Washington recalled the staple wisdom of his elders: "Study them."[13]

Yet if the outcry against the Interests simplified and moralized the political economy of the muckrakers' America, that did nothing to diminish the power of the word. The muckrakers made the everyday occurrence vivid, used the term to isolate and denounce the most shameful forms of greed, and pressed their revelations upon a middle-class readership shaken by a decade of extraordinary business consolidation and (thanks to a revolution in printing technology and cut-rate magazine prices) vastly larger than before. They created the modern form of political crusade: not the Jacksonians' dream of the permanent recapture of the government by the People but a drama in which the normally quiescent public rose in a mo-

mentary act of unified moral consciousness to force a new regula-
tory law into place. The techniques of Progressive reform—publicity, the public-interest lobby, the cultivation of a unified, issue-
conscious "public opinion"—all this hinged on a language capable
of splitting cleanly the public weal from the aims of private, interested parties. The Interests were, by definition, alien and predatory:
sores on the body politic.

Just as the Progressives' assault on the Interests particularized
evils, however, it intensified in the same breath the reality of a
common good. Even after it became clear that successful reform
politics was coalition politics, that a reform program could not be
sustained without recognition of the special grievances of labor,
farmers, small businessmen, urban dwellers, women, and on
through a score of competing claimants, the rhetoric of the moral
whole endured. This was the theme Theodore Roosevelt rode in his
increasingly furious assault on "the ferocious, scrambling rush of an
unregulated and purely individualistic industrialism." Woodrow
Wilson, promising "an unentangled government, a government that
cannot be used for private purposes," reached for the same verbal
symbols.[14] The language of the common good pervaded politics and
social thought alike. Municipal reformers crusaded for the abolition
of ward-based city councils on the grounds that a true city was no
mere federation of boss-run fiefdoms but an entity possessed of a
single will and a "common mind." School reformers lobbied for
Americanization programs to press the immigrants all the more
rapidly into the common mold. Woman suffrage advocates, abandoning feminism's earlier claims to rights, touted the special ability
of women to see society as an integrated whole. Political scientists
decried the divisive, paralyzing effects of checks and balances—"the
political science of negation," Charles Beard sneeringly called it—
and touted schemes of centralized and responsible authority.[15]

In their need for a rhetorical counterweight to the politics of mere
barter, some of the Progressives reached back to the old, radical talk
of the people's will. "These multitudes of men, mixed, of every kind
and quality, constitute somehow an organic and noble whole, a
single people," Woodrow Wilson himself declared in accepting his
party's nomination in 1912.[16] Yet for most purposes the People was
too loose-jointed, Revolution-tainted a term fully to catch the social

unity for which the Progressives yearned. Muckrakers and reformers, to be sure, wrung what they could out of the word, brought it out of disrepute, stripped the radical veneer of Populism off it, and threw it into the crusade against the Interests. When Theodore Roosevelt, to the terror of his party's conservatives, turned on the courts to denounce their latest burst of negation, the ground he took was the old Jacksonian ground of the People's sovereignty—even over the robed and learned justices of the Supreme Court. In his last volcanic campaign in 1912, an outsider now, without any party except that which he drew by his own personal magnetism, it was only fitting, given the pattern of the word's employment, that Roosevelt should have insisted that his was a crusade "sprung from . . . the people themselves," that he had nobody with him at all "except the people."[17]

But for all the Progressives' talk of a new era of popular rule, few of them were comfortable with the open, ramshackle, decentralized structure of elective offices they had inherited from the nineteenth-century champions of popular government. Among the political scientists who identified themselves with the progressive currents in politics, there ran a vigorous dislike not only of parties and bosses but (at times) voters. They warmed to the unification (rather than the dispersal) of authority, to the concentration of vastly more power in fewer, more visible hands, farther from the partisan, log-rolling considerations of elections and popularity. They were eager to clip the prerogatives of legislatures; instead they preferred strong governors and (still more) the administration of impartial, merit-appointed experts. They collaborated in the final demise of the open, volatile constitutional convention—once so potent a symbol of the People's sovereignty—through the construction of expert-staffed preparatory commissions (like that Charles Beard helped supervise in New York in 1915), designed to channel debate into narrower, more predictable directions. Unity of purpose was the desideratum: not the devolution of sovereignty into the hands of Jackson's common folk but the concentration of power in governments efficient and powerful enough to affect the common will.[18]

Nothing revealed more strikingly this inner transformation in the concept of popular government than that even those who flocked to the new devices of direct democracy—the initiative, the referendum, and the recall—should so often have joined their call for a proliferation of elections with demands for an equally startling shrinkage in the number of elective offices. The pathbreaking state in the new techniques of direct democracy was Oregon. Under the prodding of W. S. U'Ren, a quiet, insistent, ex-Populist lawyer, Oregon moved toward referenda-style politics with a speed that awed, and often worried, eastern Progressives. A decade before the passage of the Seventeenth Amendment, Oregon voters had wrested the election of United States senators into their own hands together with a good deal of the normal powers of legislation. By 1910 Oregon voters were deciding directly on over two dozen pieces of legislation a year. But if U'Ren and his People's Power League had gained the full measure of their program, the powers stripped from the legislators would have been transferred with breathtaking singleness of authority to the Oregon governor. In the polity U'Ren imagined, the governor would appoint virtually all the state offi-cials; he would concentrate in his own person the responsibilities of his administration, recommend legislation, prepare a budget, and defend his proposals in the thick of legislative debate. He would have no veto, and he could be recalled if he lost the confidence of the people before his term was out. But every appropriation bill would come from the governor; and the legislature, though it could defeat his measures, could not appropriate a penny more for any purpose than the governor had proposed.[19]

Such a vision of the people's power concentrated in its popularly elected tribune (a dream by no means singular to U'Ren) could only flow from a conviction that the people's will was one: a general will, changeable but never permanently divided. The public "mind" which the Progressives worked so skillfully to win was not to be found, they assumed, in the haggling endemic to legislatures or the chaff of the party meeting hall. "Representative government has had its long life and excellent development," Wilson wrote in 1901, "not in order that common opinion, the opinion of the street might prevail, but in order that the best opinion, the opinion generated by the best possible methods of general counsel, might rule in affairs." Call the processes of democracy (as Wilson did) the taking of the "common counsel" of the people; call them (in a phrase still heavier with import) the sounding of "public opinion"; there was no disguising the rhetorical confidence that under the cacophony of partisan, interested voices lay an undivided public will, waiting to be tapped.[20]

There were dissenters from these Rousseauian longings, to be sure. In 1908 Arthur Bentley, who had fled the abstraction-filled atmosphere of the political science seminars for a career as a Chicago political reporter, tried to bring the edifice down with a caustically witty critique of Idealist political science. There was no such thing as a public mind (a "spook," Bentley called it): only action, only "groups pressing one another, forming one another, and pushing out new groups and group representatives . . . to mediate the adjustments." But *The Process of Government* fell so far outside the conventional language of political science that the profession scarcely noticed it; even Charles Beard's first response was to chide Bentley for impertinence.[21]

Five years later, in 1913, Beard's own reduction of the debates in the federal constitutional convention of 1787 to a contest between landed and moneyed interests was far more difficult to ignore. Coming into print just as the Progressives' attack on the powers of judicial review was in full swing, at a time when corporation lawyers were heralding the Constitution as property's holy writ, *An Economic Interpretation of the Constitution* was a powerful piece of muckraking, despite Beard's laconic unwillingness to state its patent political moral. It was Beard who brought Madison's Tenth *Federalist* out of obscurity, pressing it into his argument to give a safely native tone to the suspicions Beard had derived—not from Madison's brief, trenchant comment on the inevitable presence of factions in a state—but from Bentley, E. R. A. Seligman's *The Economic Interpretation of History*, and (through Seligman) Marx.[22]

Beard's exhuming of Madison's long-forgotten essay was an event of no mean eventual consequence. Before 1913, as Douglass Adair demonstrated years ago, Madison's Tenth *Federalist* had languished in almost total obscurity, unnoticed by *The Federalist*'s commentators, ignored by Madison's biographers, rarely reprinted, and by all the weight of evidence rarely read.[23] Thirty years later Madison's contention that internal divisions in a polity were inevitable —that a republic was preserved, indeed, not by its unity but by the multitudinousness of its divisions, by its possession of so many interests that no single interest could consume the rest—all this had moved into the very core of American political science. But it would be a radical mistake to foreshorten the process by which the language of Madisonian pluralism elbowed out the language of the common good. The *Cyclopedia of American Government*'s curt entry on Interests in 1914 utterly ignored Madison to concentrate on muckraking—though perhaps it had been put in print too soon for Beard's book to take effect. Three years later when Beard resigned his Columbia professorship, the *New York Times* could barely sustain its glee at the resignation of a man so tainted by materialism (imbibed, the editors were certain in a burst of wartime patriotism, from the archenemy Germany), that he could reduce the Founding Fathers to a mere ring of land and bond speculators and profess a philosophy "which denies to man, in larger actions, the capacity of noble striving and self-sacrifice for ideals."[24]

To describe the polity as, by nature, an open market of interests, as a set of factions held together only by the politics of compromise was alien to the common talk of Progressives. It would take another generation, which had learned to squirm nervously at the sound of capitalized words, to accept that as the whole of politics. It was hardly an accident that those who rallied with such fiercely uncomplicated patriotism to Wilson's war call in 1917, who built the Committee on Public Information into a propaganda agency of unprecedented power and efficiency, who exploited so exuberantly the didactic potential of every medium from movies and posters to comic strips and historical scholarship, should have seen the war not as a contest of national interests but as a crusade for the minds of men. Nor that they should have followed Wilson so willingly up the scale of unifying, self-denying words into a "disinterested" war, waged for "ideals, and nothing but ideals." "We have been brought to one mind and purpose," Wilson declared seven months after the nation's entry into the war. "A new light shines about us. The great duties of a new day awaken a new and greater national spirit in us. We shall never again be divided or wonder what stuff we are made of." No wonder that in 1918 Wilson saw in the cheering crowds in Europe what the Progressives had so ardently wanted to see: "a great moral tide" rolling over the ancient divisions of class and ethnic rivalry. "The hearts of men," he was sure, "have never beaten so singularly in unison before."[25]

This was the rhetorical skin of the era, not its cords and muscles, but it was a rhetoric of no mean power or utility. With it the Progressives had tried to reestablish once more the distinction between the metaphors of politics and those of mere economics. It was not until the Great Crusade for Right and Civilization was over, not until the men of words found themselves in a world where opinion itself had become the grist of profitable manipulation, that (in Paul Boyer's phrase) they "got right with *Gesellschaft*," with the market-place assumptions of Madison's Tenth *Federalist*, with a polity broken in pieces.[26]

Utilitarianism Redivivus

Beneath the language of the social whole, to be sure, there were other hungers, other forms of talk. If the rhetorical secret of muck-raking lay in its urgent moral tone, the vessel of its indictment was journalistic fact. Facts of this sort had rarely counted for much in the volatile mix of axiom, principle, and metaphor which had fueled political argument since the mid-eighteenth century. The presumption that one could draw policy out of statistics and investigation —a presumption so deep in a Benthamite like Edwin Chadwick— had long breasted massive resistance in America. By the middle of the Progressive years, however, there was no mistaking the rise of a sharp, new, empirical temper in politics. One saw it in the empirical side of muckraking; in the sudden proliferation of statistical bureaus, bureaus of municipal research, and fact-finding commissions; in official bluebooks sprawling in multivolume amplitude across the shelves of the new legislative reference libraries; in legal arguments, like Louis Brandeis's famous sociological brief of 1908, crammed not with syllogism and precedent but with facts. "Facts, *facts!*" Stuart Chase remembered feeling toward the end of the Progressive years. "Here was an ear-splitting, blinding, stupefying word."[27] Here, wedging into the highbrow sonorities of politics, was a style of argument, a long-postponed utilitarianism, perhaps to empower, perhaps to eclipse, talk of the social whole.

Fact collecting in itself was hardly new. The novelty which fired the imagination of muckrakers, reformers, and younger social scientists was the possibility of replacing the familiar legal-theological wrangles over policy with the hard, determinate verdict of social science. "Statistics" was the first word to catch these ambitions. When it came into vogue in England in the mid-1830s, promoted by many of the same men to be found in the circles and subcircles around Bentham, eager "to confront the figures of speech with the figures of arithmetic" (as the Statistical Society of London put it in 1838), the word meant not the mathematics of correlation but the creation of social data. The etymological root of the word, as the early "statists" were quick to make clear, was the state: facts for enlightened state policy, state-istics.[28]

In Britain the statistical movement wedded itself quickly to health and poor law policies in a tradition that ultimately stretched from Chadwick's sanitary investigations through Charles Booth's massive surveys of London poverty, into the social insurance calculations of a William Beveridge and the architects of the early welfare state. In the United States, in contrast, the marriage of statistics and state policy proved much more difficult to contrive. There was no absence of would-be Chadwicks, no loss of zeal for counting in nineteenth-century America. Temperance crusaders worked up terrifying statistical portraits of drunkenness; Sunday school superintendents advertised the advance of Christianity by counting hymns sung and Bible verses recited; managers of public institutions classified and assiduously enumerated their inmates. Still more energy was drawn into the showpiece of American statistics, the collection of economic data. The census, responsive to calls for ever more voluminous measures of national economic progress, swelled with price and productivity figures, manufacturing and agricultural surveys, in a manner unmatched anywhere in Europe. But these mounds of facts, self-confirming and predictable, lopsidedly related to private economic life, had, in most cases, little impact on policy formation or political debate. Even at the end of the century there were no uniform health or mortality statistics in the United States, no adequate measures of poverty, no housing censuses to match those grown routine on the European continent, no central piece of legislation that could be fairly said to have had its origin in factual investigation.[29]

With the close of the Civil War, however, among many of the

men drawn from war service into the government bureaus in Washington, one begins to see signs of a state-minded empiricism of a different spirit. Many of the most talented of the new "statists" were to be found around John Wesley Powell, explorer, chief of the new Geological Survey, and pivotal figure in Washington scientific life, whose *Report on the Lands of the Arid Region of the United States* of 1878 launched a bold, ultimately futile campaign to wrest western land policy from the grip of myth and shape it to expert ecological fact. A similar knot of men was to be found in the census office around Francis A. Walker, who in 1880 engineered a dramatic expansion of the census's size and scope. Still another was to be found in the Bureau of Labor under yet another ex-Union officer, Carroll D. Wright, who (more quietly than Powell or Walker) insinuated his agency into the position of the federal government's chief investigative bureau for social phenomena. These were men of a radically different stripe than the university-based founders of academic political science. They were self-educated in the main. Walker and Wright taught themselves statistics; Powell had only a smattering of formal college learning; the brilliant polymath of Powell's agency, Lester Ward, had a night school education in belles lettres and biology. They were veterans of the war's harshly learned lessons in the primacy of expertise over abstraction, Republican in politics, scientific in temperament and ambition.[30]

Among men of this sort, so like those whom Bentham had attracted to himself a half-century earlier, the long-abused catch phrases of utilitarianism gained their first, though still precarious, foothold in America. It was one of Powell's men, W J McGee, who reworked Bentham's maxim into the conservationist slogan, "the greatest good for the greatest number for the longest time," which generations of United States Forest Service recruits were eventually to memorize. Still closer to the utilitarian mold was Lester Ward, champion of the scientifically organized, meliorist state, debunker of mere metaphorists, dreamer of organizing "happiness" with the deliberateness of a cotton mill, a man possessed by the possibilities of legislative invention and governmental expertise—as near a thing to Bentham as America had yet seen. Under the shadow of the orators, a small, home-grown utilitarian movement slowly gathered force.[31]

From these early stirrings in the post–Civil War Washington bu-

reaucracy, seeping into a few of the more advanced university seminars in the 1890s, social empiricism grew swiftly in force in the
Progressive years. In the muckrakers' wake, public and semipublic
investigators suddenly swarmed over social life. The Russell Sage
Foundation's Pittsburgh Survey, the first major adaptation of
Booth's methods to an American city, took six volumes to contain
in 1909–14; and it, in turn, was quickly dwarfed by still larger
undertakings. The Labor Bureau's *Report on Condition of Woman and
Child Wage-Earners* sprawled over nineteen volumes in 1910–12; the
City of Cleveland's investigation of its educational needs in 1915–
17, over twenty-five volumes; the Immigration Commission's report
of 1911, over forty-one volumes—giants in a veritable saturnalia of
statistical fact. In the law, Harvard's Roscoe Pound touted the beginnings of a new sociological jurisprudence. Efficiency experts like
Frederick Taylor promised utopias of empirically engineered harmony. Powell's report of 1878 had shattered on reefs of wish fulfill-
ment; a generation later facts had acquired rhetorical power and—
as the Progressive era's quantum leap in social legislation showed
—political consequence.[32]

The Progressive penchant for facts represented not simply the
yearnings of a nervous and confused public, suddenly caught in
economic forces bigger than its figures of speech could fully contain. It represented the edge of a new claim, a tool employable by
all sorts of users, though by none as sharply as the emerging new
class of experts, that legislation must be wrested from the mere
lawyers and orators, prefaced by investigation and research, made
empirical, workable, practical. New ambitions, new labels. "This is
a utilitarian country," Woodrow Wilson tried out one such in
1907. Better still, in the word that endured, it was a "pragmatic"
one. In the early 1910s, the term was just beginning to work its
way into the vocabulary of political writers. A decade later, so
deeply had the term taken root that John Dewey was struggling
hard to rebut the notion that pragmatism was nothing but another
name for Americanism.[33]

To the extent the label "pragmatism" implied that James and
Dewey were in some way responsible for the rising appeal to facts
and consequences, the term was clearly a misnomer. Pragmatism
was still a technical word for philosophers when the factual appe-

tites of the Progressive years began to show their strength, though James had been trying since the end of the 1890s, with a Chautauqua-like enthusiasm that made his philosophical colleagues wince, to spread the mental liberation gained from looking at the consequences, the "cash value" (if one must), of the ideals his friend Royce found so satisfying. Even after 1907, when the publication of *Pragmatism* vaulted James into sudden journalistic prominence, Oliver Wendell Holmes was not alone in thinking that James's strenuous dislike of system, his insistence on free will, his openness to every orphan idea, amounted to the most impractical sort of "humbug." Only in the early 1910s, and, still more so, after 1915, when John Dewey, moving beyond his popular educational tracts, made his entrance into the *New Republic* as a political writer of no mean force, did the social, instrumental implications of pragmatism clearly emerge from the impress of James's mercurial individualism.[34]

But to the extent that James and Dewey thought of themselves as locked in battle with Idealism's legion of abstractions, they shared an important kinship with the muckrakers, experts, and fact-grubbers who were leaving their stamp on politics. Dewey had fallen under the spell of Idealism at Johns Hopkins in the 1880s; he had drunk deeply of the idea of the social organism; as late as 1894 he still thought of his philosophy as an "experimental" variant of Idealism.[35] If his subsequent quarrel with Idealism was less strident than James's ("damn" the Absolute, James had cried), Dewey's pragmatism, like James's, was an effort to claw his way out of Idealism's tightly constructed cage of words. The "one great enemy" of democracy, he wrote in 1921, "is the hankering of man for unity of existence." To talk about *'the* state, *the* individual" solved none of "our particular perplexities." Such words, Dewey insisted,

do not assist inquiry. They close it. They are not instrumentalities to be employed and tested in clarifying concrete social difficulties. . . . If we talk about *the* state and *the* individual, rather than about this or that political organization and this or that group of needy and suffering human beings, the tendency is to throw the glamor and prestige, the meaning and value attached to the general notion, over the concrete situation and thereby to cover up the defects of the latter and disguise the need of serious reform.

"Wholesale creeds and all-inclusive ideals are impotent in the face of actual situations," he reiterated the theme a decade later; "for doing always means the doing of something in particular." Liberation lay in the method of science: in breaking verbal problems into concrete particulars, in hypothesis, experiment, and the weighing of consequences.[36]

This was not precisely utilitarianism, as Dewey was at pains to point out. Against the deductive and mechanistic side of Bentham's legacy, against Bentham's thin and arithmetic notion of the psyche, Dewey kept up a running quarrel. But when Dewey complained of the imprisonment of arguments within "pompous and sonorous generalities wherein controversy is as inevitable as it is incapable of solution," the voice came straight out of utilitarianism's early, critical years.[37]

Like utilitarianism, the pragmatic label entered politics as a badge of insurgency, a tool for persons eager to break the verbal dogmas which weighed so heavily in economics, politics, and the law. When the term "pragmatism" began to seep into the vocabulary of the Progressive empiricists, it entered as a gloss on an already distinct uneasiness with the pliancy, the obfuscating power of mere words. For their method of facts, too, had been a fighting creed, a strategy to pry apart the veils so thick in middle-class culture, a means of working themselves free of religious faiths grown too large and entrapping. It was characteristic of Progressive empiricists that they came to their calling with a vivid sense of liberation and release, trading in their dog-eared copies of John Ruskin, like Charles Beard, or their Christian socialism, like John Commons, for facts. Their realism never lost the marks of their quarrel with the massive verbal remains of the late nineteenth century. J. Allen Smith's often quoted remark, that "we were all Deweyites before we read Dewey," contained a precise, though frequently misunderstood, kernel of truth.[38] Political empiricism did not come naturally, out of the grain of American culture, but quickly, charged with barely hidden urgencies and rebellions.

Through the First World War and beyond, facts and ideals, lowbrow and highbrow political talk, hung together in tense and complicated balances. Nothing made it certain that the one would ultimately swallow up the other; Van Wyck Brooks was not alone in pinning his hopes on a new language of the "middle plane." The belated arrival of Bentham in America harbored promise and a multitude of possibilities. A wholesale deflation of abstractions in political talk might have led to a language closer to the skin of everyday experience than any the Americans had yet found. Out of such a vocabulary might have come a deeper, less rhetorical sense of public life: precise and vigorous talk of public utilities, words for the ways in which private lives meet in webs of interdependencies and common consequences. But such an outcome hinged on a union of the high-flown talk of the social whole with the militant new vocabulary of fact. What remained to be seen was what the reinventors of utilitarianism in its twentieth-century, American phase would do with a metaphor, as vital to politics, as difficult to pin down by empirical tests, as the public weal, the common good.

Empirical Political Science

The professional political scientists chose facts. Out from the tautologies and conundrums of Burgess's generation they rushed in the 1910s and 1920s to create an empirical political science. To the younger political scientists the crucial issue was no longer the formal structure of authority but how politics worked. They turned with relief from state theory and constitutional law to the study of government and administration, the machinery of legislation, the dynamics of party and influence.[39] Here was "real" life—the stuff of tangible power and tangible professional authority. To a public mired in words and slogans (worse yet, in antiquated words—prisoners, as the political scientists had learned to put it by the 1920s, of a massive lag between fact and culture) the political scientists would supply the realism, the expert and exact knowledge that efficient government required. If that meant leaving the discipline's big, unifying abstractions to take care of themselves, they were not particularly alarmed by the event.

The shift in professional ambition and mood was not fully visible until midway through the Progressive years. Of the seven subdisciplinary committees into which the American Political Science Association had been organized in 1903, only two (on administration and on politics) were devoted to what was to become the behavioral heart of the discipline.[40] Within a decade, however, the pressures for a more descriptive, factual political science were rapidly breaking up the familiar classroom formulas. As late as 1914, the Association's committee on college instruction was still complaining of overemphasis on such purely "abstract notions and principles" as the origins of the State or the essence of sovereignty. But by then the magisterial treatises of the 1890s and their widely employed redactions of the next decade had been all but eclipsed by textbooks in the mold of Charles Beard's enormously successful *American Government* of 1910: practical, straightforward accounts of how government worked. "American government did not originate in any abstract theories about liberty and equality," Beard's opening sentence proclaimed, but in "experience." Within another generation, an introductory text along any other lines was barely imaginable.[41]

The reconstruction of political science drew part of its intensity from the distinctive urgencies of a generational revolt. The political scientists who refashioned the profession after 1910 were more likely to have grown up in an atmosphere of debate over urban government and administration than amidst the older, Civil War-derived controversies over the nation-state. They were less likely to have spent a finishing year abroad amidst the powerful abstractions of German political science; less likely (as the declining references to foreign language books in the professional journals suggested) to care passionately about European scholarship. They hitched their fortunes not to the ebbing prestige of *Wissenschaft* but to the bright and alluring carriage of the natural sciences: hard, precise, behavioral, objective. On the eve of the First World War, similar desires ran hard through all the social sciences: through sociology, where the grand evolutionary theories of a Franklin Giddings, an Edward A. Ross, or a Thorstein Veblen were being challenged by a band of younger empiricists; through psychology, where John Watson's first statements of behaviorism burst rudely into the fray in 1912; even through economics, so long the bastion of deductive logic.[42]

In choosing facts, few of the younger political scientists intended a wholesale assault on the older rhetoric of the State. For every

Beard or Bentley, determined to liberate political science from its bondage to the "unreal," there were dozens who contrived a quieter, sometimes only half-acknowledged secession from the conceptual, integrative concerns of Burgess's generation. Typical in this regard was Charles Merriam, through whose seminars most of the most talented of the 1930s "realists" were eventually to pass. He had cut his teeth at Columbia and Berlin with a thesis on the history of the theory of sovereignty. Moving on to the University of Chicago in 1900, he was drawn into the hurly-burly of reform politics, plunging into the campaign for the open primary, running successfully for a place on the Chicago city council and from there (though he narrowly missed the prize) the mayor's seat as well. Turning from activist politics to scholarly entrepreneurship, he quickly emerged as the profession's most adroit organizer of large-scale empirical research. But it was not until 1920 that the faded outline for a comprehensive "Principles of Politics" on Burgess's scale, which Merriam had put together in a burst of intellectual ambition fifteen years earlier, finally ceased to tempt him.[43]

If in cases like Merriam's, scientism, activism, and the quest for professional authority stealthily combined to erode the turn-of-the-century science of the State, the new generation of political empiricists did not set out to dissolve the body politic into mere interests. Bentley's work, as late as the 1930s, they barely knew; his thoroughgoing animus against "soul stuff" was not yet theirs. They mounted no common crusade against the founding axioms of their discipline. They quietly laid the jargon of State and sovereignty aside on the assumption that the social whole would endure without their continued incantations.

To these tacit compromises the First World War's degradation of every species of German-derived abstraction dealt a momentarily unnerving blow. Understanding the crack-up of nineteenth-century civilization was no easy business. Nonetheless there was pathos aplenty in the stampede of the professors to pin the blame of war not merely on the kaiser or his Junkers but on still deeper, radical defects of German language and philosophy: on the "metaphysical monstrosities" of Kant, Hegel, and a century of Idealism. A handful of the German-trained American professors tried to hold out for a more balanced view—if not of Germany, at the least of the social role of ideas and Idealism. But they were no match for the sudden countertide of anti-German animus and self-doubt. Dewey threw himself into the war effort with a furious assault on Kant, who, in slicing the ideal from the material, had (Dewey charged) let loose the Pandora's box of abstractions—nation, State, *Kultur*—in whose service the German troops were now marching. Even W. W. Willoughby, backpedaling hard from his 1890s talk of State "omnipotence" in a cloud of Jeffersonian quotations, now insisted that he had meant the State to be "nothing more than a convenience of thought."[44]

If the State was unmasked as a philosophical "monster," if sovereignty was a tool of the warrior class, could one then imagine a polity without either? At its best the wartime crisis in political science provoked a furiously imaginative rethinking of the basic metaphors of politics. The effort to find a looser substitute for the sovereign State went farthest in Britain, where the syndicalist currents in the labor movement had a particularly strong influence on younger political intellectuals. As early as 1912, Beatrice Webb was noting anxiously that "syndicalism has taken the place of the old-fashioned Marxism." Two years later the Fabian Society's summer school was overrun with Oxford-trained students talking eagerly of the devolution of the state into occupational guilds, industrial syndicates, and self-governing industrial groups. The war pressed forward the dissident strain: an unhappiness with the loyalty-monopolizing State, top-heavy with concentrated authority, playing out its life in Parliamentary debates and international struggles, woefully remote from the day-to-day lives—or control—of its citizens.[45]

The most powerful writer on these lines was Harold Laski, a young, radical, Oxford-trained political theorist, compatriot of the younger British political intellectuals, who spent the war years in temporary exile as an instructor in history and political thought at Harvard. Between 1915 and 1921, in a spate of books and articles, Laski rummaged restlessly though the decentralist phases of French political thought, the writings of Tory churchmen and guild socialists, Jamesean pragmatism and the antiwar resentments of the labor left, trying to find a theoretical base for a new "pluralistic" state, which would acknowledge itself as simply one of the polity's many associations, with no more absolute claim to a citizen's allegiance than all the others. Sovereignty was a critical obstacle; "the pluralistic theory of the State . . . dissolves—what the facts themselves dissolve—the inherent claim of the State to obedience," Laski insisted. But more basic still, unavoidable as they rose to a pitch of wartime, patriotic fury, were the claims of the general will: "Whatever political problems we may consider upon this fundamental question, we shall always ultimately be driven back. How far, and in what way, is our society one? How far is there an interest of the Whole, a monistic interest, which transcends the interests of the Many who compose that whole?" Laski's answer to the wartime crisis in Idealist political theory was to call for a reconstruction of the body politic in decentralized forms, a devolution of democracy to the workplace and neighborhood, lest men be swept by "a certain grim Hegelianism . . . into the vortex of a great All which is more than ourselves."[46]

Most Americans, however, were far too deeply awhirl in the vortex of wartime patriotism to heed Laski's challenge. The American writer most closely associated with "pluralism," Mary Follett, combined a vigorous faith in the cultivation of small, grassroots, intermediary groups with an equally acute, Idealist-charged fear that *"the will to will the common will"* (the "All," Follett called it) might fall apart into an elbowing crowd of selfish interests. Among the political scientists there was a flurry of interest in ideas of functional or associational representation; but, like the brief debate over sovereignty in the political science reviews, the arguments petered out vaguely and inconclusively. The war knocked the word State, tainted with Germanism, out of the vocabulary of American political science; it hastened the flight away from theory. But into the vacuum a dozen synonyms for the common will were rushed, with patriotic urgency, into place.[47]

The Disappearing Public

The more serious blow came later, amidst the advertising-led consumer prosperity of the 1920s, suddenly filled with hucksters and opinion shapers of all sorts, when the political scientists woke up to find that the general will itself had vanished. Whatever else the war had been, it had been a massive act of will: a dramatic instance of the Progressives' faith in public opinion, united and militant. That much remained, even in the eclipse of Germanic labels. But what if the public, rising to avenge the atrocities in Belgium and crush all future seeds of war, had been duped? What if the general will could be cranked up by anyone who knew the secrets of the game? What if the "public opinion," on which the Progressives had counted so heavily, were as clay in the hands of propagandists, opinion "crystallizers," and the new horde of advertisers?

These questions flowed with massive urgency through Walter Lippmann's *Public Opinion* of 1922. A restless, frequently self-contradictory intellect, Lippmann had done his bit at the *New Republic* to stir up wartime morale. Now four years later, Lippmann was in the full tide of reconsideration—not so much of the war as of the politics of words. *Public Opinion* opened with a haunting vignette of a general staff conference, somewhere behind the French lines during the worst of the reverses at Verdun. At issue was not the morning's plan of battle but the words in which the day's events, already ended, would be reported to the press. For the critical campaign in war as in politics, Lippmann sensed, was the battle for language and morale. One waged it, Lippmann wrote in a brilliantly corrosive set of sketches, by creating "pictures" in men's heads: stereotypes, fictions, symbols, and simplifications, all masquerading as reality. In the distended societies of the twentieth century, where "the real environment is altogether too big, too complex, and too fleeting for direct acquaintance," where the ordinary citizen knew the great public events of the day only at second hand, mediated through layers of censorship and imagery, words were everything. What the public knew, it knew vicariously; imprisoned in "pseudo-environments" of symbols and rhetoric, it could at best think pseudo-thoughts. "Public Opinion, . . . a National Will, a Group Mind, a

Social Purpose, or whatever you choose to call it"—the prime movers of democracy, Lippmann wrote, all boiled down to someone else's pictures rattling through our heads.[48]

Looking back from an age saturated in advertising, it is hard to recover the shock of encounter with the propaganda-filled world *Public Opinion* helped unveil. Over the next decade the journalists worked the theme deeply and anxiously—egged on not only by accounts of the inner workings of the war propaganda machines but by the new phalanx of private hucksters, propagandists, and admen crowding into their places. For the state propaganda of war was clearly only the tip of a much larger phenomenon. The new media —tabloid press, movies, and radio—all obviously teemed with propagandistic possibilities. So, still more, did business advertising, then in its great leap forward from ads to images to "public relations" management, as business enterprises moved to increasingly deliberate assaults on potential consumers.

Propaganda, Edward Bernays boldly titled his book-length advertisement for public opinion management in 1928. It was the art not of the crude, open ad but of the disguised sell: the carefully planted editorial or newspaper story, the quietly orchestrated letter-writing campaign, the gift of one's product to the most visible of the trendsetters, and the abundant possibilities latent in the techniques of psychological association. By the end of the 1920s, one of the quickest learners, the National Electric Light Association, had flooded the nation's schoolrooms with free educational pamphlets, designed to root out any vagrant notion of publicly owned electric power. Others capitalized on the hunger of editors for prewritten copy. On the wings of the new techniques the lobbyists abandoned the back rooms, set aside the crude devices of bribe and boodle to work the levers of the public mood. Public opinion, modernized for an advertising age, had nothing to do with Rousseau or the dreams of Woodrow Wilson. It could be "crystallized" (Bernays promised), mobilized, played upon, counterfeited, indeed (if the journalists' fears and the advertisers' promises were right) bought outright.[49]

Down the tracks of the same suspicions the political scientists followed. By the end of the 1920s, the library shelves had begun to fill with studies of the techniques of the new-style pressure groups: manufacturers' associations, chambers of commerce, antisaloon and prosaloon leagues, labor unions, veterans' organizations, and on through a score of others. When the Social Science Research Council Committee on Pressure Groups and Propaganda completed its bibliographical project in 1935, it had sifted through over four thousand titles, the largest subdivision of them devoted to the propaganda activities of business groups.[50] Democracy under "pressure" was the political scientists' phrase for the new turn of events, their worries about the manipulation of public opinion for private ends made all the more acute by the simultaneous decline in the turnout of voters. By the mid-1920s, the percentage of eligible voters who bothered to cast their ballots in presidential elections had fallen almost by half from its late nineteenth-century norm, and the political scientists, who had once approved the easing of black and new immigrant voters out of the electorate, were worrying about the causes of voter apathy. An increasingly uninterested, badly informed public, joined with the rise of the skillfully orchestrated public relations campaign, was clearly a troubling phenomenon for anyone who hoped to keep the Interests and public will distinct. "The voice harkened to by the legislators is not the lone voice of a citizen crying in the wilderness of individual opinions," E. Pendleton Herring concluded the decade's most thorough investigation of the new lobbying techniques at the end of the 1920s; it was "the chorus of a cause organized for a purpose and directed by a press agent."[51]

The political scientists' premonition that they had stumbled onto a radically new phase in the history of interest politics was no illusion. In accelerating the breakup of the late nineteenth-century party system, the Progressive assault on the party bosses and narrow partisan loyalties had been a movement of hidden, far-reaching consequences. As the party organizations weakened under the pressures of the referendum, the open primary, and the widened possibilities for split-ticket voting; as the parties lost their dominance as the primary agencies through which policy was made; as the intense partisanship which had drawn nineteenth-century Americans to the polls in massive numbers began to erode, swamped in a bombardment of new stimuli and appeals, the political arena was thrown open to extraparty pressure groups of all sorts. The spectacular success of the prohibition lobby, the appearance of a congressional farm bloc organized across party lines, the Progressives' own skill at issue-building politics, all heralded the reformation of political loyalties into much more fluid, fractionated patterns, in which the interested groups were free to work the machinery of opinion and publicity.[52]

Where the constitutional convention had symbolized the nineteenth-century reign of the people, the gist of the new politics was most clearly to be seen in the legislative hearing. Rare in the nineteenth century, except where the tariff was at stake, hearings had become an indispensable, ritualistic part of the process of legislation by the eve of the First World War. At times they roamed the country, the very symbol of a government in search of the common counsel of the people. But in fact legislative hearings quickly turned into a forum for the interested, organized associations to have their say—for reformers, pressure group spokesmen, and (most prominently of them all) business lobbyists to make their statements, bid for influence, and act out in the open the fragmented nature of the social will.[53]

In this cave of interested voices, propaganda-fueled sentiments, and veiled words, where was the "public" to be found? In 1922 Lippmann had hoped that an expert, disinterested agency for news and intelligence might provide the basis on which a soberly informed public opinion, worthy of the name, might grow. Within another three years, however, Lippmann had grown sour even on that. "We have been taught to think of society as a body, with a mind, a soul and a purpose," he wrote in *The Phantom Public* in 1925. Political theory had built its foundations on a "mythical entity, called Society, the Nation, the Community." But they were all phantoms. The metaphor of the common will offered no sound basis for action. Even under the best of circumstances public opinion could be nothing but the voice of "the interested spectators of action," taken up now and then by a trampling, bewildered herd. A sober politics, Lippmann now concluded, was a frankly fragmented politics, a politics of "accommodation" and adjustment, in which "the conflicting interests merely find a way of giving a little and taking a little, and of existing together without too much bad blood."[54]

Not every student of politics was willing to dismiss the public as merely a badly turned figure of speech. Dewey, for one, never let go the conviction that some better organization of news, some forthright seizure of the information-disseminating function from the commercial interests, would bring the voice of the public back to life. Publics there were, Dewey pleaded, not in the Idealist sense of the word but as communities of persons drawn together in common webs of tangible consequences. In modern societies, however, where interdependence was at once inescapable and opaque, publics of this sort were normally too diffuse, too little conscious of their common experience, to act as a whole. News was consciousness, and, in the making of active publics out of passive relations, consciousness was everything. With a better organization of intelligence, Dewey hoped, the "great society" might be reconstructed as "a Great Community: a society in which the ever-expanding and intricately ramifying consequences of associated activities shall be known in the full sense of that word, so that an organized, articulate Public comes into being."[55]

Through the New Deal, Dewey kept up the plea for a "Great Community" bigger than the mere play of interests. But none of this —begging as it did so many questions of control—was easy to make clear. The political scientists, by and large, turned their anxieties into proposals to better register and regulate the lobbyists: simpler solutions than Dewey's, though patently inadequate to the conditions they had found. Let the big words collapse, and it was no easy matter to find in the wreckage the middle-sized, practical language of community to take their place.

The voice of new-style realism was Lippmann's: that the public was a metaphor, and a botched one at that. When the voters spoke, they spoke not as a whole but in a "babel" of interested voices, competing in the political marketplace. "The only opinion, the only will, that exists is the opinion, the will, of special groups," John Dickinson wrote in the *American Political Science Review* in 1930. The best, then, a government could do was to pick with some intelligence and sanity "the special interest which, in any particular case, it will allow to win." Interests were tangible. Beard, writing history now which seethed with power and interests ("the rough stuff of reality," he proudly called it), put them at the heart of the American experience.[56]

For most political scientists at the end of the 1920s, the disappearance of the social whole remained a suspicion rather than a certainty. Their allegiance lay to realism, not yet to Madison's language of counterbalanced interests. But the closer, the more skeptically one looked, in this new world of propaganda and appearances, the less one found. What lay beyond the individual but the inescapable press of interests? When the rhetoric of the State and the social whole, loaded with so much freight of significance, became suspect as a sham, what was left but fragments?

The Rhetoric of Realism

Between the inner doubts of the political scientists and the certainties of popular politics there remained, as yet, a major chasm. Talk of the common good and the common interest survived the propagandists, the aftershocks of overheated war patriotism, and the skepticisms of a Lippmann. The vogue of the word "service" was an example. A synonym for heroic sacrifice during the war (not by whim was the military draft called the "selective service"), the word was appropriated by business publicists in the 1920s to trumpet the end of capitalism's cutthroat phase and the opening of an era in which business served nothing but the commonweal. Herbert Hoover in the Commerce secretariat in the 1920s developed a scheme of industrial associationalism which mimicked from the political right much of the decentralist, pluralistic rhetoric of Laski and the guild socialists. But the keywords in Hoover's public speeches were unifying words: the mutual interests of labor and capital, universal prosperity, and cooperation.[57]

Franklin Roosevelt, too, swept into office on a rhetoric of the common good. Wilsonian talk of "vision," "discipline," and "sacrifice" saturated his first inaugural and left its stamp deeply on the public rhetoric of the National Recovery Administration. "There is a unity in this country which I have not seen and you have not seen since April 1917," Roosevelt declared in the springtime of the NRA's fortunes late in 1933. In the New Dealers' opening war against the "money changers," the "self-seekers," and the "Interests," the biggest rhetorical weapon they possessed was the Progressive imperative of "the great whole."[58]

Even after the collapse of the NRA, after the dream of restoring the integrated wartime economy through some combination of state power and business patriotism had evaporated, after the New Deal planners were forced on to piecemeal approaches to economic recovery, Roosevelt never abandoned the rhetoric of the common good. "Interdependence" was his favorite word for the theme. To raise the fortunes and the purchasing power of any depressed sector of the economy was automatically to raise the fortunes of them all —pulling the common boat up on a self-willed tide of higher consumer spending. Farmers, miners, industrial workers, businessmen: "the factory worker, the store keeper, the gas station man, the manufacturer, the merchant—big and small—the banker." However the list went, "they are all part and parcel of a rounded whole."[59]

And yet there were limits to the New Dealers' willingness to use the Wilsonian strain they knew so well. In the 1930s, as Richard Hofstadter once acutely noted, it was the conservatives who wrung the most effect out of the Progressives' "traffic in moral absolutes" and their "exalted moral tone."[60] The anti-New Deal lobbies cranked up the old abstractions—the Declaration, the hallowed principles of constitutional law, the Revolutionary talk of trampled rights—in hopes that the words would save the familiar order of a reasonably unchecked capitalism. Their fortress of power, if they were to find one, was the courts, as full of potent abstractions as ever and of power sufficient to come within a hairsbreadth of skewering the New Deal on the words of constitutional formalism.

The rhetoric which soon came to dominate the New Deal, partly in response, was hard-boiled, pragmatic, realist. Nothing was more characteristic of the New Dealers than suspicion of the diversionary, mystifying functions of words. They had no faith in the business puffery of the 1920s, the verbal jugglery of the courts, the stiff, dogmatic side of Woodrow Wilson, or the legal and moral shibboleths onto which the New Deal's opponents had retrenched. It was no accident that the tone of Roosevelt's fireside chats was explanatory and deliberately unoratorical. Words were the trouble—the bigger the words, the more evasive of facts and straightforward solutions. This was the theme of Stuart Chase's *The Tyranny of Words* of 1938, a politically charged popularization of semantics, designed to rend the veil from the "fantastic wonderland" of grandiose, referent-free noises that passed for political speech. *The Deflation of American Ideals,* Edgar Kemler titled his New Deal call-to-arms three years later; the phrase, which spoke volumes about the ambitions of the hard-boiled experimentalists in the New Deal, was not a lament but a manifesto.[61]

Not surprisingly it was among the New Deal lawyers that the assault on words, on the verbal ghosts of Idealism, found its sharpest expression. Legal realism, as the attack on the notion of a logically coherent Law behind the law was known, was hardly organized enough to form a school, much less a legal philosophy. It was an experiment in the politics of satire, which bristled with wit and skepticism. If the legal realists possessed a creed, however, it was the phrase they lifted from Oliver Wendell Holmes: "We must think things not words." Only men with the "thought-ways" of children, desperate for harmony, chancelessness, and security, really believed in the law as a thing of logic, Jerome Frank laid down the realists' challenge in 1930. "The whole confused, shifting helter-skelter of life" parades before the law. One could not make rules for so unpredictable a reality with "word-magic." The task required an "avowedly pragmatic" sense of the law, Frank urged, a willingness to entertain chance and pliancy, and a legal language close to the vernacular of everyday experience. To Thurman Arnold, whom Frank brought from the Yale Law School into the New Deal, the blubber of abstractions and principle lay thick over every aspect of governance. "Every one distrusts direct methods of solving the problem immediately at hand," Arnold protested, in the decade's wittiest, most caustic book on politics; everyone pleaded principles. What was needed instead, Arnold countered, was a social philosophy which would free men to experiment, to "do practical and humanitarian things in government" without worrying overly hard about the cosmos—a social philosophy which would "give them an understanding of the world, undistorted by the thick prismatic lenses of principles and ideals."[62]

The New Dealers had their own ideals, to be sure, hidden behind what Richard Hofstadter approvingly styled "the new opportunism" of the 1930s. In the rhetoric of a Henry Wallace there were five-dollar words enough to dilute the skeptical pose of several Thurman Arnolds. Even Arnold, in truth, recognized the indispensability of symbols strong enough to bind men together in common loyalties.[63] Indeed in collectivist symbols, from the NRA's blue-eagle parades to the great public power dams, the New Deal was unabashedly fertile. Most powerful of them all, once more, was the People. Out of the New Deal agencies came Art for the People, a People's Theater, and a spectacularly ambitious program of public works. The People stood revealed in the government murals now, muscles rippling, reaping, sowing, trading, forging iron, driving steel rivets, bearing children—the flow of the separate groups of workers massing in a common strength.[64] But the very realism of the New Dealers, their preoccupation with hard, tangible properties like interests, the submerged effects of 1920s political science together with the din in their ears from Beard's histories, where workers, employers, and farmers clashed in open, constant battle, all worked against the notion of the People as a single whole. By the mid-1930s a distinctive figure of speech had begun to work its way into the rhetoric of the New Deal realists. The People was a plural noun: a phalanx of the fundamental interests—farmers, labor, and capital—adrift in a common boat.

When the metaphor of the People as a tensely poised balance of interests took root in the New Deal realists' heads is not easy to pin down. One early hint came in the flurry of planning proposals that flooded the magazines at the nadir of the Depression in 1931–32, when anything, including a wholesale reconstruction of the Constitution, seemed better than to drift into economic chaos. The debate over planning was, at bottom, a debate over who should seize the helm of the broken economy. Beard himself proposed a scheme of wholesale industrial syndicalization. Others urged that the economic machine be given over entirely to a general staff of experts, who would know what to do with it. Closer to the mainstream, however, was Stuart Chase's proposal for a general economic board which would gather representatives of the major social interests together in a new supradirectorate: government, industry, labor, farmers, and the professors, with a neutral expert as chairman. Similar notions soon found their way into the NRA, after its initial fling with business self-association was over. In its 1934 reorganization, the NRA gained a new board of overseers composed of two representatives from industry, one from labor, and two (college professors both) to represent the consumers and the public. A year later, the representatives of labor's interests were given parity with the others. Nullities in practice, the NRA reorganizations reflected a quiet reconstruction in the ways the polity was to be perceived: as a bundle of competing, yet inter-related interest groups. In the Agricultural Adjustment Adminis-tration and its producers' associations, the farmers' interest had already found formal, political representation. By the midpoint of the New Deal, as Ellis Hawley has shown, the planners had scat-tered in a dozen directions to prop up the weaker industries and raise the fortunes of labor by promoting the development of labor organizations strong enough to counterbalance the concentration of capital, in a policy Hawley has called economic "counterorgani-zation."[65]

This was not the pluralistic state Laski had imagined, radically decentralized and democratized down to the grass roots and the shop floor. The New Deal realists of the late 1930s accepted the basic social interests pretty much as given; the benefits of govern-ment-sponsored "counterorganization" bypassed most farm labor-ers, black sharecroppers, and the poorest of the poor. Their essential job, as the New Dealers increasingly saw it, was to keep the craft of state, leaky and unevenly loaded, in balance. "For decades," Alan Brinkley writes, reformers had dreamed "of creating a smoothly functioning, ordered, harmonious whole out of the clashing parts of modern capitalism." By the late 1930s, however, the New Dealers had concluded that

Americans would . . . have to accept the inevitability, even the desirability of constant conflict and instability in economic life. . . . Government would be a constantly vigilant, constantly active referee, a "traffic manager," stepping into the market to correct imbalances, remove "bottlenecks," protect efficiency, restore competition. It would operate from no "master plan," and it would seek no fundamental structural reform. It would work, rather, to keep the machinery of American capitalism running smoothly and productively.[66]

To the New Deal's opponents, that meant a policy without a center. Ray Stannard Baker, speaking for many of the old Progressives grown sour on New Deal experimentalism, wrote in his diary on Election Day 1936, that "in this dreary campaign there was almost no call to any kind of unselfish service; everywhere group demands for special favors, and career politicians promising to grant them." Among the political scientists, it was a cliché to say that the New Deal spoke with the most extraordinary confusion of tongues. "If there is leadership," the American Political Science Association's president complained in 1934, "it is the leadership of mounting one's horse and dashing off in every direction at once."[67]

Not until 1940 did the tactics of piecemeal intervention acquire a name, popularized by the onetime radical journalist, John Chamberlain, on his way toward the anti-New Deal right. For the moment, however, Chamberlain was full of praise for Franklin Roosevelt—not as the man of "vision" of 1933 but as the master realist, a "master broker" of politics. Roosevelt's "Broker State" stood for no Common Good, Chamberlain wrote.

The labor union, the consumers' or producers' co-operative, the "institute," the syndicate—these are the important things in a democracy. If their power is evenly spread, if there are economic checks and balances to parallel the political checks and balances, then society will be democratic. For democracy is what results when you have a state of tension in society that permits no one group to dare bid for the total power.

Chamberlain nowhere cited Madison, but this was the point of Madison's Tenth *Federalist,* translated into the slangy accents of mid-twentieth-century realism.[68]

"A social historian in the future, seeking to describe the mood of the 1940 intellectuals, will find [Chamberlain's] *The American Stakes* a first-rate starting point," Max Lerner wrote in the *New Republic.* "There runs through the book a monistic obsession with whatever is pluralist, pragmatic, full of loose ends, in the nature of compromise. . . . If intellectuals sat on crackerboxes, they would talk as Chamberlain does in this book." Chamberlain's "pragmatic liberalism" (as Lerner styled it), his fusion of the language of trade and the language of politics, was not entirely fair to the New Dealers. The metaphors in Roosevelt's own speeches tacked back and forth with the occasion and the speechwriter. The function of government was to "strike the equitable balance between conflicting interests," Roosevelt claimed when in one mood; to express the needs of the "whole Nation," when in another.[69] Even the patchwork makers, the architects of "counterorganization," who moved into Roosevelt's inner circles with the collapse of the NRA, harbored a notion of the public interest bigger than mere compromise. They had no particular sympathy for the haggling of the economic marketplace, whose umpires and regulators they proposed to be. Their pump priming was a Keynesianism of *public* works—dams, post office murals, reforestation schemes, or rural electrification—not the market-dominated Keynesianism of tax cuts and heightened consumer spending. There was no little irony, then, in the fact that it was those most deeply skeptical of the pretensions of business who finally merged the language of governance and brokerage, polity and marketplace, so fully that there was to be no easy unscrambling of them.

Part of the explanation for the new respect for the disunities of American politics was to be found abroad. When the international shocks of the late 1930s hit home—the emergence of German-style fascism, stripped of the corporatist veneer of Mussolini's Italy to bare the iron reality of a centralized military state, together with the collapse of liberal hopes for the Soviet Union under the repressive centralization of Stalin—it was little wonder that political observers should have been eager for John Chamberlain's loose-ended pluralism. By the middle of the decade, political scientists had already pulled "totalitarian" out of the lexicon of fascist slogans to describe the nightmare of a body politic in which there was no friction, no interest but that of the state itself. In response, the political science texts of the late 1930s swelled with a newfound celebration of the maneuvers, contentions, and inconclusiveness of American politics. Barter filled as the American system was, it did what it needed to do, E. Pendleton Herring now wrote: provide for a certain amount of compromise and adjustment and a reasonable "balance of interests." In totalitarianism's reflection, the genius of American democracy now seemed to lie in its very disunity, the absence of anything like the general will for which the Progressives had yearned.[70]

For the New Dealers the dissolution of the polity into interests was also profoundly liberating. It rescued them from the paralysis of excessive principles, which had finally left Herbert Hoover preaching impotently of the imperatives of Individualism. Perceiving the body politic as a bundle of interest groups freed the New Deal realists to patch what needed patching without waiting until they had comprehended the polity whole or traced the thread of potential precedent through the entire social fabric. In these circumstances, the language of marketplace realism was a language of action.

But the still deeper forces which edged the New Deal realists toward the suspect language of the marketplace were to be found in their realism itself. For what was their pragmatism, their hardboiled, skeptical talk, but words with the trail of past arguments all over them? Wedded to a notion of fact forged in quarrel with the inflated verbal constructs of the past, their talk shaped in recoil against a vocabulary of the Ideal which seemed to have come to the end of its tether as an apologetics for the status quo, their distrust of words honed still sharper by the hucksters and propagandists of the 1920s, they were not to be taken in readily by cheap verbal unifications. Behind the noise of politics, behind a misty phrase like Dewey's "Great Community," what could there really be but advantages and interests? Having spent so many words in the crusade to puncture words, the New Deal realists had not much left but economic words—the lowbrow banter of trade and barter—out of which to fashion the rhetoric of realist political science.

Into the intellectual breach they swept the snippet they knew of Madison. They seized on the Tenth *Federalist* as reassurance that they were still right with the Founders and the American political tradition. But the result was hardly history or (for that matter) realism. In Lippmann's terms, the upshot was to insinuate a new picture inside men's heads. The basic ingredients of politics—call them a triad of labor, capital, and agriculture or call them a shifting bundle of economic groups—were not the Revolutionary pamphleteers' rights-bearing individuals or Madison's property holders or the People or the social whole—but interests. By the late 1930s the political scientists had abandoned their laments at the growth of pressure groups and dropped their reformist hopes that the lobbyists and propaganda makers could somehow be resisted and controlled. The "pressure groups," John Chamberlain too had insisted, were not to be decried. "The pressure group has long since become the new democratic unit," he wrote, the essential "watchdog" of society.[71] The Interests were no longer alien to the body politic. The roiling, inconclusive contest of interested groups *was* politics.

It was to take another generation for the political scientists to take the full measure of the figure of speech they had invented. Only in the mid-1950s, with a Bentley revival in full swing, with Madison apotheosized as the prophet of countervailing powers, did the rhetoric of 1930s realism harden into an orthodoxy as firm as the highbrow political science it had supplanted. Within another decade, however, it was the language of insurgency to complain of "the scientific pluralist's scientific dread of such poetic terms as 'public interest,' 'the state,' and 'sovereignty.' "[72] The word Interests was the residuum of the debates and disillusionments of the first third of the century. It was a label no one claimed for themselves. It was not, like Natural Rights, a term to fight over. The story of the word Interests was the story of the failure of other words, a lexicon of bigger, public words—stretched too taut, to be sure, and too often used for obscurantist purposes—which eroded (tumbling over Dewey's middle ground) into a jargon in which the real was a bundle of competing, partial utilities. Roosevelt's talk of economic interdependence remained, but the public the Progressives had held in their mind's eye was gone. There was no public will, no common good above the working compromise of private goods. The integrative abstractions of the nineteenth century were stuffed into the closet. What endured was Interests.

Epilogue

The Conflations of Freedom

Of the making of words there is no end. Since independence the keywords of political talk had risen and receded in crises and cycles. None of them had been the work of particularly profound invention. In the making of grand political theory the Americans had played only a minor role. Rather, in the teeth of crisis the talkers had reached into the ample, preexisting vocabulary of politics to seize a word and press it into new service. From the declaration writers' overhauling of the rhetoric of natural law to the Jacksonians' reemployment of one of the key radical slogans of the seventeenth-century English revolution to the efforts of the late nineteenth-century middle class to take shelter in that still older word, the State, the investment of an ancient phrase with powerfully new meaning had been a central, recurrent event in political debate. Novelty counted for little in these matters; the crucial contest was over meaning. For every effort to alter the root metaphors of politics inaugurated a furiously intense struggle over the control of words. In the crisis the talkers rushed to lay claim to phrases grown suddenly slippery and indeterminate: to expand their meaning, to make them carriers of radically new demands, to puncture or to co-opt them. It is this recurrent struggle over a relatively small number of words that has shaped political talk in America, disguised its powerful conflicts under a misleading veneer of sameness, and propelled it forward.

Even talk of Interests met its challenge. As the nation slipped once more into war in the 1940s—this time not merely into a single, cataclysmic contest but (as it turned out) a future of war, quasi-war, and unbroken war readiness—the rhetoric of interest group pluralism temporarily gave way before an urgent need for new abstractions. We live within the continuing reverberations of that event still, our political vocabulary stocked beyond our ken with the verbal products of the 1940s. Even now on the trailing edge of the Reagan years, the outcome of the war and Cold War reconstitution of the language of politics remains uncertain—too much so for more than a rough and tentative epilogue. But clearly the keyword of the moment was Freedom, and the conflicts over the term's possession as deep as any of the contests that had come before. Pushed to the front of the American political vocabulary for deeply conservative ends—a war word, a unifying cry—Freedom turned out to be a tool capable of powerfully divergent purposes, unstable in meaning, open to radical redefinition from below: a word (like so many abstract words before it) to fight over.

War framed this last cycle of word making. Free of the tightening vise of international events, the hard-boiled, piecemeal humanitarianism of New Dealers like Arnold might have found room to flourish. But war strains language to the utmost, pitches it sharply toward the dualistic and abstract slogans with which loyalty is most readily bought. In this the Second World War was no exception. The New Deal realists had scarcely found their marketplace metaphor when the collapse of Europe sent Americans of all sorts scrambling once again for grander phrases. The first sign of the demands the war would place on language was a rush for restatements of political fundamentals. Amidst angry debate over the moral bankruptcy of a merely pragmatic politics, 1940s political scientists began suddenly to rummage hard through their discipline's back drawers for a nobler heritage to defend than skeptical, pluralist realism. The most prominent case in point was Charles Beard. By the middle of the war, he had come round full circle from his muckraking past to celebrate the Constitution and its framers in a book whose subtitle, *Conversations on Fundamentals,* caught the widely shared mood. Many of the same forces drew Walter Lippmann into an awkward but serious flirtation with a natural law philosophy he could neither fully believe nor, in the war crisis, fully do without.

In a world careening toward dictatorship, blitzkrieg, and terror, the mere looseness of American politics was no longer comfort enough. The hard coin of political responsibility once again was principle.[1]

The sharply altered tone of the political science journals was mirrored, with much greater effect, in the New Deal vocabulary. By 1939 the abstractions were multiplying rapidly in Roosevelt's speeches as he hunted for rhetorical tools capable of cementing a new, interventionist coalition together. Despite the New Dealers' determination not to repeat the propaganda excesses of 1917–18, they could not resist the need for principles to bring the urgencies of the moment home. This time the keyword in the clash of forces was not to be "civilization" (a term shattered beyond repair in 1919) nor the defense of "democracy"—though Roosevelt's speeches of 1939 and early 1940 tended strongly in that direction. This time the rallying cry of the war was to be Freedom. Pulled shrewdly out of the core vocabulary of the New Deal's domestic opponents, stretched (with convenient elasticity) over the deep fissures within the antifascist alliance, the word swelled with new power in the 1940s. It resounded through Roosevelt's "four freedoms" rhetoric, through the claims of a dozen exile committees to speak for what remained of "free Europe," through talk of the wartime alliance of the "freedom-loving nations," through Roosevelt's promise of a postwar "free world."[2]

At the grass roots, too, talk of Freedom in 1940s America found a powerful response. Two years after the close of the war when a group of business and political leaders hit on the idea of packing the nation's core documents into a "Freedom Train" for a solemn processional tour through the land, the exhibit was swamped with deeply affected visitors. Some three million people visited the Freedom Train between 1947 and 1949, standing patiently in line for a glimpse at the pieces of paper on which the meaning of their freedom was putatively inscribed: Jefferson's first draft of the Declaration of Independence, the Constitution annotated in Washington's own hand, Hamilton's reports on the American economy, Lincoln's scrawled Gettysburg Address, all joined (in a symbolic union no one could miss) to a car carrying the final documents of the German and Japanese surrender.[3] Freedom bundled them all together: Jefferson and Hamilton, General Dwight Eisenhower and Admiral William

Halsey. Freedom had won the war. However differently an economic or geopolitical realist might have put it, that formulation of the war's meaning, sweat, and sacrifice worked its way deep into the patterns of everyday speech.

Thus when the rivalries in the wartime alliance gave way to a new kind of quasi-war in Europe between the United States and the Soviet Union, it was not surprising that the policy makers should have tried to transfer the antifascist rhetoric of Freedom wholesale into the new cause. Or that the rapid switch of labels should have succeeded so brilliantly. By the end of the 1940s the incorporation was complete. Roosevelt's 1941 image of a world rent down the middle—"divided between human slavery and human freedom"— had been slipped unchanged into place as the controlling metaphor of the Cold War. The words defined the unnerving events of the late 1940s in the clarifying language of the past; they threw over the nation's new quasi-war posture and its nervous armament drive the legitimating mantle of the war just won. The cause of the United States was once more the cause of freedom, threatened by yet another malignant form of "slavery." Once more its armies defended no mere sphere of influence against a rival power, but the "free world." Through the cold war declarations of a Harry Truman, a John Foster Dulles, a John F. Kennedy, or a Ronald Reagan, the phrases have rumbled into our own political age with extraordinary continuity and effect.[4]

Powerful words, capable of holding the chaos of experience in a massive, reassuring lock, they nonetheless obscured a lot. For in postwar America, the rhetoric of Freedom drew its primary power not from its specificity but its all-pervasiveness, its ability to bind together the confusions and discordancies of American life with a single, powerfully flexible noun. Freedom in mainstream postwar talk was not this or that list of rights. It was bigger and vaguer. It was the obverse of the twentieth century's new totalitarianisms; it was, in a word, everything that fascism and communism were not.

The spokesmen of the political center quickly learned to employ it to bundle together every facet of postwar life. One learned to talk of the United States' leadership of the "free world," of free and "captive" Europe, of Free and Red China, and of the alliance of "freedom-loving nations"—some of which parceled out freedom to their citizens with what in other circumstances might have seemed a conspicuously stingy hand. Cold War intellectuals gathered in government-sponsored congresses for the defense of "cultural freedom." At home one learned to talk of economic relations in terms of the "free market" and the bounties of the "free enterprise system." The latter term, put into currency toward the end of the 1930s by anti-New Deal businessmen who sensed the defects of their earlier (though more honest) talk of "private" enterprise, and still uncertainly used during the war years, had become a fixture of both parties' platform rhetoric by the early 1950s.[5] Free world, free enterprise: the word Freedom cut across all boundaries. In its conflations no mere political system but what the talkers now increasingly called the American way of life was evoked, defended, legitimized.

Every abstraction conflates; that is the essence of open, accordion-like phrases. But none of the earlier metaphors of politics had been employed so deliberately to bundle in a word the institutions of the status quo—or so fully efface the boundary between economic and political life. One of the strengths of American political talk had been a sense that the keywords of politics must somehow be different from those which undergirded the mere "expediencies" of economic relations. Even the realist political scientists of the 1930s had felt the need to hedge their marketplace metaphors. But now, under the rubric of Freedom, capitalism and democracy were finally, confidently folded into a common entity.

The trick turned in large part on the very abstractness of the new terms of cold war debate. Certainly the "free enterprise" system was free in the sense that it was not state run or (for most purposes) publicly planned. Still it was no easy matter to equate the postwar economy, dominated by a score or two of giant corporations, with the town meeting ideal which still passed for freedom in the sphere of politics. The term "freedom of choice" with which the jugglery was done was accordingly fuzzy and indistinct. It bound in a phrase the consumer benefits of postwar prosperity with the political fact of choice in open, reasonably contested elections. It did so, however, at the expense of what everyone knew, once the words moved closer to the grain of experience: that private choices of economic opportunities and public choices of policy were not really the same thing at all, that the heaping of one's shopping cart to overflowing in the supermarkets of postwar America and the collective strain and furor of democratic decision making (whether the issue be the weight of next year's school tax or the paving of the county's roads or the relative worth of social security and aircraft carriers) were hardly subsumable under a single word, even as big a word as Freedom. But under the pressures of foreign events, amidst the Americans' new willingness to define themselves in the reflex of other nation's systems, amidst an urgent need for words large enough to justify their rise to world dominance, the word Freedom took shape as a synonym for everything the Americans already had—for the way of life (however many compromises of freedom it might contain) that they were prepared to defend.

Rights Without Retrospection

Freedom was America: its refrigerators, its elections, its alliances, its swelling patriotism. No word as heavy with multiple meanings as this, however, could be easily contained. Let the mission and destiny of the United States be defined as freedom, and there were bound to be Americans, possessed of sharper, dissident notions of what freedom might mean, eager to claim the word and, with it, force open the contradictions between the Cold War slogans and the postwar way of life. The transformation of the term Freedom from a unifying cry to a protest slogan required the unbundling of the word into the hard, specific language of rights. That happened quickly and, as so often before, not in the centers of power but on its margins. Within twenty years after the war's end, Americans found themselves in an era of rights making more vigorous than ever before in their history. The rhetoric of Freedom had slipped its moorings to be returned, like so many abstract words before it, radically transformed from below.

Even in the 1940s the radical potential in the wartime talk of Freedom had not been lost on the New Deal left. In 1944 Roosevelt himself had translated his generalized "four freedoms" rhetoric into the startling specificity of a new "economic bill of rights": the right to a useful and remunerative job, to a decent home and adequate income, to medical care, and to security from the economic terrors of unemployment and old age. Four years later Henry Wallace's Progressive party and the labor unions were still playing hard on those promises, despite the scuttling of the political centrists toward safer ground. Other New Deal liberals, Eleanor Roosevelt conspicuous among them, turned their energies to the drafting of a Universal Declaration of Human Rights: a bold, new international bill of rights and freedoms (complete with a controversial section on economic security) which they steered through the new United Nations in 1947–48.

But it was where talk of Freedom ran up against the post-Reconstruction mores of race that the slogans of patriotic assurance turned sharply and momentously unstable. The effort to turn the antitotalitarian rhetoric of the war into a vehicle for the grievances of black Americans had begun well before the war was over. By 1948, black leaders had forced the phrase "civil rights" from the margins of political argument, to which it had been shunted (like most radical forms of rights talk) with the collapse of Reconstruction, into the eye of presidential election politics, where it was to stay, to the acute discomfort of party leaders, for a generation. Even the Freedom Train in that year found itself embroiled in the erupting, postwar debate over racism when city officials in Memphis and Birmingham demanded Jim Crow lines and separate visiting hours for blacks and whites, in keeping with what most Americans had long been accustomed to call freedom. The organizers refused; and where the Freedom Train's integrated lines were permitted in the South, observers commented on the quiet, intent seriousness of the exhibit's black visitors.

All this was carried home with profound, submerged effect. Within a decade, talk of rights and Freedom—spinning off the war and Cold War sloganeering, running with new intensity through the black South and the segregated ghettoes of the urban North, fused with the humiliations of segregation and with a Freedom talk deep in black experience, forced with new readiness into the courts where (thanks to the justices' own absorption of the war's demand for fundamentals) it began to get an increasingly sympathetic hearing —exploded in a rights crusade on a scale the nation had never seen before. From the beginning the civil rights campaign was a movement of several tongues. But politically its most telling rhetoric worked by exploiting the massive, barely veiled contradiction between the official postwar rhetoric of Freedom and customary practice. It contrived to turn the newly professed faith of the nation back upon itself, with glaring literalness. Segregation, fixed in the southern law codes at the end of the nineteenth century, had promised order. The war's encounter with the horrors of Nazi racism and the extravagant postwar rhetoric of free world leadership, however, put the system of black subcitizenship to a much sharper test. It could not but make the customary arrangements of American-style apartheid problematic and, if the tactics of protest were skillfully designed, acutely embarrassing. The civil rights movement swept up rights and Freedom into a common cry of protest and threw it back at mainstream America in a score of nervy, ingenious ways: in freedom rides, freedom schools, freedom songs, a counter Freedom Democratic party. "The peoples wants freedom," Stokely Carmichael began a workshop in Mississippi in the wake of what civil rights workers had pointedly called the "freedom summer" of 1964.[6] Here was no strange political tongue, no language easily turned aside as alien to American politics, as politicians and presidents noted with visible confusion. This was the core rhetoric of the Cold War translated into black vernacular, specified, sharpened into radically destabilizing demands, appropriated by the most marginal of Americans.

The practical test of Freedom was rights. Not since the antislavery crusade had a movement so saturated with popular rights claims pushed so hard against power and custom. But the potency of the civil rights movement's blend of language and tactics was not solely to be found in what historians soon began to call the "second Reconstruction" of the mid-1960s. Still more remarkable was the tidal wave of rights invention it set in motion. By the mid-1970s, though the civil rights movement itself had shattered into fragments, Americans all over the social landscape were pressing their grievances into a revived language of rights: women's rights, gay rights, children's rights, the rights of control over one's body, the rights of the unborn, ethnic rights, Native American rights, welfare rights, consumers' rights, human rights, rights of privacy and rights of expression, criminal defendants' rights, prisoners' rights, the rights of the ill, the right to die.[7]

Nothing in the eighteenth- or nineteenth-century past matched this avalanche of multiplying rights claims. Out of the extraordinarily contagious effects of the civil rights movement, out of a new, militant sense of the potential diversity of American life, out of resentment at the concentration of private and public power in ever more distant, bureaucratic forms, out of a new sense of the social power of litigation (and of language shaped for legal action), out of a myriad divergent grievances and desires the new rights revival flowed. The Declaration of Independence reappeared as a protest anthem; in the late 1960s you could hear it on your car radio, the words now electric with revolutionary meaning. A decade later moral conservatives angry at the Supreme Court's abortion decision and libertarians somewhere to the right of the Republican party, radical feminists, and American Civil Liberties-style liberals were all talking heatedly, at a score of cross purposes, of rights. In the last quarter of the twentieth century, the language of rights has proved to be the most volatile, flexible language of protest we have.

But unlike eighteenth- and nineteenth-century Americans almost no one now talks of Natural Rights. The eccentricity of a John Rawls in the early 1970s, reimagining the principles that should have ruled the formation of the social contract, had men been lucky enough ever to have made one, is proof enough of the distance rights talk had traveled.[8] We hammer home our rights and freedoms without pause for retrospection or much puzzlement (like Channing's) about the essence of human nature. The common coin of rights claims now seems simpler. Rights claims channel an extraordinary variety of desires and grievances into a language prickly (as always) with implicit individualism and justiciable in the law—for the judges to do with them what they can.

Even the keenest defenders of the postwar courts readily admit that the judges, burdened with sorting out this mounting cacophony of rights talk, have not found consistency easy. Imaginative, quicksilver rights inventors like William O. Douglas have appealed to the logical "penumbras" and "emanations" surrounding the Constitution's formally enumerated rights—though the evanescent phrases betrayed a nervousness that might well have made the manifesto writers of the eighteenth and early nineteenth centuries, with their tangible sense of dispossession, wince. Others like Hugo Black tried with much simpler literalism to inject the entire federal Bill of Rights into the corpus of state law, though they never carried the full court with them. The majority of the justices on the Warren and Burger courts chose instead to carve out piecemeal a new list of "basic" and "fundamental" rights, creating case by case what amounted to a second, common law bill of rights. Out of the twists and turns of the judges and the shifting pressures from below came new fundamental rights of suffrage (in the poll tax and reapportionment cases), of privacy (in the contraception and abortion cases), of education (in the school desegregation cases), and of protection against the prosecutory powers of the state. Not noticeably strong in the logical relations between its parts, its freedoms couched in language heavy with the marks of compromise, this second, postwar bill of rights has nonetheless proved in fits and moments to be a tool of profound political effects.[9]

But by the middle of the 1980s no one could miss the accumulating strain on the words, fraying out under the wear of so many divergent uses. The rights revival, as it spread through the vastly more diverse America of the late twentieth century, resulted finally in a certain blurring of the line between rights and desires. Mainstream political scientists, who had begun to move back in force to the old terrain of "realism" in the 1950s, were more than ever inclined to call them both simple statements of interest. Vastly more rights and an extraordinary proliferation of rights talk, together with an increasing inability on the part of judges, plaintiffs, and professional political scientists to restate the new logic of rights for a people no longer as certain as before about the intentions of the Creator—all this added up to no simple picture. But amidst the growing confusion in rights talk, one increasingly heard the old, nervous voices of outright repudiation. If self-professed conservatives still tried their hand at rights invention, the conservative justices on the Supreme Court seemed more wary than ever of that sort of volatile, destabilizing talk. A straw in the wind was the announcement of the Supreme Court's conservative majority in a sodomy case in 1986 that in a controversial matter like sexuality it was dead set against allowing any new basic rights to be smuggled into the Constitution under the cover of "fundamental" human rights or the "penumbras" of privacy.[10] Two decades after the rights explosion began, the counterforce of resistance was once more running hard and, apparently, successfully.

From a centrist cry to a tool of radical social reconstruction to the butt of nervous compromise and repudiations, the rhetoric of Freedom, transmuted into rights, seems once more on the track of a familiar arc. Over and over again a keyword—Natural Rights, the People, and now Freedom—had slipped its established place. Appropriated by Americans far outside the corridors of power, it had been thrust back into political talk, outwardly unchanged, as the tool of radically transformed purposes—only to be blunted and spent at last. This sort of political debate in a hall of abstract mirrors has its share of deceptions and confusions. It has repeatedly misled those who have mistaken the outer noise of talk for inner consensus. Samuel Huntington's term, "the politics of creedal passion," however, is surely the more accurate one.[11] Freedom was an open abstraction: its ambiguities and its power inextricable from one another. A word which rose on the crest of its historic moment, wrenched from purpose to purpose, fillable and refillable with meaning, tugged at by ever more sets of hands, it reiterated in its career the central dynamics of our political talk. Ask not what Freedom is, for if it is worth much it is never static. Ask what the word is being used to do.

Public Talk

But Freedom cannot be the whole of public talk. Nor Interests—the tough, residual, lowbrow talk that in the erosion of the rhetoric of Freedom once again fills the legislative corridors and the pages of the centrist journals. A democracy must also have strong and generous words for its common life and common wants.

If there had been a distinctive pattern to the vocabulary of political argument in America, however, it had been the distance between its collective words, pitched so far above the affairs of daily life, and its liberating words, so close to the skin of the individual self. Along this rift, the keywords of American politics had for a long time been starkly divided. Many of the most potent and volatile of its words had been employed for vigorously, subversively individualistic ends. Natural Rights, Freedom, even the People—each was used at the crest of its historical moment to thrust back the claims of other people's power, to break the injustices of custom, to whittle down the scope of government, and to expand the possessions and possibilities of the self. The ineradicability of rights talk, despite the repeated efforts to root it out, endowed American speech with a powerfully individualistic set of tools. No other political culture has had a vocabulary of individual liberation quite like it.

But what Americans had found much harder to come by were clear ways in which to talk about the common bonds and responsibilities of public life. Not that American political talk had showed any shortage of integrative words; those, too, had risen and fallen in spectacular arcs since independence. But the biggest of them, carriers of so many desires and intentions, had worked on a plane strikingly remote from common experience. The partisans of early nineteenth-century majoritarian democracy, with their notion of possessive sovereignty, had had a surprisingly difficult time putting the purposes of the People's collective power into words. Those who pushed the counterclaims of Government, their eyes bent on the sovereignty of God, rarely talked very specifically about political relationships among human beings. The late nineteenth-century seers of the State, propelled by the metaphysics of their Protestantism and the anxieties of their class, soared Icarus-like into still more extravagant levels of abstraction. Even the nation-obsessed rhetoricians of the Cold War rarely had a much clearer sense—beyond military readiness and individual prosperity—of what the common threads in the American way of life entailed. We have used our words for public life most easily when the phenomena—nation, State, the Free World—are farthest away from us. The result has been a public talk at once shrill and shallow: top-heavy with abstract terms for the nation and the political whole but skeletally thin in everyday, middle-level phrases for common, collective action. That, too, has endured, etched in our keywords.

To say as much is to put once more the complaint that has run so hard, and ineffectually, through insurgent political science since the 1960s.[12] That decade, in addition to its revival of rights talk, also reinvented language for common life: community, neighborhood, participational democracy, the public interest group, the "beloved community" of Martin Luther King. But none in the end endured well. When the civil rights crusade moved beyond issues of rights to issues of power, it could not sustain the bonds that had held it in tense, effective relationship to mainstream political talk. The term "community," to be sure, is everywhere now, in entities we casually refer to as the business community, the black community, the real estate community, or the medical community—but no one doubts that they are interest groups under another name. Talk of power once more spirals down on Interests. Interest group pluralism, revived in the 1950s, reigns in the political science textbooks as never before. "Our concern must be for a special interest group that has been too long neglected," Ronald Reagan promised in his first inaugural, groping for a synonym for the People.[13] Savvy above power and rhetoric, we know the source of his difficulty.

But a public life without a strong, deeply rooted repertoire of public words carries consequences. When the metaphors fail, legitimacy erodes. As Robert Bellah and his co-observers of contemporary America note, we have an embarrassingly hard time finding words to explain even to ourselves our enduring sense of common responsibility. Our "first language," they write, is individualistic; our "second language," reflective of our actual public commitments, is weakly connected to ourselves—though the brass bands of patriotism will bring it out powerfully.[14]

The richness and the poverty of our keywords is not fixed. Political talk might be an arena in which we talk seriously about public goods, about the resources and needs we possess not individually but in common, about what we want from the policemen, schoolteachers, garbage collectors, drivers' license examiners, pothole fixers, highway planners, missile launchers, and lawmakers who compose our governments. We might talk specifically about what we want our collective life to be, what we desire in common, and the common consequences of our getting it. That was what Bentham meant in the best of his antimetaphysical moods. That was what the turn-of-the-century British socializers of utilitarianism had in mind. That, still more so, was what Dewey meant by the "Great Community." But the old, heated quarrel with Bentham's language of consequences is not over. The words for common happiness still elude us. Open as the language of American politics has been to so many uses, swept as it has been with so much energy, so much liberating force, so many anxious desires for coherence, so many contested truths, that sort of public talk has not come easily.

NOTES

Prologue

1. Marvin Meyers, *The Jacksonian Persuasion: Politics and Belief* (1957; new ed., New York: Vintage Books, 1960), p. v.

2. On the multiplicity of such uses: Murray Edelman, *The Symbolic Uses of Politics* (Urbana: University of Illinois Press, 1964).

3. Quoted in John P. Diggins, *The Lost Soul of American Politics: Virtue, Self-Interest, and the Foundations of Liberalism* (New York: Basic Books, 1984), p. 114.

4. "Schematic images of social order," Clifford Geertz has labeled these figures of speech. I have preferred, avoiding Morgan's implication that such images are by their nature false and Geertz's assumption of a necessarily high degree of logical (ideological) order among them, to call them metaphors. Edmund S. Morgan, "Government by Fiction: The Idea of Representation," *Yale Review* 72 (1983): 321–39; Clifford Geertz, *The Interpretation of Cultures: Selected Essays* (New York: Basic Books, 1973), p. 218.

5. The term "keywords" is borrowed from Raymond Williams's rich and illuminating *Keywords: A Vocabulary of Culture and Society*, rev. ed. (New York: Oxford University Press, 1985).

6. Albert B. Hart, "Growth of American Theories of Popular Government," *American Political Science Review* 1 (1907): 560; Hannah Arendt, *On Revolution* (New York: Viking, 1963); Daniel J. Boorstin, *The Genius of American Politics* (Chicago: Chicago University Press, 1953).

7. Quoted in Sacvan Bercovitch, "The Biblical Basis of the American Myth," in *The Bible and American Arts and Letters,* ed. Giles B. Gunn (Philadelphia: Fortress Press, 1983), p. 219.

8. Clinton Rossiter, *Conservatism in America: The Thankless Persuasion* (1955; 2d ed., New York: Vintage Books, 1962), pp. 67–68; Louis Hartz, *The Liberal Tradition in America: An Interpretation of American Political Thought since the Revolution* (New York: Harcourt, Brace, 1955). The notion of a consensual political "creed," made up of some combination of Locke, Jefferson, Protestant Christianity, and entrepreneurial capitalism still remains strong among political scientists. See, for example, Samuel P. Huntington, *American Politics: The Promise of Disharmony* (Cambridge: Harvard University Press, 1981), chap. 2.

9. For example: Sacvan Bercovitch, *The American Jeremiad* (Madison: University of Wisconsin Press, 1978).

10. Gordon S. Wood, *The Creation of the American Republic, 1776–1787* (Chapel Hill: University of North Carolina Press, 1969); J. G. A. Pocock, *The Machiavellian Moment: Florentine Political Thought and the Atlantic Republican Tradition* (Princeton: Princeton University Press, 1975); Joyce Appleby, "Republicanism in Old and New Contexts," *William and Mary Quarterly,* 3d ser., 43 (1986): 20–34.

11. Karl Marx, *The Eighteenth Brumaire of Louis Bonaparte* (1852; New York: International Publishers, 1963), p. 15.

12. Quoted in Rossiter, *Conservatism,* p. 5.

Chapter 1. *Utility*

1. Frederick Jackson Turner, *The Frontier in American History* (New York: Henry Holt, 1921), p. 37; Daniel J. Boorstin, *The Genius of American Politics* (Chicago: University of Chicago Press, 1953); *The Papers of Woodrow Wilson,* ed. Arthur S. Link (Princeton: Princeton University Press, 1966–), 17: 570.

2. For an overview of Bentham's life and ideas, the essential starting places are Mary P. Mack, *Jeremy Bentham: An Odyssey of Ideas* (New York: Columbia University Press, 1963); James Steintrager, *Bentham* (Ithaca: Cornell University Press, 1977); and H. L. A. Hart, *Essays on Bentham: Studies in Jurisprudence and Political Theory* (Oxford: Oxford University Press, 1982).

3. Jeremy Bentham, *A Fragment on Government; or, A Comment on the Commentaries* (1776), in *The Works of Jeremy Bentham,* ed. John Bowring, 11 vols. (Edinburgh: William Tait, 1843), 1: 260–95.

4. Jeremy Bentham, *Theory of Legislation,* ed. Richard Hildreth, 2 vols. (Boston: Weeks, Jordan, 1840), 1: 87–110. The "Mother Goose" line is quoted in Stefan Collini, Donald Winch, and John Burrow, *That Noble Science of Politics: A Study in Nineteenth-Century Intellectual History* (Cambridge: Cambridge University Press, 1983), p. 94.

5. John Austin, *Lectures on Jurisprudence; or, The Philosophy of Positive Law,* ed. Robert Campbell, 4th ed., 2 vols. (London: John Murray, 1873), 1: 123, 122; Bentham, *Theory of Legislation,* 1: 110.

6. Robert Shackleton, "The Greatest Happiness of the Greatest Number: The History of Bentham's Phrase," *Studies on Voltaire and the Eighteenth Century* 90 (1972): 1461–82; Bentham, *Theory of Legislation,* 1: 90, 15.

7. Quoted in Alan Bullock and Maurice Shock, eds., *The Liberal Tradition, from Fox to Keynes* (New York: New York University Press, 1957), p. xxvi.

8. Hart, *Essays on Bentham,* chap. 3; J. R. Dinwiddy, "Bentham's Transition to Political Radicalism, 1809–10," *Journal of the History of Ideas* 36 (1975): 683–700.

9. Bentham, *Theory of Legislation,* 1: 66; Bentham, *A Defense of Usury* (1787; Philadelphia: Mathew Carey, 1796). Marx's characterization of Bentham is quoted in Hart, *Essays on Bentham,* p. 24.

10. Eric Stokes, *The English Utilitarians and India* (Oxford: Clarendon Press, 1959); L. J. Hume, *Bentham and Bureaucracy* (Cambridge: Cambridge University Press, 1981); Gertrude Himmelfarb, "The Haunted House of Jeremy Bentham," in her *Victorian Minds* (New York: Knopf, 1968).

11. Bentham, *An Introduction to the Principles of Morals and Legislation,* ed. J. L. Burns and H. L. A. Hart (1789; London: University of London, 1970), p. 12.

12. A. V. Dicey, *Lectures on the Relations between Law and Public Opinion in England during the Nineteenth Century* (London: Macmillan, 1905); Robert Nisbet, *Twilight of Authority* (New York: Oxford University Press, 1975), pp. 242, 245; Sheldon S. Wolin, *Politics and Vision: Continuity and Innovation in Western Political Thought* (Boston: Little, Brown, 1960), chap. 9; J. Bartlet Brebner, "Laissez Faire and State Intervention in Nineteenth-Century Britain," *The Tasks of Economic History* 8 (1948): 59–73.

13. John Stuart Mill, "Bentham" (1838), in *The Collected Works of John Stuart Mill,* ed. John M. Robson (Toronto: University of Toronto Press, 1963–), 10: 75–115.

14. Bentham, *Theory of Legislation,* ed. Richard Hildreth, 2 vols. (Boston: Weeks, Jordan, 1840).

15. William Thomas, *The Philosophical Radicals: Nine Studies in Theory and Practice, 1817–1841* (Oxford: Oxford University Press, 1979), chap. 1; Bentham, *Works,* 11: 76–83.

16. Bentham, *Works,* 4: 474. On his codification efforts: Frederick Rosen, *Jeremy Bentham and Representative Democracy: A Study of the Constitutional Code* (Oxford: Oxford University Press, 1983).

17. Thomas, *Philosophical Radicals,* p. 158; Thomas Carlyle, "Signs of the Times" (1829), in *The Works of Thomas Carlyle,* Centenary ed. (New York: Charles Scribner's Sons, 1898–1901),

27: 56–82; Charles Dickens, *Hard Times* (1854), *The Writings of Charles Dickens,* 32 vols. (Boston: Houghton, Mifflin, 1894), vol. 26.

18. Jerome B. Schneewind, "Moral Problems and Moral Philosophy in the Victorian Period," *Victorian Studies* 9 supplement (1965): 29–46; Collini et al., *Noble Science,* p. 346.

19. Harold Perkin, *The Origins of Modern English Society, 1780–1880* (London: Routledge and Kegan Paul, 1969); S. E. Finer, "The Transmission of Benthamite Ideas, 1820–1850," in *Studies in the Growth of Nineteenth Century Government,* ed. Gillian Sutherland (London: Routledge and Kegan Paul, 1972).

20. Thomas, *Philosophical Radicals,* p. 6; Dicey, *Law and Public Opinion.* Dicey's claims have been the gist of continued controversy: David Roberts, "Jeremy Bentham and the Victorian Administrative State," *Victorian Studies* 2 (1959): 193–210; Henry Parris, "The Nineteenth-Century Revolution in Government: A Reappraisal Reappraised," *Historical Journal* 3 (1960): 17–37; Jenifer Hart, "Nineteenth-Century Social Reform: A Tory Interpretation of History," *Past and Present* 31 (1965): 39–61; Thomas, *Philosophical Radicals;* David Roberts, "The Utilitarian Conscience," in *The Conscience of the Victorian State,* ed. Peter Marsh (Syracuse: Syracuse University Press, 1979).

21. Joseph Chamberlain et al., *The Radical Programme,* ed. D. A. Hamer (1885; Brighton, England: Harvester Press, 1971), p. lviii; Beatrice Webb, *Our Partnership* (1948; Cambridge: Cambridge University Press, 1975), p. 210; W. Stanley Jevons, *The State in Relation to Labour* (1882; London: Macmillan, 1887), p. 12; L. T. Hobhouse, *Liberalism* (London: Williams and Norgate, 1911).

22. John Stuart Mill, *Considerations on Representative Government* (1861), *On Liberty* (1859), *Utilitarianism* (1863).

23. John Adams, *Thoughts on Government* (1776), in *The Works of John Adams,* ed. Charles F. Adams, 10 vols. (Boston: Little, Brown, 1850–56), 4: 193. For other examples: Howard M. Jones, *The Pursuit of Happiness* (Cambridge: Harvard University Press, 1953), p. 4; Garry Wills, *Inventing America: Jefferson's Declaration of Independence* (Garden City, N.Y.: Doubleday, 1978), chap. 18.

24. William Paley, *Paley's Moral and Political Philosophy, as Condensed by A. J. Valpy* (Philadelphia: Uriah Hunt, 1835). On Paley's influence: Wilson Smith, "William Paley's Theological Utilitarianism in America," *William and Mary Quarterly,* 3d ser., 11 (1954): 402–24; Daniel W. Howe, *The Unitarian Conscience: Harvard Moral Philosophy, 1805–1861* (Cambridge: Harvard University Press, 1970), pp. 64–67.

25. Bentham, *Theory of Legislation;* John H. Burton, ed., *Benthamiana; or, Select Extracts from the Works of Jeremy Bentham* (Philadelphia: Lea and Blanchard, 1844).

26. Paul A. Palmer, "Benthamism in England and America," *American Political Science Review* 35 (1941): 855–71; Peter J. King, "Utilitarian Jurisprudence in America: The Influence of Bentham and Austin on American Legal Thought in the Nineteenth Century" (Ph.D. diss., University of Illinois, 1961), chaps. 2–4; J. Parton, *The Life and Times of Aaron Burr* (New York: Mason Brothers, 1858), pp. 519–24; *The Private Journal of Aaron Burr, during his Residence of Four Years in Europe,* ed. Matthew L. Davis, 2 vols. (New York: Harper and Brothers, 1838), 1: 88; Charles F. Adams, ed., *Memoirs of John Quincy Adams, Comprising Portions of His Diary from 1795 to 1848,* 12 vols. (Philadelphia: J. B. Lippincott, 1874–77), 3: 51, 536–39, 563–65.

27. "Jeremy Bentham," *United States Magazine and Democratic Review* 8 (1840): 251–71; Arthur M. Schlesinger, Jr., *The Age of Jackson* (Boston: Little, Brown, 1945), pp. 330–31; Thomas Cooper, "Slavery," *Southern Literary Journal* 1 (1835): 188–93; Dumas Malone, *The Public Life of Thomas Cooper, 1783–1839* (New Haven: Yale University Press, 1926).

28. William M. Armstrong, *E. L. Godkin: A Biography* (Albany: State University of New York, 1978); Edward H. Madden, *Civil Disobedience and Moral Law in Nineteenth-Century American Philosophy* (Seattle: University of Washington Press, 1968), chaps. 12–13.

29. [Hugh S. Legaré], "Jeremy Bentham and the Utilitarians," *Southern Review* 7 (1831): 284, 292; Drew G. Faust, *A Sacred Circle: The Dilemma of the Intellectual in the Old South, 1840–1860* (Baltimore: Johns Hopkins University Press, 1977), p. 55; Wendell Phillips, "Bentham's *Theory*

of Legislation," *North American Review* 51 (1840): 384–96; W. H. Dilworth, "Extreme Utilitarianism," *Arena* 28 (1902): 281–84.

John Stuart Mill's reputation suffered from the same anti-utilitarian animus. The evangelical reviews, *The Princeton Review* in the lead, were as bitterly opposed to Mill's version of utilitarianism as to Bentham's. In liberal journals he tended to be described, with unmistakable condescension, as a preternaturally talented thinker who, with no clear systematic idea to guide him, had wandered into deeper and deeper confusions. For example: Edward E. Hale, "John Stuart Mill," *Old and New* 9 (1874): 128–35; Percy F. Bicknell, "John Stuart Mill," *Popular Science Monthly* 69 (1906): 451–57.

30. Bernard Crick, *The American Science of Politics: Its Origins and Conditions* (Berkeley: University of California Press, 1959), p. 9.

31. On the accordionlike expansion and contraction of state activities: Carter Goodrich, "State In, State Out—A Pattern of Development Policy," *Journal of Economic Issues* 2 (1968): 365–83; Louis Hartz, *Economic Policy and Democratic Thought: Pennsylvania, 1776–1860* (Cambridge: Harvard University Press, 1948); J. Mills Thornton III, *Politics and Power in a Slave Society: Alabama, 1800–1860* (Baton Rouge: Louisiana State University Press, 1978); Morton Keller, *Affairs of State: Public Life in Late Nineteenth Century America* (Cambridge: Harvard University Press, 1977); Harry N. Scheiber, "Property Law, Expropriation, and Resource Allocation by Government: The United States, 1789–1910," *Journal of Economic History* 33 (1973): 232–51.

32. James Bryce, *The American Commonwealth,* 2 vols. (London: Macmillan, 1888), chap. 92. On the force of instrumentalism in the law: Morton J. Horwitz, *The Transformation of American Law, 1780–1860* (Cambridge: Harvard University Press, 1977).

33. William S. Jenkins, *Pro-Slavery Thought in the Old South* (Chapel Hill: University of North Carolina Press, 1935), p. 62; Merrill D. Peterson, ed., *Democracy, Liberty, and Property: The State Constitutional Conventions of the 1820s* (Indianapolis: Bobbs-Merrill, 1966), p. 96.

34. Perry Miller, *The Life of the Mind in America: From the Revolution to the Civil War* (New York: Harcourt, Brace, and World, 1965), bk. 2; Charles G. Haines, *The Revival of Natural Law Concepts* (Cambridge: Harvard University Press, 1930).

35. John E. Keeler, "Survival of the Theory of Natural Rights in Judicial Decisions," *Yale Law Journal* 5 (1895): 14–25; Harold M. Hyman and William M. Wiecek, *Equal Justice under Law: Constitutional Development, 1835–1875* (New York: Harper & Row, 1982), pp. 97–98.

36. James D. Richardson, ed., *A Compilation of the Messages and Papers of the Presidents, 1789–1897,* 10 vols. (Washington, D.C.: U.S. Government Printing Office, 1896–99), 2: 491; *Proceedings and Debates of the Virginia State Convention of 1829–30* (Richmond: Ritchie and Cooke, 1830), pp. 55, 129.

37. *Register of the Debates and Proceedings of the Virginia Reform Convention* (Richmond: Robert H. Gallaher, 1851), p. 298; *Proceedings and Debates of the Constitutional Convention of the State of New York, held in 1867 and 1868,* 5 vols. (Albany: Weed, Parsons, 1868), 1: 238–39.

38. *Debates and Proceedings of the Virginia Reform Convention,* p. 199; *Debates of the Convention to Amend the Constitution of Pennsylvania, Convened at Harrisburg, November 12, 1872,* 9 vols. (Harrisburg, 1873), 1: 583.

39. Theodore Parker, *The Rights of Man in America,* ed. F. B. Sanborn (1911; reprint ed., New York: Negro Universities Press, 1969), p. 365.

40. *The Letters of Sidney and Beatrice Webb,* ed. Norman MacKenzie, 3 vols. (Cambridge: Cambridge University Press, 1978), 3: 387; Stanley Weintraub, ed., *Shaw: An Autobiography,* 2 vols. (New York: Weybright and Talley, 1969–70), 1: 113–14; *Fabian News* 19 (July 1908): 66.

41. Sacvan Bercovitch, "The Biblical Basis of the American Myth," in *The Bible and American Arts and Letters,* ed. Giles B. Gunn (Philadelphia: Fortress Press, 1983); Catherine L. Albanese, *Sons of the Fathers: The Civil Religion of the American Revolution* (Philadelphia: Temple University Press, 1976).

42. Grant Gilmore, *The Ages of American Law* (New Haven: Yale University Press, 1977), pp. 10–11.

43. Lawrence M. Friedman, *A History of American Law* (New York: Simon and Schuster, 1973),

p. 265. On the lawyer-orators: Barnet Baskerville, *The People's Voice: The Orator in American Society* (Lexington: University Press of Kentucky, 1979), chap. 2.

44. J. A. Thomas, "The House of Commons, 1832–67: A Functional Analysis," *Economica* 5 (1925): 49–61; William L. Barney, *The Secessionist Impulse: Alabama and Mississippi in 1860* (Princeton: Princeton University Press, 1974), p. 53; Clement Eaton, "Henry A. Wise: A Liberal of the Old South," *Journal of Southern History* 7 (1941): 488; Friedman, *History of American Law*, p. 560.

45. David A. Shannon, ed., *Beatrice Webb's American Diary, 1898* (Madison: University of Wisconsin Press, 1963), p. 149.

46. Alan D. Gilbert, *Religion and Society in Industrial England: Church, Chapel and Social Change, 1740–1914* (London: Longman, 1976). On the transatlantic Protestant network: Charles I. Foster, *An Errand of Mercy: The Evangelical United Front, 1790–1837* (Chapel Hill: University of North Carolina Press, 1960).

47. Michael Sanderson, ed., *The Universities in the Nineteenth Century* (London: Routledge and Kegan Paul, 1975).

48. Alexis de Tocqueville, *Democracy in America*, ed. Phillips Bradley, 2 vols. (New York: Knopf, 1945), 2: 74.

49. Frederick Pollock, *An Introduction to the History of the Science of Politics* (1890; new and rev. ed., London: Macmillan, 1911), p. 107.

Chapter 2. *Natural Rights*

1. Timothy L. S. Sprigge, ed., *The Correspondence of Jeremy Bentham* (London: University of London Press, 1968–), 1: 341–44; John Bowring, ed., *The Works of Jeremy Bentham*, 11 vols. (Edinburgh: William Tait, 1843), 2: 501.

2. John Adams, "A Dissertation on the Canon and Feudal Law" (1765), in *The Works of John Adams*, ed. Charles F. Adams, 10 vols. (Boston: Little, Brown, 1850–56), 3: 449.

3. The radical potential of the appeal to natural rights—a point obscured in recent historical debate—is powerfully argued in Staughton Lynd's *Intellectual Origins of American Radicalism* (New York: Pantheon, 1968).

4. Carl L. Becker, *The Declaration of Independence: A Study in the History of Political Ideas* (1922; New York: Knopf, 1942), p. 25.

5. Bernard Bailyn, *The Ideological Origins of the American Revolution* (Cambridge: Harvard University Press, 1967); Pauline Maier, *From Resistance to Revolution: Colonial Radicals and the Development of American Opposition to Britain, 1765–1776* (New York: Knopf, 1972).

6. Bernard Bailyn, ed., *Pamphlets of the American Revolution* (Cambridge: Harvard University Press, 1965), p. 474.

7. Edmund S. Morgan, ed., *Prologue to Revolution: Sources and Documents on the Stamp Act Crisis, 1764–1766* (Chapel Hill: University of North Carolina Press, 1959), p. 56; John Dickinson, *An Address to the Committee of Correspondence in Barbados* (1766), quoted in Bailyn, *Ideological Origins*, p. 187.

8. On the limits of the natural law tradition, David Brion Davis's volumes are indispensable: *The Problem of Slavery in Western Culture* (Ithaca: Cornell University Press, 1966) and *The Problem of Slavery in the Age of Revolution, 1770–1823* (Ithaca: Cornell University Press, 1975).

9. *Blackstone's Commentaries, with Notes of Reference to the Constitution and Laws of the Federal Government of the United States and of the Commonwealth of Virginia by St. George Tucker*, 5 vols. (1803; reprint ed., New York: Augustus M. Kelley, 1969), 1: 51.

10. On the reputation of European writers in the colonies: Donald S. Lutz, "The Relative Influence of European Writers on Late Eighteenth-Century American Political Thought," *American Political Science Review* 78 (1984): 189–97; Donald Lundberg and Henry F. May, "The

Enlightened Reader in America," *American Quarterly* 28 (1976): 262ff; Henry F. May, *The Enlightenment in America* (New York: Oxford University Press, 1976).

The assumption that the ideological framework of the American Revolution must have been lifted, virtually intact, from one or another of the books in the patriot leaders' libraries —from Locke (as generations of historical scholarship had it) or the Scots moral philosophers (Garry Wills) or the Swiss jurist Jean Jacques Burlamaqui (Morton White)—is surprisingly hard to down. But the assumption that any of these writers provide a back-door entry into what the Americans really thought—so wildly implausible on the face of it and so clearly at odds with the eclectic untidiness with which even as philosophical a man as Thomas Jefferson stirred his authorities together under the press of events—disintegrates when one moves beyond isolated, borrowed passages. On the central question of resistance to Parliamentary law and taxation, none of these writers lent any support to the patriot cause at all. Cf. Garry Wills, *Inventing America: Jefferson's Declaration of Independence* (Garden City, N.Y.: Doubleday, 1978); Morton White, *The Philosophy of the American Revolution* (New York: Oxford University Press, 1978); Ronald Hamowy, "Jefferson and the Scottish Enlightenment: A Critique of Garry Wills's *Inventing America: Jefferson's Declaration of Independence,*" *William and Mary Quarterly,* 3d ser., 36 (1979): 503–23.

11. David Hume, "Of the Original Contract" (1748), in *Social Contract: Essays by Locke, Hume, and Rousseau,* ed. Ernest Barker (New York: Oxford University Press, 1948); Adam Ferguson, *An Essay on the History of Civil Society,* ed. Duncan Forbes (1767; Edinburgh: Edinburgh University Press, 1966), p. 8. Of the widely quoted Scots writers, the last to take the notion of a state of nature seriously was Francis Hutcheson, whose *Short Introduction to Moral Philosophy* came out in 1747, a year before the publication of Hume's essay.

12. H. T. Dickinson, *Liberty and Property: Political Ideology in Eighteenth-Century Britain* (London: Weidenfeld and Nicolson, 1977), chap. 2; Richard Ashcraft, *Revolutionary Politics and Locke's Two Treatises of Government* (Princeton: Princeton University Press, 1986). Cf. John Dunn, "The Politics of Locke in England and America in the Eighteenth Century," in *John Locke: Problems and Perspectives,* ed. John W. Yolton (Cambridge: Cambridge University Press, 1969); J. G. A. Pocock, "The Myth of John Locke and the Obsession with Liberalism," in *John Locke,* ed. J. G. A. Pocock and Richard Ashcraft (Los Angeles: University of California, 1980).

13. James Otis, *The Rights of the British Colonies Asserted and Proved* (1764), in Bailyn, *Pamphlets,* pp. 419–23; Richard Bland, "An Inquiry into the Rights of the British Colonies" (1766), in *Tracts of the American Revolution,* ed. Merrill Jensen (Indianapolis: Bobbs-Merrill, 1967), pp. 112–13. Scattered earlier manifestations of this line of argument are noted in Lawrence H. Leder, *Liberty and Authority: Early American Political Ideology, 1689–1763* (Chicago: Quadrangle, 1968) and Thaddeus W. Tate, Jr., "The Theory of the Social Contract in the American Revolution, 1776–1787" (Ph.D. diss., Brown University, 1960). But, as Tate notes, they were far from the center of the colonists' accustomed political talk.

14. Harry A. Cushing, ed., *The Writings of Samuel Adams,* 4 vols. (New York: G. P. Putnam's Sons, 1904–8), 2: 210, 258, 298–300, 354–55. The assertion that men are "by Nature, all free, equal and independent" was Locke's. In Virginia, George Mason altered it to "equally free and independent."

15. Robert A. Rutland, ed., *The Papers of George Mason,* 3 vols. (Chapel Hill: University of North Carolina, 1970), 1: 274–91.

16. Julian Boyd et al., eds., *The Papers of Thomas Jefferson* (Princeton: Princeton University Press, 1950–), 1: 141.

17. Bland, "Inquiry," p. 113; Leonard Labaree et al., eds., *The Papers of Benjamin Franklin* (New Haven: Yale University Press, 1959–), 17: 400; 20: 303; 16: 318; Samuel Adams, *Writings,* 2: 351; Wills, *Inventing America,* chap. 6.

18. Paul H. Smith, ed., *Letters of the Delegates to Congress, 1774–1789* (Washington, D.C.: Library of Congress, 1976–), 1: 46–49.

19. Jefferson, *Papers,* 6: 247–49; Tate, "Theory of the Social Contract," p. 204.

20. Thomas Paine, *The Rights of Man* (1791–92), in *Thomas Paine: Representative Selections,* ed. Harry H. Clark, rev. ed. (New York: Hill and Wang, 1961), pp. 85–86.

21. Lutz, "Relative Influence of European Writers," p. 192.

22. Virginia, Pennsylvania, Maryland, Delaware, and North Carolina adopted bills of rights in 1776; Massachusetts followed in 1780, New Hampshire in 1784. The authors of the Vermont constitution of 1777, following the Pennsylvania example, likewise included a bill of rights in their work.

23. Even the reiterations of the colonists' common law rights were initially hit or miss, executed (in Leonard Levy's words) in "an incredibly haphazard fashion that verged on ineptness." Leonard W. Levy, *Emergence of a Free Press* (New York: Oxford University Press, 1985), p. 324. The texts of the state bills of rights are collected in William F. Swindler, ed., *Sources and Documents of United States Constitutions,* 10 vols. (Dobbs Ferry, N.Y.: Oceana, 1973–79).

24. J. E. Crowley, *This Sheba, Self: The Conceptualization of Economic Life in Eighteenth Century America* (Baltimore: Johns Hopkins University Press, 1974); J. G. A. Pocock, *The Machiavellian Moment: Florentine Political Thought and the Atlantic Republican Tradition* (Princeton: Princeton University Press, 1975). The quoted passage is from Eric Foner, *Tom Paine and Revolutionary America* (New York: Oxford University Press, 1976), pp. 169–70.

25. "Americans creating a new society could not conceive of the state in any other terms than organic unity," Gordon Wood wrote, with his eye on this sort of rhetoric, in his massively influential *Creation of the American Republic.* "The important liberty" in 1776 was not private liberty but "public or political liberty"; and only a "fundamental transformation of political culture," a casting off of the preconceptions "that had imprisoned men's minds for centuries," woke them up to the fact that the body politic was no "body" at all but an agglomeration of often jarring, rights-bearing individuals. But from the beginning, expansive talk of individual rights ("What a man hath honestly acquired is absolutely his own," the Massachusetts House of Representatives had declared in 1768) and expansive claims for the public good were thoroughly mixed together. To generate an organized resistance to the British designs on private property both languages were from the outset indispensable (Gordon S. Wood, *The Creation of the American Republic* [Chapel Hill: University of North Carolina Press, 1969], pp. 59, 61, viii, 614; Samuel Adams, *Writings,* 1: 185).

The controversy initiated by Pocock and Wood and fueled by a subsequent excess of misplaced polarities is summed up in John P. Diggins, *The Lost Soul of American Politics: Virtue, Self-Interest and the Foundations of Liberalism* (New York: Basic Books, 1984); Joyce Appleby, *Capitalism and a New Social Order: The Republican Vision of the 1790s* (New York: New York University Press, 1984); and most sensibly in Robert E. Shalhope, "Republicanism and Early American Historiography," *William and Mary Quarterly,* 3d ser., 39 (1982): 334–56.

26. Tate, "Theory of the Social Contract," chaps. 6–7; Oscar and Mary Handlin, eds., *Popular Sources of Political Authority: Documents on the Massachusetts Constitution of 1780* (Cambridge: Harvard University Press, 1966), pp. 330–32.

27. Bailyn, *Ideological Origins,* chap. 6; Handlin, *Popular Sources,* pp. 231, 254, 302, 309, 375.

28. See, more generally, Forrest McDonald, *Novus Ordo Seclorum: The Intellectual Origins of the Constitution* (Lawrence: University of Kansas Press, 1985), pp. 13–36.

29. Edmund Burke, *Reflections on the Revolution in France* (1790), in *The Works of the Right Honorable Edmund Burke,* 5th ed., 12 vols. (Boston: Little, Brown, 1877), 3: 313.

30. Dickinson, *Liberty and Property,* chap. 6; John Brewer, *Party Ideology and Popular Politics at the Accession of George III* (Cambridge: Cambridge University Press, 1976); Colin Bonwick, *English Radicals and the American Revolution* (Chapel Hill: University of North Carolina Press, 1977); E. P. Thompson, *The Making of the English Working Class* (London: Gollancz, 1963), pt. 1.

The English and American radical movements of the last third of the eighteenth century were deeply intertwined. The Wilkes affair of the 1760s had repercussions up and down the colonies. But the explosion of natural rights manifestoes in England in the mid-1770s— Granville Sharp's *A Declaration of the People's Natural Right to a Share in the Legislature* (1774), Thomas Spence's *The Real Rights of Man* (1775), Richard Price's *Observations on the Nature of Civil Liberty* (1776)—suggests that a good deal of the argument had come back into the language of English radicalism via America. Cf. Isaac Kramnick, "Republican Revisionism Revisited," *American*

Historical Review 87 (1982): 629–64; and Margaret Jacob and James Jacob, eds., *The Origins of Anglo-American Radicalism* (London: George Allen and Unwin, 1984).

31. Burke, *Reflections on the Revolution in France*, in his *Works*, 3: 240.

32. Gareth Stedman Jones, "Rethinking Chartism," in his *Languages of Class: Studies in English Workingclass History, 1832–1982* (Cambridge: Cambridge University Press, 1983); Herbert Spencer, *Social Statics; or, The Conditions Essential to Human Happiness Specified, and the First of them Developed* (London: Chapman, 1851); Herbert Spencer, *The Man versus the State*, ed. Truxton Beale (New York: Mitchell Kennerly, 1916); J. A. Hobson, "The Influence of Henry George in England," *Fortnightly Review* 68 (1897): 841.

33. John Morley, *Recollections* (New York: Macmillan, 1917), p. 158.

34. Edward Dumbauld, *The Bill of Rights, and What It Means Today* (Norman, Oklahoma: University of Oklahoma Press, 1957), pp. 4–6, 9–10.

35. Mason, *Papers*, 3: 1068–71. The final result of the Virginia convention, together with the drafts debated in Congress, are reprinted in Dumbauld, *Bill of Rights*, app.

36. Marvin Meyers, ed., *The Mind of the Founder: Sources of the Political Thought of James Madison* (Indianapolis: Bobbs-Merrill, 1973), pp. 206, 224; Dumbauld, *Bill of Rights*, pp. 206–9.

37. *The Debates and Proceedings in the Congress of the United States* (Washington, D.C.: Gales and Seaton, 1834), 1: 774; William W. Henry, *Patrick Henry: Life, Correspondence, and Speeches*, 3 vols. (1891; reprint ed., New York: Burt Franklin, 1969), 3: 398.

38. Philip S. Foner, ed., *The Democratic-Republican Societies, 1790–1800: A Documentary Sourcebook of Constitutions, Declarations, Addresses, Resolutions, and Toasts* (Westport, Conn.: Greenwood, 1976); William B. Scott, *In Pursuit of Happiness: American Conceptions of Property from the Seventeenth to the Twentieth Century* (Bloomington: Indiana University Press, 1977), chap. 7; Bailyn, *Ideological Origins*, chap. 6. On the subsequent history of the natural rights defense of property, see herein pp. 122–30.

39. Wills, *Inventing America*, chaps. 24–26; Smith, *Letters of the Delegates*, vol. 4.

40. Philip F. Detweiler, "The Changing Reputation of the Declaration of Independence: The First Fifty Years," *William and Mary Quarterly*, 3d ser., 19 (1962): 557–74; Charles Warren, "Fourth of July Myths," ibid., 3d ser., 2 (1945): 237–72; Howard H. Martin, "Orations on the Anniversary of Independence, 1776–1876" (Ph.D. diss., Northwestern University, 1955).

41. Michael Kammen, *A Season of Youth: The American Revolution and the American Historical Imagination* (New York: Alfred A. Knopf, 1978), pp. 43–46; Merrill D. Peterson, *The Jefferson Image in the American Mind* (New York: Oxford University Press, 1960), chap. 1; Pauline Maier, "The Road Not Taken: Nullification, John C. Calhoun, and the Revolutionary Tradition in South Carolina," *South Carolina Historical Magazine* 82 (1981): 1–19.

42. Martin, "Orations"; Donald B. Johnson, ed., *National Party Platforms*, 2 vols. (Urbana: University of Illinois Press, 1978), 1: 5. The first state to borrow the sentence beginning "All men are created equal" was Indiana in 1851. A much smaller fragment ("life, liberty, and the pursuit of happiness") had appeared in the Wisconsin constitution of 1848.

43. The most widely copied southern formula came (via the Kentucky constitutions of the 1790s) out of the Mississippi constitutional convention of 1817: "All free men, when they form a social compact are equal in rights." That avoided specifying the natural rights of the contractors (and their slaves) altogether.

44. Of the nine southern states admitted to the Union between 1789 and the Civil War, seven incorporated the right to "abolish" government as a natural right. None of the twelve northern states organized in the same period did so. In Ohio in 1802, and in Michigan (1835) and Oregon (1857), where Democrats dominated the constitutional conventions, the right to "abolish" government was preserved but demoted to an ordinary, not a natural, right.

45. Martin, "Orations," p. 146; Edward Pessen, *Most Uncommon Jacksonians: The Radical Leaders of the Early Labor Movement* (Albany: State University of New York Press, 1967), p. 103.

46. Sean Wilentz, *Chants Democratic: New York City and the Rise of the American Working Class, 1788–1850* (New York: Oxford University Press, 1984); Alan Dawley, *Class and Community: The*

Industrial Revolution in Lynn (Cambridge: Harvard University Press, 1976); Bruce Laurie, *Working People of Philadelphia, 1800–1850* (Philadelphia: Temple University Press, 1980), chap. 4.

47. James D. Richardson, ed., *A Compilation of the Messages and Papers of the Presidents, 1789–1897,* 10 vols. (Washington, D.C.: U. S. Government Printing Office, 1896–99), 2: 295.

48. Philips S. Foner, ed., *We, The Other People: Alternative Declarations of Independence by Labor Groups, Farmers, Woman's Rights Advocates, Socialists, and Blacks, 1829–1975* (Urbana: University of Illinois Press, 1976), pp. 48, 72.

49. John R. Commons et al., eds., *A Documentary History of American Industrial Society,* 10 vols. (Cleveland: Arthur H. Clark, 1910–11), 6: 94; 5: 86; Thomas Skidmore, *The Rights of Man to Property!* (New York: Alexander Ming, 1829), pp. 58–63, 3.

50. Thomas Paine, *Agrarian Justice* (1797), in Paine, *Representative Selections,* p. 338. Remnants of this sort of talk survived for a time in the New York Equal Rights party. F. Byrdsall, *History of the Loco-Foco or Equal Rights Party* (1842; reprint ed., New York: Burt Franklin, 1967), pp. 57–58.

51. Skidmore, *Rights of Man,* pp. 33, 127, 116; Marvin Meyers, *The Jacksonian Persuasion: Politics and Belief,* new ed. (New York: Vintage, 1960), p. 193.

52. Lynd, *Intellectual Origins of American Radicalism,* passim.

53. *William Lloyd Garrison, 1805–1879: The Story of His Life Told by His Children,* 4 vols. (Boston: Houghton, Mifflin, 1889), 1: 412.

54. Angelina E. Grimke, *Letters to Catherine E. Beecher, in Reply to An Essay on Slavery and Abolitionism* (Boston: Isaac Knapp, 1838), p. 119.

55. Eric Foner, *Free Soil, Free Labor, Free Men: The Ideology of the Republican Party before the Civil War* (New York: Oxford University Press, 1970), p. 133; Roy P. Basler, ed., *The Collected Works of Abraham Lincoln,* 8 vols. (New Brunswick: Rutgers University Press, 1953), 4: 240.

56. Ibid., 3: 376.

57. Clinton Rossiter, *Seedtime of the Republic: The Origin of the American Tradition of Political Liberty* (New York: Harcourt Brace, 1953), p. 375.

Chapter 3. *The People*

1. Page Smith, *John Adams,* 2 vols. (Garden City: Doubleday, 1962), 2: 1129–30; Hugh B. Grigsby, "Sketches of Members of the Constitutional Convention of 1829–1830," *Virginia Magazine of History and Biography* 61 (1953): 331; Hugh R. Pleasants, "Sketches of the Virginia Convention of 1829–30," *Southern Literary Messenger* 17 (1851): 147–54.

2. Charles F. Adams, ed., *The Works of John Adams,* 10 vols. (Boston: Little, Brown, 1850–56), 10: 398.

3. *Journal of the Debates and Proceedings in the Convention of Delegates, Chosen to Revise the Constitution of Massachusetts, begun and holden at Boston, Nov. 15, 1820,* new ed. (Boston: Boston Daily Advertiser, 1853); William W. Story, ed., *Life and Letters of Joseph Story,* 2 vols. (Boston: Charles C. Little and James Brown, 1851), 1: 395.

4. *Proceedings and Debates of the Virginia State Convention of 1829–30* (Richmond: Ritchie and Cook, 1830), pp. 54, 55, 159, 137. On the background of the convention: Dickson D. Bruce, Jr., *The Rhetoric of Conservatism: The Virginia Convention of 1829–30 and the Conservative Tradition in the South* (San Marino: Huntington Library, 1982).

5. M. A. DeWolfe Howe, *The Life and Letters of George Bancroft,* 2 vols. (New York: Charles Scribner's Sons, 1908), 1: 181.

6. *Blackstone's Commentaries, with Notes of Reference to the Constitution and Laws of the Federal Government of the United States and of the Commonwealth of Virginia, by St. George Tucker,* 5 vols. (1803; reprint ed., New York: Augustus M. Kelley, 1969), 1: 48.

7. Robert G. McCloskey, ed., *The Works of James Wilson,* 2 vols. (Cambridge: Harvard University Press, 1967), 1: 77–81; John Adams, *Works,* 6: 469. Trumbull is quoted in Robert A. Ferguson, *Law and Letters in American Culture* (Cambridge: Harvard University Press, 1984), p. 109.

8. Jack P. Greene, *All Men Are Created Equal: Some Reflections on the Character of the American Revolution* (Oxford: Oxford University Press, 1976); Robert H. Wiebe, *The Opening of American Society: From the Adoption of the Constitution to the Eve of Disunion* (New York: Knopf, 1984), pp. 35–41; Edmund S. Morgan, "Government by Fiction: The Idea of Representation," *Yale Review* 72 (1983): 323.

9. R. R. Palmer, *The Age of Democratic Revolution: A Political History of Europe and America, 1760–1880,* 2 vols. (Princeton: Princeton University Press, 1959–64), 1: chap. 8; Gordon S. Wood, *The Creation of the American Republic, 1776–1787* (Chapel Hill: University of North Carolina Press, 1969), chaps. 8–9.

10. Albert L. Sturm, *Methods of State Constitutional Reform,* Michigan Governmental Studies, no. 28 (Ann Arbor: University of Michigan, 1954), pp. 10–11. Outside New England at the end of the 1820s, only the constitutions of Louisiana (1812) and New York (1821) had been popularly ratified. In the 1830s Delaware, Mississippi, and Arkansas, all put new constitutions into effect without a popular vote; but between 1836 and secession, popular ratification was the rule.

11. Walter F. Dodd, *The Revision and Amendment of State Constitutions* (Baltimore: John Hopkins University Press, 1910), pp. 42, 63.

12. Richard P. McCormick, "New Perspectives on Jacksonian Politics," *American Historical Review* 65 (1960): 288–301. The era's most celebrated debate over the suffrage, in the New York constitutional convention of 1821, was the work of a small knot of obstructionists, whose case was clearly lost before they began. By the end of the 1820s, only in Rhode Island, Louisiana, Virginia, and North Carolina (which retained a special freehold electorate for the state senate) did property barriers still significantly hem in the suffrage.

13. Nathaniel H. Carter and William L. Stone, *Reports of the Proceedings and Debates of the Convention of 1821, Assembled for the Purpose of Amending the Constitution of the State of New York* (Albany: E. E. Hosford, 1821), pp. 223–24; S. Croswell and R. Sutton, *Debates and Proceedings in the New-York State Convention for the Revision of the Constitution* (Albany: Albany Argus, 1846), p. 162.

14. James D. Richardson, ed., *A Compilation of the Messages and Papers of the Presidents, 1789–1897,* 10 vols. (Washington, D.C.: U.S. Government Printing Office, 1896–99), 2: 448.

15. Ibid., 3: 3.

16. John Ashworth, *"Agrarians" & "Aristocrats": Party Political Ideology in the United States, 1837–1846* (London: Royal Historical Society, 1983); Rush Welter, *The Mind of America, 1820–1860* (New York: Columbia University Press, 1975), chaps. 7, 9.

17. Marvin Meyers, *The Jacksonian Persuasion: Politics and Belief,* new ed. (New York: Vintage, 1960), pp. 18–19; William J. Cooper, Jr., *The South and the Politics of Slavery, 1828–1856* (Baton Rouge: Louisiana State University Press, 1978), p. 80.

18. Jean H. Baker, *Affairs of Party: The Political Culture of Northern Democrats in the Mid-Nineteenth Century* (Ithaca: Cornell University Press, 1983), chap. 7; William E. Gienapp, " 'Politics Seem to Enter into Everything': Political Culture in the North, 1840–1860," in *Essays on American Antebellum Politics, 1840–1860,* ed. Stephen E. Maizlish and John J. Kushma (College Station: Texas A & M Press, 1982).

19. Abel P. Upshur, "The True Theory of Government" (1841), *Southern Literary Messenger* 22 (1856): 401–10; *Register of the Debates and Proceedings of the Virginia Reform Convention* (Richmond: Ro. H. Gallaher, 1851), p. 221.

20. *The Writings and Speeches of Daniel Webster,* National ed., 18 vols. (Boston: Little, Brown, 1903), 6: 54; Theodore Parker, *The Slave Power,* ed. James K. Hosmer (1916; reprint ed., New York: Arno, 1969), p. 250; *Debates and Proceedings of the Virginia Reform Convention,* p. 173.

21. John William Ward, *Andrew Jackson: Symbol for an Age* (New York: Oxford University Press, 1955).

22. George Bancroft, "The Office of the People," in his *Literary and Historical Miscellanies* (New York: Harper and Brothers, 1855). In the early 1840s, Orestes Brownson, lurching uncertainly from Democratic partisanship to his own version of Catholic statism, peppered the *Democratic Review* with long critiques of majoritarian democracy, berating the absurdity of a polity in

which, everyone being sovereign, there were no subjects. But the editors preferred to let Brownson run out his contract and depart, cringing at their readers' defections, rather than sustain a systematic rebuttal. Orestes A. Brownson, "Democracy and Liberty," *United States Magazine and Democratic Review* 12 (1843): 374–91; Brownson, "Popular Government," ibid. 12 (1943): 529–44; Brownson, "Origin and Ground of Government," ibid. 13 (1843): 129–47, 241–62, 353–77.

23. Sturm, *Methods of State Constitutional Reform,* lists the conventions on pp. 114–15.

24. Gordon S. Wood, "The Democratization of Mind in the American Revolution," in *Leadership in the American Revolution: Papers Presented at the Third Library of Congress Symposium on the American Revolution* (Washington, D.C.: Library of Congress, 1974).

25. *Official Report of the Debates and Proceedings in the State Convention, Assembled May 4th, 1853, to Revise and Amend the Constitution of the Commonwealth of Massachusetts,* 3 vols. (Boston: White and Potter, 1853), 1: 45–50, 72–188; Arthur C. Cole, ed., *The Constitutional Debates of 1847,* in *Collections of the Illinois State Historical Library,* vol. 14 (Springfield, 1919), pp. 9–41; Croswell and Sutton, *Debates and Proceedings in the New-York State Convention* (1846), pp. 129–222; *Debates and Proceedings of the Virginia Reform Convention,* pp. 88–236.

26. Charles F. Adams, *Richard Henry Dana,* 2 vols. (Boston: Houghton, Mifflin, 1891), 1: 235.

27. Alabama (1868), Arkansas (1864), Missouri (1865), Mississippi (1869), North Carolina (1868), and South Carolina (1868), all received their first popularly ratified constitutions under the pressure of their northern military occupiers.

28. Dodd, *Revision and Amendment,* chap. 3.

29. John A. Jameson, *The Constitutional Convention: Its History, Powers, and Modes of Proceeding* (New York: Charles Scribner, 1867), p. 292.

30. *Debates and Proceedings in the [Massachusetts] State Convention* (1853) 1: 78–79; Jameson, *Constitutional Convention,* p. 292.

31. Stephen A. Channing, *Kentucky: A Bicentennial History* (New York: W. W. Norton, 1977), chap. 3.

32. *Report of the Debates and Proceedings of the Convention for the Revision of the Constitution of the State of Kentucky, 1849* (Frankfort: Hodges, 1849), pp. 857, 811–12.

33. James Guthrie, the convention's president who turned a fortune in Louisville real estate investments into railroad and bank promotion, and William D. Mitchell, eloquent in his enthusiasm for Kentucky's urban, commercial progress, were examples of the type.

34. "Radicalism," *United States Magazine and Democratic Review* 3 (1838): 111; Ashworth, *"Agrarians" & "Aristocrats",* p. 24; Welter, *Mind of America,* chap. 7.

35. *Proceedings and Debates of the [New York] Convention of 1821,* p. 199.

36. Donald B. Johnson, ed., *National Party Platforms,* 2 vols. (Urbana: University of Illinois Press, 1978), 1: 12; G. D. Lillibridge, *Beacon of Freedom: The Impact of American Democracy upon Great Britain, 1830–1870* (Philadelphia: University of Pennsylvania Press, 1955), p. 42; Gareth Stedman Jones, "Rethinking Chartism," in his *Languages of Class: Studies in English Working Class History, 1832–1982* (Cambridge: Cambridge University Press, 1983). Burke is quoted in H. T. Dickinson, *Liberty and Property: Political Ideology in Eighteenth-Century Britain* (London: Weidenfeld and Nicolson, 1977), p. 290.

37. The standard account is Marvin E. Gettleman, *The Dorr Rebellion: A Study in American Radicalism, 1833–1849* (New York: Random House, 1973).

38. George M. Dennison, *The Dorr War: Republicanism on Trial, 1831–1861* (Lexington: University Press of Kentucky, 1976), p. 115; Webster, *Writings,* 11: 222, 225; William M. Wiecek, "Popular Sovereignty in the Dorr War: Conservative Counterblast," *Rhode Island History* 32 (1973): 35–51.

39. John Quincy Adams, *The Social Compact Exemplified in the Constitution of the Commonwealth of Massachusetts* (Providence: Knowles and Vose, 1842).

40. Webster, *Writings,* 11: 221.

41. "Right of the People to Form a Constitution: Statement of Reasons," in *Rhode Island Historical Tracts,* no. 11 (Providence: Sidney Rider, 1880), pp. 68–92; U. S. House of Representa-

tives, *Interference of the Executive in the Affairs of Rhode Island* (1844), 28 Cong., 1 sess., H.R. 546, pp. 267, 83; Benjamin Hallett, *The Right of the People to Establish Forms of Government: Mr. Hallett's Argument in the Rhode Island Cases before the Supreme Court of the United States, January 1848* (Boston: Beals and Greene, 1848).

42. William M. Wiecek, *The Guarantee Clause of the United States Constitution* (Ithaca: Cornell University Press, 1972), pp. 94–95.

43. U. S. House of Representatives, *Interference of the Executive,* pp. 42–43.

44. Croswell and Sutton, *Debates and Proceedings in the New-York State Convention* (1846), pp. 211–12.

45. *Dred Scott* v. *Sandford,* 19 Howard 393 (1857); E. A. Pollard, ed., *Echoes from the South, Comprising the Most Important Speeches, Proclamations, and Public Acts Emanating from the South during the Late War* (1866; reprint ed., Westport, Conn.: Negro Universities Press, 1970); Charles R. Lee, *The Confederate Constitutions* (Chapel Hill: University of North Carolina Press, 1963), p. 171; Roy P. Basler, ed., *The Collected Works of Abraham Lincoln,* 8 vols. (New Brunswick: Rutgers University Press, 1953), 4: 438.

46. Robert W. Johannsen, *Stephen A. Douglas* (New York: Oxford University Press, 1973), p. 725.

47. Paul M. Angle, ed., *Created Equal? The Complete Lincoln-Douglas Debates of 1858* (Chicago: University of Chicago Press, 1958), p. 12.

48. Jefferson Davis, *The Rise and Fall of the Confederate Government,* 2 vols. (New York: D. Appleton, 1881), 1: 569–91; Angle, *Created Equal?,* p. 2.

Chapter 4. *Government*

1. Edmund Burke, *Reflections on the Revolution in France* (1790), in *The Works of the Right Honorable Edmund Burke,* 5th ed., 12 vols. (Boston: Little, Brown, 1877), 3: 359. On the Federalist temper: David H. Fischer, *The Revolution of American Conservatism: The Federalist Party in the Era of Jeffersonian Democracy* (New York: Harper & Row, 1965); Linda K. Kerber, *Federalists in Dissent: Imagery and Ideology in Jeffersonian America* (Ithaca: Cornell University Press, 1970).

2. Rufus Choate, "The Position and Functions of the American Bar, as an Element of Conservatism in the State" (1845), in *The Works of Rufus Choate,* 2 vols. (Boston: Little, Brown, 1862), 1: 423–24.

3. Louis Hartz, *The Liberal Tradition in America: An Interpretation of American Political Thought since the Revolution* (New York: Harcourt, Brace, 1955), pt. 4.

4. Quoted in Benjamin F. Wright, *American Interpretations of Natural Law* (Cambridge: Harvard University Press, 1931), p. 192.

5. Paul E. Johnson, *A Shopkeepers' Millennium: Society and Revivals in Rochester, New York, 1815–1837* (New York: Hill and Wang, 1978); Timothy L. Smith, *Revivalism and Social Reform in Mid-Nineteenth-Century America* (New York: Abingdon Press, 1957); Donald G. Mathews, *Religion in the Old South* (Chicago: University of Chicago Press, 1977); Clifford S. Griffin, *Their Brothers' Keepers: Moral Stewardship in the United States, 1800–1865* (New Brunswick: Rutgers University Press, 1960).

6. Noah Webster, *An American Dictionary of the English Language* (New York: S. Converse, 1828), "Government."

7. Robert Kelley, *The Cultural Pattern in American Politics: The First Century* (New York: Knopf, 1979); Daniel W. Howe, *The Political Culture of the American Whigs* (Chicago: University of Chicago Press, 1979). The rush to wedge a newfangled shred of piety into the state constitutions was a northern phenomenon, which bypassed the South until after the Civil War. Statements of this sort had been almost exclusively a New England phenomenon before 1840; after that date it was an extraordinarily rare northern state constitutional convention which dared to omit such a clause from its work. The exceptions, Michigan in 1850 and Oregon in 1857, were (not surprisingly) conventions dominated by Democratic majorities.

8. Anne C. Loveland, *Southern Evangelicals and the Social Order, 1800–1860* (Baton Rouge: Louisiana State University Press, 1980), pp. 108–29; John B. Boles, *The Great Revival, 1787–1805: The Origins of the Southern Evangelical Mind* (Lexington: University Press of Kentucky, 1972); Donald M. Scott, *From Office to Profession: The New England Ministry, 1750–1850* (Philadelphia: University of Pennsylvania Press, 1978).

9. Wilson Smith, *Professors and Public Ethics: A Study of Northern Moral Philosophers before the Civil War* (Ithaca: Cornell University Press, 1956); D. H. Meyer, *The Instructed Conscience: The Shaping of the American National Ethic* (Philadelphia: University of Pennsylvania Press, 1972). A particularly revealing glimpse into the character of the early moral philosophy courses can be found in *President Dwight's Decisions of Questions Discussed by the Senior Class in Yale College in 1813 and 1814,* ed. Timothy Dwight, Jr. (New York: Jonathan Leavitt, 1833).

10. John Witherspoon, *Lectures on Moral Philosophy* (1800; Princeton: Princeton University Press, 1912), pp. 67–72; Francis Wayland, *The Elements of Moral Science,* ed. Joseph L. Blau (1837; Cambridge: Harvard University Press, 1963), pp. 198–99; Charles C. Cole, Jr., *The Social Ideas of the Northern Evangelists, 1826–1860* (New York: Columbia University Press, 1954), pp. 144–51.

11. Laurens P. Hickok, *A System of Moral Science* (1853; 3d ed., New York: Ivison, Phinney, Blakeman, 1869), p. 153; Wayland, *Elements of Moral Science,* p. 182; Francis Bowen, "Dr. Lieber's *Political Ethics,*" *Christian Examiner and General Review* 26 (1839): 36. See also Daniel W. Howe, *The Unitarian Conscience: Harvard Moral Philosophy, 1805–1861* (Cambridge: Harvard University Press, 1970), chap. 5.

12. Thomas Paine, *The Rights of Man* (1791–92), in *Thomas Paine: Representative Selections,* ed. Harry H. Clark (New York: Hill and Wang, 1961), p. 176; Yehoshua Arieli, *Individualism and Nationalism in American Ideology* (Cambridge: Harvard University Press, 1964), chap. 6.

13. Joseph Haven, *Moral Philosophy, Including Theoretical and Practical Ethics* (1859; Boston: Gould and Lincoln, 1873); J. L. Dagg, *The Elements of Moral Science* (New York: Sheldon, 1860). The "duties of reciprocity" phrase was Dagg's.

14. Mark Hopkins, *Lectures on Moral Science* (Boston: Gould and Lincoln, 1862), p. 256; "Inaugural Address of Francis Lieber," in *Addresses of the Newly-Appointed Professors of Columbia College, February 1858* (New York: Columbia College, 1858), p. 97.

15. Joseph B. Burleigh, *The American Manual* (1848; 2d ed., Philadelphia: Grigg and Elliot, 1850), p. 49; Hickok, *System of Moral Science,* p. 153; Francis Lieber, *Manual of Political Ethics,* 2 vols. (Boston: Little and Brown, 1838–39), 1: 171; Tayler Lewis, "Human Rights According to Modern Philosophy," *American Review* 2 (1845): 447.

16. Charles F. Adams, *Richard Henry Dana,* 2 vols. (Boston: Houghton, Mifflin, 1891), 1: 246; Francis Bowen, "The Recent Contest in Rhode Island," *North American Review* 58 (1844): 421.

17. Quoted in Philip S. Paludan, *A Covenant with Death: The Constitution, Law, and Equity in the Civil War Era* (Urbana: University of Illinois Press, 1975), p. 75.

18. John Locke, *Two Treatises of Government,* ed. Peter Laslett, 2d ed. (Cambridge: Cambridge University Press, 1967), p. 304.

19. Charles G. Haines, *The Revival of Natural Law Concepts* (Cambridge: Harvard University Press, 1930); William B. Scott, *In Pursuit of Happiness: American Conceptions of Property from the Seventeenth to the Twentieth Century* (Bloomington: Indiana University Press, 1977), chap. 7.

20. Francis Bowen, "Wayland's *Political Economy,*" *Christian Examiner and General Review* 24 (1838): 58; James McClellan, *Joseph Story and the American Constitution: A Study in Political and Legal Thought* (Norman: University of Oklahoma Press, 1971), p. 320; Bernard E. Brown, *American Conservatives: The Political Thought of Francis Lieber and John W. Burgess* (New York: Columbia University Press, 1951), p. 64; Calvin Colton, ed., *The Works of Henry Clay,* 10 vols. (New York: G. P. Putnam's Sons, 1904), 8: 152. For a hint of the dismay of the artisan radicals: "What Is the Reason?" *United States Magazine and Democratic Review* 16 (1845): 17–30.

21. Harry N. Scheiber, "Public Economic Policy and the American Legal System: Historical Perspectives," *Wisconsin Law Review* (1980): 1159–89; Morton J. Horwitz, *The Transformation of American Law, 1780–1860* (Cambridge: Harvard University Press, 1977).

22. Harry A. Cushing, ed., *The Writings of Samuel Adams,* 4 vols. (New York: G. P. Putnam's Sons, 1904–8), 1: 190.

23. *The Writings of Thomas Jefferson*, 20 vols. (Washington, D.C.: Thomas Jefferson Memorial Association, 1903), 13: 333. On John Taylor: Paul K. Conkin, *Prophets of Prosperity: America's First Political Economists* (Bloomington: Indiana University Press, 1980), chap. 3.

24. Albert T. Bledsoe, *An Essay on Liberty and Slavery* (Philadelphia: J. B. Lippincott, 1856), p. 34.

25. Ibid., p. 111; Jenkins, *Pro-Slavery Thought*, pp. 107–24; Kenneth S. Greenberg, "Revolutionary Ideology and the Proslavery Argument: The Abolition of Slavery in Antebellum South Carolina," *Journal of Southern History* 42 (1976): 365–84. The "powder-cask abstractions" line was George Fitzhugh's, quoted in Merrill D. Peterson, *The Jefferson Image in the American Mind* (New York: Oxford University Press, 1960), p. 214.

26. *Blackstone's Commentaries, with Notes of Reference to the Constitution and Laws of the Federal Government of the United States and of the Commonwealth of Virginia, by St. George Tucker*, 5 vols. (1803; reprint ed., New York: Augustus M. Kelley, 1969); N. Beverly Tucker, *A Series of Lectures on the Science of Government* (Philadelphia: Carey and Hart, 1845), p. 255; *Proceedings and Debates of the Virginia State Convention of 1829–30* (Richmond: Ritchie and Cook, 1830), pp. 69–70.

27. Richard Crallé, ed., *The Works of John C. Calhoun*, 6 vols. (New York: D. Appleton, 1883), 6: 222; 1: 58, 1 (italics added).

28. Carl L. Becker, *The Declaration of Independence: A Study in the History of Political Ideas* (1922; New York: Knopf, 1942), pp. 262–63.

29. *Journal of the Debates and Proceedings in the Convention of Delegates, Chosen to Revise the Constitution of Massachusetts, begun and holden at Boston, Nov. 15, 1820*, new ed. (Boston: Boston Daily Advertiser, 1853), pp. 275–76, 285–87; Timothy Dwight, *Travels in New-England and New-York* (1821–22), quoted in Arieli, *Individualism*, p. 252; Francis Lieber, *Essays on Property and Labour as Connected with Natural Law and the Constitution of Society* (1841; New York: Harper and Brothers, 1847), p. 192.

30. Timothy Walker, *Introduction to American Law, Designed as a First Book for Students* (Philadelphia: Nicklin and Johnson, 1837), p. 190.

31. C. B. Macpherson, *The Political Theory of Possessive Individualism: Hobbes to Locke* (Oxford: Oxford University Press, 1962).

32. *The Works of William Ellery Channing*, 7th complete ed., 6 vols. (Boston: James Munroe, 1847), 6: 31; Arieli, *Individualism*, p. 268.

33. Channing, *Works*, 2: 39, 42.

34. Ibid., 2: 44; 6: 244, 68–73; William H. Channing, *The Life of William Ellery Channing* (Boston: American Unitarian Association, 1880), p. 598.

35. Theodore Parker, *The Rights of Man in America*, ed. F. B. Sanborn (1911; reprint ed., New York: Negro Universities Press, 1969), p. 360; William Goodell, *The Rights and Wrongs of Rhode Island* (Oneida: Press of the Oneida Institute, 1842), p. 117. Wendell Phillips is quoted in Staughton Lynd, *Intellectual Origins of American Radicalism* (New York: Pantheon, 1968), p. 123.

36. Ronald G. Walters, *The Antislavery Appeal: American Abolitionism after 1830* (Baltimore: Johns Hopkins University Press, 1976), p. 55; William Goodell, *Views of American Constitutional Law in Its Bearing upon American Slavery*, 2d ed. (Utica: Lawson and Chaplin, 1845), p. 154; Theodore Parker, *The Slave Power*, ed. James K. Hosmer (1916; reprint ed., New York: Arno, 1969), pp. 295–96; George M. Fredrickson, ed., *William Lloyd Garrison* (Englewood Cliffs, N.J.: Prentice-Hall, 1968), pp. 54–55; Lewis Perry, *Radical Abolitionism: Anarchy and the Government of God in Antislavery Thought* (Ithaca: Cornell University Press, 1973).

37. Charles Beecher, *The Duty of Disobedience to Wicked Laws: A Sermon on the Fugitive Slave Law* (New York: John A. Gray, 1851), pp. 22, 16.

38. [E. A. Pollard], ed., *Echoes from the South, Comprising the Most Important Speeches, Proclamations, and Public Acts Emanating from the South during the Late War* (1866; reprint ed., Westport, Conn.: Negro Universities Press, 1970); Jefferson Davis, *The Rise and Fall of the Confederate Government*, 2 vols. (New York: D. Appleton, 1881). On the force of southern particularism: David Donald, "Died of Democracy," in Donald, ed., *Why the North Won the Civil War* (Baton Rouge: Louisiana State University Press, 1960); Harry P. Owens and James J. Cooke, eds., *The Old South in the Crucible of War* (Jackson: University Press of Mississippi, 1983).

39. James H. Moorhead, *American Apocalypse: Yankee Protestants and the Civil War, 1860–1869* (New Haven: Yale University Press, 1978), pp. 134, 139, 141; Henry W. Bellows, *The State and the Nation—Sacred to Christian Citizens* (New York: James Miller, 1861), p. 11; and more generally George M. Fredrickson, *The Inner Civil War: Northern Intellectuals and the Crisis of the Union* (New York: Harper & Row, 1965), chaps. 5, 9.

40. Roy P. Basler, ed., *The Collected Works of Abraham Lincoln*, 8 vols. (New Brunswick: Rutgers University Press, 1953), 4: 269.

41. The right to the fruits of one's labor, nowhere guaranteed in this way in the North, was written into the constitutions of Maryland (1864), Missouri (1865), and North Carolina (1868). On the law: William E. Nelson, "The Impact of the Antislavery Movement upon Styles of Judicial Reasoning in Nineteenth Century America," *Harvard Law Review* 87 (1974): 513–66. On the freedmen: Eric Foner, *Nothing But Freedom: Emancipation and Its Legacy* (Baton Rouge: Louisiana State University Press, 1983), chap. 2.

42. *Congressional Globe*, 39 Cong., 1 sess. (1866), p. 309; George W. Julian, *Speeches on Political Questions* (New York: Hurd and Houghton, 1872), pp. 294, 291.

43. *The Debates and Proceedings of the Constitutional Convention of the State of Virginia, Assembled at the City of Richmond, December 3, 1867* (Richmond: New Nation, 1868), 1: 454–550. The black delegates are listed in David L. Pulliam, *The Constitutional Conventions of Virginia from the Foundation of the Commonwealth to the Present Time* (Richmond: John T. West, 1901), pp. 141–43.

44. On the political background of the convention: James C. Mohr, *The Radical Republicans and Reform in New York during Reconstruction* (Ithaca: Cornell University Press, 1973).

45. *Proceedings and Debates of the Constitutional Convention of the State of New York, held in 1867 and 1868*, 5 vols. (Albany: Weed, Parsons, 1868), 1: 238–39, 310–11, 333–35.

46. Ibid., 1: 221, 266–67, 243, 200; *The Miscellaneous Writings of Francis Lieber*, 2 vols. (Philadelphia: J. B. Lippincott, 1881), 1: 205–6.

47. *Proceedings and Debates of the Constitutional Convention of the State of New York*, 1: 335–36.

48. Ibid., 1: 200, 203, 213, 246, 382.

49. Ibid., 1: 336–37.

50. Ibid., 1: 239.

Chapter 5. *The State*

1. For example: William Sullivan, *The Political Class Book: Intended to Instruct the Higher Classes in Schools in the Origin, Nature, and Use of Political Power* (1830; new ed., Boston: Charles J. Hendee, 1841); Andrew W. Young, *Introduction to the Science of Government, and Compend of the Constitutional and Civil Jurisprudence of the United States, with a Brief Treatise on Political Economy, Designed for the Use of Families and Schools* (1835; 10th ed., Rochester, N.Y.: William Alling, 1843); Joseph B. Burleigh, *The American Manual* (1848; 2d ed., Philadelphia: Grigg, Elliot, 1850).

2. Bernard Crick, *The American Science of Politics: Its Origins and Conditions* (Berkeley: University of California Press, 1959), pp. 26–31, 95–101.

3. Alexis de Tocqueville, *Democracy in America*, ed. Phillips Bradley, 2 vols. (New York: Knopf, 1945), 1: 282–90.

4. William E. Nelson, "Changing Conceptions of Judicial Review: The Evolution of Constitutional Theory in the States, 1790–1860," *University of Pennsylvania Law Review* 120 (1972): 1166–85; Margaret V. Nelson, *A Study of Judicial Review in Virginia, 1798–1928* (New York: Columbia University Press, 1947), p. 35; James M. Rosenthal, "Massachusetts Acts and Resolves Declared Unconstitutional by the Supreme Judicial Court of Massachusetts," *Massachusetts Law Quarterly* 1 (1916): 303–13; Edward S. Corwin, "The Extension of Judicial Review in New York, 1793–1905," *Michigan Law Review* 15 (1917): 281–313. Prior to 1865, the United States Supreme Court had overturned 60 state laws. Between 1865 and 1898 it invalidated 171; between 1899 and 1930, over 300. Benjamin F. Wright, *The Growth of American Constitutional Law* (Boston: Houghton Mifflin, 1942), pp. 77, 82, 86, 113.

5. David Montgomery, *Beyond Equality: Labor and the Radical Republicans, 1862–1872* (New York: Knopf, 1967); Morton Keller, *Affairs of State: Public Life in Late Nineteenth Century America* (Cambridge: Harvard University Press, 1977), pt. 1; William R. Brock, *Investigation and Responsibility: Public Responsibility in the United States, 1865–1900* (Cambridge: Cambridge University Press, 1984). On Bentham: *Official Report of the Proceedings and Debates of the Third Constitutional Convention of Ohio, 1873*, 2 vols. (Cleveland, 1873–74), 2: 2583, 2585.

6. John A. Jameson, *The Constitutional Convention: Its History, Powers, and Modes of Proceeding* (New York: Charles Scribner, 1867), pp. 3–11.

7. Walter F. Dodd, *The Revision and Amendment of State Constitutions* (Baltimore: Johns Hopkins University Press, 1910), chap. 3; *Revised Record of the Constitutional Convention of the State of New York, 1894*, 5 vols. (Albany, 1900).

8. Thomas M. Cooley, *A Treatise on the Constitutional Limitations which Rest upon the Legislative Power of the States* (1868; 4th ed., Boston: Little, Brown, 1878). On Cooley's influence: Clyde E. Jacobs, *Law Writers and the Courts: The Influence of Thomas M. Cooley, Christopher G. Tiedeman, and John F. Dillon upon American Constitutional Law* (Berkeley: University of California Press, 1954); Phillip S. Paludan, *A Covenant with Death: The Constitution, Law, and Equality in the Civil War Era* (Urbana: University of Illinois Press, 1975).

9. Robert G. McCloskey, *American Conservatism in the Age of Enterprise, 1865–1910: A Study of William Graham Sumner, Stephen J. Field, and Andrew Carnegie* (Cambridge: Harvard University Press, 1951); William E. Nelson, "The Impact of the Antislavery Movement upon Styles of Judicial Reasoning in Nineteenth Century America," *Harvard Law Review* 87 (1974): 513–66.

10. For example: David J. Brewer, "Protection to Private Property from Public Attack," *New Englander* 55 (1891): 96–110.

11. Frederick Saunders, ed., *Our National Centennial Jubilee: Orations, Addresses and Poems Delivered on the Fourth of July, 1876, in the Several States of the Union* (New York: E. B. Treat, 1877); Donald B. Johnson, ed., *National Party Platforms*, 2 vols. (Urbana: University of Illinois Press, 1978).

12. Cooley, *Constitutional Limitations*, p. 204. *"What is property?"* Cooley wrote. "That is property which is recognized as such by the law, and nothing else is or can be." (Thomas M. Cooley, *The General Principles of Constitutional Law in the United States of America* [1880; 3d ed., Boston: Little, Brown, 1898], p. 345.)

13. Arnold M. Paul, *Conservative Crisis and the Rule of Law: Attitudes of Bar and Bench, 1887–1895* (Ithaca: Cornell University Press, 1960).

14. Corwin, "Extension of Judicial Review"; Lawrence M. Friedman, *A History of American Law* (New York: Simon and Schuster, 1973), pp. 311–18, 484–94; Keller, *Affairs of State*, chap. 9.

15. Quoted in Paul, *Conservative Crisis*, p. 81.

16. On the flexible (and often erratic) course of late nineteenth-century judicial opinion: Charles W. McCurdy, "Justice Field and the Jurisprudence of Government-Business Relations: Some Parameters of Laissez-Faire Constitutionalism, 1863–1897," *Journal of American History* 61 (1975): 970–1005; Alan Jones, "Thomas M. Cooley and 'Laissez-Faire Constitutionalism': A Reconsideration," ibid. 53 (1967): 751–71; John E. Semonche, *Charting the Future: The Supreme Court Responds to a Changing Society, 1890–1920* (Westport, Conn.: Greenwood, 1978); Melvin I. Urofsky, "State Courts and Protective Legislation during the Progressive Era: A Reevaluation," *Journal of American History* 72 (1985): 63–91.

Of the efforts to discern a reigning logic in this mass of opinion, the best are Michael Les Benedict's "Laissez-Faire and Liberty: A Re-Evaluation of the Meaning and Origins of Laissez-Faire Constitutionalism," *Law and History Review* 3 (1985): 293–331, and Robert W. Gordon's much more powerful "Legal Thought and Legal Practice in the Age of American Enterprise, 1870–1920," in *Professions and Professional Ideologies in America*, ed. Gerald L. Geison (Chapel Hill: University of North Carolina Press, 1983).

17. Robert Stevens, *Law School: Legal Education in America from the 1850s to the 1980s* (Chapel Hill: University of North Carolina Press, 1983), chaps. 1–4.

18. Albert Somit and Joseph Tanenhaus, *The Development of American Political Science: From Burgess*

to Behavioralism (Boston: Allyn and Bacon, 1967), chap. 3; R. R. Bowker and George Iles, *The Reader's Guide in Economic, Social and Political Science* (New York: Society for Political Education, 1891), pp. 129–37; "Report on Instruction in Political Science in Colleges and Universities," *Proceedings of the American Political Science Association* 10 (1914): 250.

19. *Catalogue of the College of William and Mary, Session 1891–92* (Richmond, 1892), p. 26; *Calendar of the University of Michigan for 1883–84* (Ann Arbor, 1884), p. 49; *Catalogue of the Officers and Students of Yale College, with a Statement of the Course of Instruction in the Various Departments, 1885–86* (New Haven, 1885), pp. 58–59; H. B. Adams, *The Study of History in American Colleges and Universities,* U. S. Bureau of Education, Circular of Information, vol. 6, no. 2 (Washington, D.C., 1887), pp. 114–23; John W. Burgess, "The Study of the Political Sciences in Columbia College," *International Review* 12 (1882): 346–51. The eclectic character of the discipline in its formative years is well illustrated in "Social Science Instruction in Colleges," *Journal of Social Science* 22 (1887): 7–27.

20. Raymond G. Gettell, *Introduction to Political Science* (Boston: Ginn, 1910), p. 100; A. Lawrence Lowell, *Essays on Government* (Boston: Houghton, Mifflin, 1889), p. 193; George L. Scherger, *The Evolution of Modern Liberty* (New York: Longmans, Green, 1904), p. 11.

21. Theodore D. Woolsey, *Political Science; or, The State, Theoretically and Practically Considered,* 2 vols. (New York: Charles Scribner's Sons, 1877), 1: 216, 198.

22. John J. Lalor, ed., *Cyclopaedia of Political Science, Political Economy, and the Political History of the United States,* 3 vols. (Chicago: Rand, McNally, 1881–84). The trend was already advanced enough in the early 1880s that William W. Crane and Bernard Moses's *Politics: An Introduction to the Study of Comparative Constitutional Law* (New York: G. P. Putnam's Sons, 1883) dismissed the question of rights as outside the sphere of theoretical political science altogether.

23. Arthur S. Link, ed., *The Papers of Woodrow Wilson* (Princeton: Princeton University Press, 1966–   ), 8: 564; Woodrow Wilson, *Mere Literature and Other Essays* (Boston: Houghton, Mifflin, 1896), p. 198.

24. John W. Burgess, *Political Science and Comparative Constitutional Law,* 2 vols. (Boston: Ginn, 1890), 1: 88, 54; Jeremiah W. Jenks, *Principles of Politics, from the Viewpoint of the American Citizen* (1909; New York: Columbia University Press, 1916), p. 44.

25. Gettell, *Introduction to Political Science,* p. 89; W. W. Willoughby, *An Examination of the Nature of the State* (1896; New York: Macmillan, 1922), chap. 6.

26. Ibid., p. 309; Burgess, *Political Science,* 1: 52, 56; James Q. Dealey, *The Development of the State: Its Governmental Organization and Its Activities* (New York: Silver, Burdett, 1909), pp. 57, 65; Stephen Leacock, *Elements of Political Science* (1906; rev. ed., Boston: Houghton Mifflin, 1913), p. 53.

27. John Austin, *Lectures on Jurisprudence; or, The Philosophy of Positive Law,* 4th ed., 2 vols. (London: John Murray, 1873), 1: 264–68; James Bryce, "The Nature of Sovereignty," in his *Studies in History and Jurisprudence,* 2 vols. (New York: Oxford University Press, 1901); David G. Ritchie, "On the Conception of Sovereignty," *Annals of the American Academy of Political and Social Science* 1 (1891): 385–411.

28. Woodrow Wilson, *The State: Elements of Historical and Practical Politics* (1889; Boston: D. C. Heath, 1895), p. 597; Woodrow Wilson, "Political Sovereignty," in his *An Old Master and Other Political Essays* (New York: Charles Scribner's Sons, 1893).

29. For example: Philemon Bliss, *Of Sovereignty* (Boston: Little, Brown, 1885); Charles M. Platt, "A Triad of Political Conceptions: State, Sovereign, Government," *Political Science Quarterly* 10 (1895): 292–323. At Harvard, A. Lawrence Lowell likewise resisted much of the conceptual framework on the ascent at Columbia and Johns Hopkins. Burgess, in particular, made intellectual enemies easily; between Willoughby, Wilson, and Burgess (the discipline's three most ambitious theorizers) little love, or deference, was manifest. But these were arguments within a narrow fold. Although the political science fraternity was never monolithic, the repetitive, formulaic quality of the textbooks published before the First World War is striking evidence of the way a handful of quasi-theoretical words had been made to define the subject matter of political science and give accounts of politics professional authority.

30. Dealey, *Development of the State,* p. 300.

31. Charles E. Merriam, Jr., *History of the Theory of Sovereignty since Rousseau,* Columbia University Studies in History, Economics, and Public Law, vol. 12, no. 4 (New York: Columbia University Press, 1900). The quotation is from Jameson, *Constitutional Convention,* p. 47.

32. Somit and Tanenhaus, *Development of American Political Science,* p. 32; Mary O. Furner, *Advocacy and Objectivity: A Crisis in the Professionalization of American Social Science, 1865–1905* (Lexington: University Press of Kentucky, 1975), pp. 278–91.

33. John W. Burgess, *Reminiscences of an American Scholar* (New York: Columbia University Press, 1934).

34. John W. Burgess, "The Ideal of the American Commonwealth," *Political Science Quarterly* 10 (1895): 404–25; Burgess, *The German Emperor and the German Government* (New York: Germanistic Society of America, 1909); Burgess, *The Reconciliation of Government with Liberty* (New York: Charles Scribner's Sons, 1915), p. 379.

35. Burgess, *Recent Changes in American Constitutional Theory* (New York: Columbia University Press, 1923), pp. 1–2.

36. Crick, *American Science of Politics,* p. 99.

37. Platt, "Triad of Political Conceptions," p. 306.

38. Frank S. Hoffman, *The Sphere of the State; or, The People as a Body-Politic* (New York: G. P. Putnam's Sons, 1894), p. 7; *Political Science Quarterly* 10 (1895): 164–65.

39. Charles A. Beard, "Political Science in the Crucible," *New Republic* 13 (Nov. 17, 1917): pt. 2, p. 3; *Educational Review* 35 (1908): 202.

40. J. K. Bluntschli, *The Theory of the State,* trans. D. G. Ritchie, P. E. Matheson, and R. Lodge (Oxford: Clarendon Press, 1885); Herbert B. Adams, *Bluntschli's Life-Work* (Baltimore, 1884).

41. Merriam, *History of the Theory of Sovereignty;* Rupert Emerson, *State and Sovereignty in Modern Germany* (New Haven: Yale University Press, 1928).

42. For example: Georg Jellinek, *The Declaration of the Rights of Man and of Citizens: A Contribution to Modern Constitutional History,* trans. Max Farrand (New York: Henry Holt, 1901); Jellinek, *Allgemeine Staatslehre* (1900; 2d ed., Berlin: O. Häring, 1905).

43. Alan Trachtenberg, *The Incorporation of America: Culture and Society in the Gilded Age* (New York: Hill and Wang, 1982), p. 19.

44. William James, *Pragmatism: A New Name for Some Old Ways of Thinking* (New York: Longmans, Green, 1907), p. 22; Bruce Kuklick, *The Rise of American Philosophy: Cambridge, Massachusetts, 1860–1930* (New Haven: Yale University Press, 1977); Ralph B. Perry, *The Present Conflict of Ideals: A Study of the Philosophical Background of the World War* (New York: Longmans, Green, 1919), p. 199.

45. Richard T. Ely, *The Social Law of Service* (New York: Eaton and Mains, 1896), p. 162; Eleanor H. Woods, *Robert A. Woods: Champion of Democracy* (Boston: Houghton Mifflin, 1929), pp. 105–6. In the 1880s, as Dorothy Ross has demonstrated, the language of insurgent economists like Ely had veered very close to that of socialism. Woods came back from a trip to England full of Fabian inspirations. But the hard times and heightened academic pressures of the 1890s dulled the radical edge of their politics and brought their yearning for social coherence increasingly to the fore. (Dorothy Ross, "Socialism and American Liberalism: Academic Social Thought in the 1880's," *Perspectives in American History* 11 [1977–8]: 5–79.)

46. The phrases are from William James's *Pragmatism,* p. 22.

47. Melvin Richter, *The Politics of Conscience: T. H. Green and His Age* (Cambridge: Harvard University Press, 1964); Stefan Collini, "Hobhouse, Bosanquet and the State: Philosophical Idealism and Political Argument in England, 1880–1918," *Past and Present* 72 (1976): 86–111.

48. Johnson, *National Party Platforms,* 1: 90; Philip S. Foner, ed., *We, The Other People: Alternative Declarations of Independence by Labor Groups, Farmers, Woman's Rights Advocates, Socialists and Blacks, 1829–1975* (Urbana: University of Illinois Press, 1976); Elizabeth C. Stanton et al., eds., *History of Woman Suffrage,* 6 vols. (New York and Rochester, 1881–1922), 5: 151, 193; Aileen S. Kraditor, *The Ideas of the Woman Suffrage Movement, 1890–1920* (New York: Columbia University Press, 1965), chap. 3.

49. James C. Carter, *Law: Its Origin, Growth and Function* (New York: G. P. Putnam's Sons, 1907), pp. 191–93, 344–45; John F. Dillon, *The Laws and Jurisprudence of England and America* (Boston: Little, Brown, 1894), p. 16.

50. Leacock, *Elements of Political Science*, p. 228; Frank J. Goodnow, *Politics and Administration* (New York: Macmillan, 1900).

51. Burgess, *Political Science*, 1: 56.

52. *Official Proceedings of the Constitutional Convention of the State of Alabama, May 21st, 1901 to September 3rd, 1901*, 4 vols. (Wetumpka, Ala., 1940), 1: 12.

53. Arthur F. Bentley, *The Process of Government: A Study of Social Pressures* (1908; reprint ed., Cambridge: Harvard University Press, 1967), p. 264.

Chapter 6. *Interests*

1. Charles Dickens, *American Notes for General Circulation* (1842), in *The Writings of Charles Dickens*, 32 vols. (Boston: Houghton, Mifflin, 1894), vol. 11; H. G. Wells, *The Future in America: A Search after Realities* (New York: Harper and Brothers, 1906).

2. Van Wyck Brooks, *America's Coming-of-Age* (1915), in *Van Wyck Brooks: The Early Years. A Selection from His Works, 1908–1921,* ed. Claire Sprague (New York: Harper & Row, 1968), pp. 82–83, 92, 88, 93.

3. Arthur F. Bentley, *The Process of Government: A Study of Social Pressures* (1908; reprint ed., Cambridge: Harvard University Press, 1967).

4. Harold D. Lasswell, *Politics: Who Gets What, When, How* (New York: McGraw Hill, 1936).

5. Clifford Geertz, *The Interpretation of Cultures: Selected Essays* (New York: Basic Books, 1973), p. 316.

6. Arthur S. Link, ed., *The Papers of Woodrow Wilson,* (Princeton: Princeton University Press, 1966–), 24: 204; Samuel I. Rosenman, ed., *The Public Papers and Addresses of Franklin D. Roosevelt,* 13 vols. (New York: Random House, 1938–50), 2: 157; David B. Truman, *The Governmental Process: Political Interests and Public Opinion* (New York: Knopf, 1951), pp. 50–51.

7. I have given a fuller sketch of the era's competing political languages in "In Search of Progressivism," *Reviews in American History* 10 (1982): 113–32.

8. H. G. Wells, *Experiment in Autobiography,* 2 vols. (London: Victor Gollancz, 1934), 2: 755. The World War altered the rhetoric of British politics and pushed it into a realm of super-charged abstractions—Honor, Duty, Patriotism, Sacrifice—every bit as powerful as those of a Theodore Roosevelt or a Woodrow Wilson. But in the decade before 1914, the contrast is unmistakable. Compare, for example, L. T. Hobhouse, *Liberalism* (London: Williams and Norgate, 1911) with Herbert Croly, *The Promise of American Life* (New York: Macmillan, 1909) or David Lloyd George, *Better Times* (London: Hodder and Stoughton, 1910) with Woodrow Wilson, *The New Freedom: A Call for the Emancipation of the Generous Energies of a People* (New York: Doubleday, Page, 1913). Paul F. Bourke makes a similar point in "The Status of Politics, 1909–1919: *The New Republic,* Randolph Bourne and Van Wyck Brooks," *Journal of American Studies* 8 (1974): 171–202.

9. Richard Hofstadter, *The Age of Reform, from Bryan to F.D.R.* (New York: Knopf, 1955), p. 203.

10. Richard L. McCormick, "The Discovery that 'Business Corrupts Politics': A Reappraisal of the Origins of Progressivism," *American Historical Review* 86 (1981): 247–74.

11. Lincoln Steffens, *The Shame of the Cities* (New York: McClure, Phillips, 1904); David G. Phillips, *The Treason of the Senate* (1906; Chicago: Quadrangle, 1964); *The Works of Theodore Roosevelt,* Memorial ed., 24 vols. (New York: Charles Scribner's Sons, 1923–26), 19: 15–16; Wilson, *Papers,* 22: 75. For the prehistory of the word: Albert O. Hirschman, *The Passions and the Interests: Political Arguments for Capitalism before Its Triumph* (Princeton: Princeton University Press, 1977).

12. Richard L. McCormick, "The Party Period and Public Policy: An Exploratory Hypothesis," *Journal of American History* 66 (1979): 279–98; Wallace D. Farnham, "'The Weakened Spring of Government': A Study in Nineteenth-Century American History," *American Historical Review* 68 (1963): 662–80.

13. Quoted in Grant McConnell, *Private Power and American Democracy* (New York: Knopf, 1966), p. 30.

14. John A. Gable, *The Bull Moose Years: Theodore Roosevelt and the Progressive Party* (Port Washington, N.Y.: Kennikat, 1978), p. 125; Wilson, *Papers,* 25: 18.

15. Michael H. Ebner and Eugene M. Tobin, eds., *The Age of Urban Reform: New Perspectives on the Progressive Era* (Port Washington, N.Y.: Kennikat, 1977), p. 22; David B. Tyack, *The One Best System: A History of American Urban Education* (Cambridge: Harvard University Press, 1974), pt. 5; Aileen S. Kraditor, *The Ideas of the Woman Suffrage Movement, 1890–1920* (New York: Columbia University Press, 1965), chap. 3; Charles A. Beard, "Reconstructing State Government," *New Republic* 4 (Aug. 21, 1915), pt. 2, p. 5.

16. Wilson, *Papers,* 25: 7.

17. *Works of Theodore Roosevelt,* 19: 362, 284.

18. Charles A. Beard, "The Ballot's Burden," *Political Science Quarterly* 24 (1909): 589–614; "Revision of the State Constitution," *Proceedings of the Academy of Political Science* 5 (1914–15), nos. 1–2; Frank J. Goodnow, *The American Conception of Liberty and Government* (Providence: Standard Printing Co., 1916).

19. Frederic C. Howe, "Oregon: The Most Complete Democracy in the World," *Hampton's Magazine* 26 (1911): 459–72; Burton J. Hendrick, "The Initiative and Referendum, and How Oregon Got Them," *McClure's Magazine* 37 (1911): 235–48; W. S. U'Ren, "State and County Government in Oregon and Proposed Changes," *Annals of the American Academy of Political and Social Science* 47 (1913): 271–73; Herbert Croly, *Progressive Democracy* (New York: Macmillan, 1914), pp. 292–302.

20. Wilson, *Papers,* 12: 8. Still more revealing, because it was the work of a man trying to extricate himself from the rhetoric of the general will, was A. Lawrence Lowell's *Public Opinion and Popular Government* (New York: Longmans, Green, 1913).

21. Bentley, *Process of Government,* p. 269; *Political Science Quarterly* 23 (1908): 739–41. A similar incident took place among the economists when John R. Commons, then in his radical phase, tried to dismiss the claims of the public good as a veil over tangible class interests (John R. Commons et al., "Discussion of the President's Address," *Publications of the American Economic Association,* 3d ser., 1 (1900): 62–88).

22. Charles A. Beard, *An Economic Interpretation of the Constitution of the United States* (New York: Macmillan, 1913); Ellen Nore, *Charles A. Beard: An Intellectual Biography* (Carbondale: Southern Illinois University Press, 1983), chap. 3.

23. Douglass Adair, "The Tenth Federalist Revisited," *William and Mary Quarterly,* 3d ser., 8 (1951): 48–67.

24. "Interests," *Cyclopedia of American Government,* ed. Andrew C. McLaughlin and Albert B. Hart, 3 vols. (New York: D. Appleton, 1914); "Columbia's Deliverance," *New York Times,* Oct. 10, 1917, p. 10.

25. George Creel, *How We Advertised America* (New York: Harper and Brothers, 1920); Woodrow Wilson, *War and Peace: Presidential Messages, Addresses and Public Papers (1917–1924),* ed. Ray S. Baker and William E. Dodd, 2 vols. (New York: Harper and Brothers, 1927), 1: 436, 111–12, 338.

26. Paul Boyer, *Urban Masses and Moral Order in America, 1820–1920* (Cambridge: Harvard University Press, 1978), chap. 20.

27. Stuart Chase, "Portrait of a Radical," *Century* 108 (1924): 301.

28. *Journal of the Statistical Society of London* 1 (1839): 8. More generally, T. S. Ashton, *Economic and Social Investigations in Manchester, 1833–1933: A Centenary History of the Manchester Statistical Society* (London: P. S. King and Son, 1934); and M. J. Cullen, *The Statistical Movement in Early Victorian Britain: The Foundations of Empirical Social Research* (Hassocks, Sussex, England: Harvester, 1975).

29. Patricia C. Cohen, *A Calculating People: The Spread of Numeracy in Early America* (Chicago:

University of Chicago Press, 1982); James H. Cassedy, *American Medicine and Statistical Thinking, 1800–1860* (Cambridge: Harvard University Press, 1984); S. N. D. North, "Seventy-Five Years of Progress in Statistics," in *The History of Statistics: Their Development and Progress in Many Countries,* ed. John Koren (New York: Macmillan, 1918). It was indicative of the main thrust of the statistical movement in the United States that the short-lived *American Statistical Review* of 1879, "Devoted to the Revival of American Industries: Not One, but All," offered up a straight digest of export statistics.

30. Wallace Stegner, *Beyond the Hundredth Meridian: John Wesley Powell and the Second Opening of the West* (Boston: Houghton Mifflin, 1954); Bernard Newton, *The Economics of Francis Amasa Walker: American Economics in Transition* (New York: Augustus M. Kelley, 1968), chap. 12; James Leiby, *Carroll Wright and Labor Reform: The Origin of Labor Statistics* (Cambridge: Harvard University Press, 1960).

31. Gifford Pinchot, *Breaking New Ground* (New York: Harcourt, Brace, 1947), pp. 326, 358–60; Whitney R. Cross, "W J McGee and the Idea of Conservation," *Historian* 15 (1953): 148–62; Lester F. Ward, "Hegel on the State," *Social Economist* 7 (1894): 32–37; Ward, *Dynamic Sociology,* 2 vols. (New York: D. Appleton, 1883).

32. Robert H. Wiebe, *The Search for Order, 1877–1920* (New York: Hill and Wang, 1967), chap. 6.

33. Wilson, *Papers,* 17: 570; John Dewey, "The Development of American Pragmatism," in *John Dewey: The Later Works, 1925–1953,* ed. Jo Ann Boydston (Carbondale: Southern Illinois University Press, 1981–), 2: 18–21; David A. Hollinger, "The Problem of Pragmatism in American History," *Journal of American History* 67 (1980): 88–107.

34. James first introduced the word "pragmatism" in 1898, but it was not until the enormous burst of publicity given James's *Pragmatism* in 1907–8 that the word gained general currency. Even then, as Finley Peter Dunne's mock-encounter between James and the man in the street made clear, it was far from easy for most readers to figure out what pragmatism was all about. Roscoe Pound (as early as 1908), Simon Patten, and Frank Goodnow (both by 1911) had grasped the affinity between their brands of social science and pragmatism. But the vogue of the term in political discourse did not really begin, under the prodding of William E. Walling, Dewey, Walter Lippmann, and others, until the mid-1910s.

Max H. Fisch, "American Pragmatism Before and After 1898," in *American Philosophy from Edwards to Quine,* ed. Robert W. Shahan and Kenneth R. Merrill (Norman, Oklahoma: University of Oklahoma Press, 1977); F. P. Dunne, "Mr. Dooley on Philosophers," *American Magazine* 65 (1908): 540–44; Roscoe Pound, "Mechanical Jurisprudence," *Columbia Law Review* 8 (1908): 608–10; Simon N. Patten, "Pragmatism and Social Science" (1911), in his *Essays in Economic Theory,* ed. Rexford G. Tugwell (New York: Knopf, 1924); Frank J. Goodnow, *Social Reform and the Constitution* (New York: Macmillan, 1911), pp. 3–4; William E. Walling, *The Larger Aspects of Socialism* (New York: Macmillan, 1913), chap. 1.

For Holmes's opinion of pragmatism: Mark DeWolfe Howe, ed., *Holmes-Pollock Letters: The Correspondence of Mr. Justice Holmes and Sir Frederick Pollock, 1874–1932,* 2 vols. (Cambridge: Harvard University Press, 1941), 2: 139.

35. Neil Coughlan, *Young John Dewey: An Essay in American Intellectual History* (Chicago: University of Chicago Press, 1975); George Dykhuizen, *The Life and Mind of John Dewey* (Carbondale: Southern Illinois University Press, 1973).

36. John Dewey, *Characters and Events: Popular Essays in Social and Political Philosophy,* 2 vols. (New York: Henry Holt, 1929), 2: 726; Dewey, *Reconstruction in Philosophy* (1920; enl. ed., Boston: Beacon Press, 1957), pp. 188, 189, 190; Dewey, *Individualism, Old and New* (1930; New York: G. P. Putnam's Sons, 1962), p. 165.

37. Dewey, *Reconstruction,* p. 199. For Dewey and his circle, Bentham was "in the camp of the enemy," Morton White wrote in his influential *Social Thought in America: The Revolt against Formalism,* new ed. (Boston: Beacon Press, 1957), p. 14. But to emphasize only the Progressive intellectuals' quarrel with Bentham's psychology is to miss the complex mix of both attraction and antipathy in their relationship to utilitarianism.

38. Quoted in Eric F. Goldman, *Rendezvous with Destiny: A History of Modern American Reform* (New York: Knopf, 1952), p. 159.

39. Bernard Crick, *The American Science of Politics: Its Origins and Conditions* (Berkeley: University of California Press, 1959); Albert Somit and Joseph Tanenhaus, *The Development of American Political Science: From Burgess to Behavioralism* (Boston: Allyn and Bacon, 1967).

40. The other five committees were devoted to comparative legislation, comparative jurisprudence, international law and diplomacy, constitutional law, and political theory. *Proceedings of the American Political Science Association* 1 (1904): 14–15.

41. "Report on Instruction in Political Science in Colleges and Universities," ibid. 10 (1914): 264; Charles A. Beard, *American Government and Politics* (New York: Macmillan, 1910), p. 1.

42. Somit and Tanenhaus, *Development of American Political Science,* pp. 61–62; Dorothy Ross, "The Development of the Social Sciences," in *The Organization of Knowledge in Modern America, 1860–1920,* ed. Alexandra Oleson and John Voss (Baltimore: Johns Hopkins University Press, 1979); Mary O. Furner, *Advocacy and Objectivity: A Crisis in the Professionalization of American Social Science, 1865–1905* (Lexington: University of Kentucky Press, 1975). Edward A. Purcell, Jr., stresses (and exaggerates) the amoralism of the new political science in *The Crisis of Democratic Theory: Scientific Naturalism and the Problem of Value* (Lexington: University Press of Kentucky, 1973).

43. Charles E. Merriam, "The Education of Charles E. Merriam," in *The Future of Government in the United States,* ed. Leonard D. White (Chicago: University of Chicago Press, 1942); Barry D. Karl, *Charles E. Merriam and the Study of Politics* (Chicago: University of Chicago Press, 1974).

44. Franklin H. Giddings, *The Responsible State: A Reexamination of Fundamental Political Doctrines in the Light of World War and the Menace of Anarchism* (Boston: Houghton Mifflin, 1918); John Dewey, *German Philosophy and Politics* (New York: Henry Holt, 1915); Westel W. Willoughby, *Prussian Political Philosophy: Its Principles and Implications* (New York: D. Appleton, 1918), p. 56; Carol S. Gruber, *Mars and Minerva: World War I and the Uses of the Higher Learning in America* (Baton Rouge: Louisiana State University Press, 1975), chap. 2.

45. L. P. Carpenter, *G. D. H. Cole: An Intellectual Biography* (Cambridge: Cambridge University Press, 1973); A. W. Wright, *G. D. H. Cole and Socialist Democracy* (Oxford: Oxford University Press, 1979). Beatrice Webb is quoted in Wright, *Cole,* p. 32n.

46. Harold J. Laski, *Studies in the Problem of Sovereignty* (New Haven: Yale University Press, 1917); Laski, *Authority in the Modern State* (New Haven: Yale University Press, 1919); Laski, "Democracy," *Yale Review,* n.s. 9 (1920): 788–803; Laski, *The Foundations of Sovereignty and Other Essays* (New York: Harcourt, Brace, 1921). The quoted passages are from *Studies in the Problem of Sovereignty,* pp. 23, 3, 208.

47. Mary P. Follett, *The New State: Group Organization the Solution of Popular Government* (1918; reprint ed., Gloucester, Mass.: Peter Smith, 1965), pp. 49, 7; "Functional Representation," *Encyclopaedia of the Social Sciences,* ed. E. R. A. Seligman, 15 vols. (New York: Macmillan, 1930–35). Cf. Paul F. Bourke, "The Pluralist Reading of James Madison's Tenth *Federalist,"* *Perspectives in American History* 9 (1975): 271–95.

48. Walter Lippmann, *Public Opinion* (New York: Harcourt, Brace, 1922), pp. 16, 30.

49. Edward L. Bernays, *Propaganda* (New York: Liveright, 1928) and Bernays, *Crystallizing Public Opinion* (New York: Boni and Liveright, 1923). On the private power lobby: U. S. Congress, Senate Committee on the Judiciary, *Lobby Investigation,* 4 vols., 71 Cong., 1 sess., 1929–31.

50. Peter H. Odegard, *Pressure Politics: The Story of the Anti-Saloon League* (New York: Columbia University Press, 1928); William B. Munro, *The Invisible Government* (New York: Macmillan, 1928); E. Pendleton Herring, *Group Representation before Congress* (Baltimore: Johns Hopkins University Press, 1929); Edward B. Logan, "Lobbying," *Annals of the American Academy of Political and Social Science* 144 suppl. (July 1929); Harwood L. Childs, *Labor and Capital in National Politics* (Columbus: Ohio State University Press, 1930); Peter H. Odegard, *The American Public Mind* (New York: Columbia University Press, 1930); Frederick E. Lumley, *The Propaganda Menace* (New York: Century, 1933); Harold D. Lasswell et al., *Propaganda and Promotional Activities: An Annotated Bibliography* (Minneapolis: University of Minnesota Press, 1935).

51. Charles E. Merriam and Harold F. Gosnell, *Non-Voting: Causes and Methods of Control* (Chicago: University of Chicago Press, 1924). The quoted passage is from Herring, *Group Representation*, p. 7.

52. Rodgers, "In Search of Progressivism," pp. 114–17.

53. At the turn of the century, observers of Congress had thought the hearing system a new and hopeful departure in politics. By the end of the 1920s, the realists were intent on stripping the facade from that now thoroughly routinized institution. Lauros G. McConachie, *Congressional Committees: A Study of the Origin and Development of Our National and Local Legislative Methods* (New York: Thomas Y. Crowell, 1898), pp. 61–64; E. E. Schattschneider, *Politics, Pressures and the Tariff: A Study of Free Private Enterprise in Pressure Politics, as Shown in the 1929–1930 Revision of the Tariff* (New York: Prentice-Hall, 1935).

54. Walter Lippmann, *The Phantom Public* (New York: Harcourt, Brace, 1925), pp. 156, 197, 99.

55. John Dewey, *The Public and Its Problems* (New York: Holt, 1927), p. 184. Dewey responded directly to Lippmann in "Public Opinion," *New Republic* 30 (1922): 286–88, and "Practical Democracy," ibid. 45 (1925): 52–54.

56. John Dickinson, "Democratic Realities and Democratic Dogma," *American Political Science Review* 24 (1930): 291, 292; Charles A. Beard, "English Political Thought," *New Republic* 24 (1920): 303.

57. Ellis W. Hawley et al., *Herbert Hoover and the Crisis of American Capitalism* (Cambridge: Schenkman, 1973), pp. 3–33; Herbert Hoover, *The New Day: Campaign Speeches of Herbert Hoover, 1928* (Stanford: Stanford University Press, 1928).

58. *Public Papers of Franklin D. Roosevelt*, 2: 345, 157.

59. Ibid., 7: 248; 5: 481.

60. Hofstadter, *Age of Reform*, p. 315.

61. Stuart Chase, *The Tyranny of Words* (New York: Harcourt, Brace, 1938); Edgar Kemler, *The Deflation of American Ideals: An Ethical Guide for New Dealers* (Washington, D.C.: American Council on Public Affairs, 1941).

62. Jerome Frank, *Law and the Modern Mind* (1930; New York: Coward-McCann, 1949), pp. 124, 6; Frank, "The Speech of Judges: A Dissenting Opinion" (1943), in *A Man's Reach: The Philosophy of Judge Jerome Frank,* ed. Barbara F. Kristin (New York: Macmillan, 1965); Thurman W. Arnold, *The Symbols of Government* (New Haven: Yale University Press, 1935), pp. 110, 234, 258. Karl Llewellyn put the complaint in the same terms: "The traditional approach [in the law] is in terms of words; it centers on words; it has the utmost difficulty in getting beyond words." Quoted in Purcell, *Crisis of Democratic Theory,* p. 81.

63. "I tried to express a philosophy which permitted an idealistic use of the opinion which can only be obtained in a skeptical frame of mind," Thurman Arnold wrote Harold Laski soon after *The Symbols of Government* appeared (*Voltaire and the Cowboy: The Letters of Thurman Arnold,* ed. Gene M. Gressley [Boulder: Colorado Associated University Press, 1977], p. 217).

64. Warren I. Susman, *Culture as History: The Transformation of American Society in the Twentieth Century* (New York: Pantheon, 1984), pp. 211–12; Richard H. Pells, *Radical Visions and American Dreams: Culture and Social Thought in the Depression Years* (New York: Harper & Row, 1973). On the other hand, Roosevelt himself, for whatever combination of reasons and doubts, only rarely played on the term "the people."

65. Charles A. Beard, "A 'Five-Year Plan' for America," *Forum* 86 (1931): 1–11; Stuart Chase, "A Ten Year Plan for America," *Harper's Magazine* 163 (1931): 1–10; Ellis W. Hawley, *The New Deal and the Problem of Monopoly: A Study in Economic Ambivalence* (Princeton: Princeton University Press, 1966). In the matter of control, the paper schemes of 1931–32 differed markedly from the brief experience with centralized economic management during the First World War. Though the War Industries Board had had a token labor representative, it was overwhelmingly dominated by businessmen (Robert D. Cuff, *The War Industries Board: Business-Government Relations during World War I* [Baltimore: Johns Hopkins University Press, 1973]).

66. Alan Brinkley, "The Concept of New Deal Liberalism, 1937–1945," paper presented at the Woodrow Wilson International Center for Scholars (Washington, D.C., June 1985), quoted with permission of the author.

67. Otis L. Graham, Jr., *An Encore for Reform: The Old Progressives and the New Deal* (New York: Oxford University Press, 1967), p. 70; Walter J. Shepard, "Democracy in Transition," *American Political Science Review* 29 (1935): 11.

68. John Chamberlain, *The American Stakes* (New York: Carrick and Evans, 1940), pp. 31–32.

69. Max Lerner, "The Broker State," *New Republic* 102 (1940): 477; *Public Papers of Franklin D. Roosevelt*, 3: 126; 5: 570.

70. E. Pendleton Herring, *The Politics of Democracy: American Parties in Action* (New York: Norton, 1940). Representative of the same vein were Peter H. Odegard and E. Allen Helms, *American Politics: A Study in Political Dynamics* (New York: Harper and Brothers, 1938) and V. O. Key, *Politics, Parties, and Pressure Groups* (New York: Thomas Y. Crowell, 1942). Herring had begun his career with a study of congressional pressure politics, Odegard with a study of the lobbying work of the Anti-Saloon League, Key with a study of the techniques of graft. But now the key term was no longer "pressure" but the continuous, dynamic adjustment of conflicts.

71. Chamberlain, *American Stakes*, p. 28.

72. R. Booth Fowler, *Believing Skeptics: American Political Intellectuals, 1945–1964* (Westport, Conn.: Greenwood, 1978). The quoted passage is from Theodore J. Lowi, *The End of Liberalism: Ideology, Policy, and the Crisis of Public Authority* (New York: Norton, 1969), p. 48.

Epilogue

1. Charles A. Beard, *The Republic: Conversations on Fundamentals* (New York: Viking, 1943); Walter Lippmann, *Essays in the Public Philosophy* (Boston: Little, Brown, 1955); and more generally Edward A. Purcell, Jr., *The Crisis of Democratic Theory: Scientific Naturalism and the Problem of Value* (Lexington: University Press of Kentucky, 1973).

2. Samuel I. Rosenman, ed., *The Public Papers and Addresses of Franklin D. Roosevelt*, 13 vols. (New York: Random House, 1938–50), 9: 671–72; 13: 33; 10: 477.

3. Gilbert Bailey, "Why They Throng to the Freedom Train," *New York Times*, Jan. 25, 1948, pt. 6, pp. 18ff.

4. *Public Papers of Franklin D. Roosevelt*, 10: 192. The rhetoricians of the Cold War not only absorbed the key slogans of the world war but exaggerated them to the point of cartoonlike —and enormously effective—melodrama. For one of the key examples: NSC 68 (1950), in Thomas H. Etzold and John L. Gaddis, eds., *Containment: Documents on American Policy and Strategy, 1945–1950* (New York: Columbia University Press, 1978).

5. Wendell L. Willkie, *Free Enterprise* (Washington, D.C.: National Home Library Foundation, 1940).

6. Paul Jacobs and Saul Landau, eds., *The New Radicals: A Report with Documents* (New York: Vintage, 1966), p. 131.

7. On the rights revival: Norman Dorsen's collection of essays in honor of the American Civil Liberties Union's fiftieth anniversary, *The Rights of Americans: What They Are—What They Should Be* (New York: Pantheon, 1971); Ronald Dworkin, *Taking Rights Seriously* (Cambridge: Harvard University Press, 1977); Richard E. Morgan's polemical *Disabling America: The "Rights Industry" in Our Time* (New York: Basic Books, 1984); and Stuart A. Scheingold, *The Politics of Rights: Lawyers, Public Policy, and Political Change* (New Haven: Yale University Press, 1974).

8. John Rawls, *A Theory of Justice* (Cambridge: Harvard University Press, 1971).

9. Kenneth L. Karst, "Invidious Discrimination: Justice Douglas and the Return of the 'Natural-Law-Due-Process-Formula,' " *UCLA Law Review* 16 (1969): 716–50; Alexander M. Bickel, *The Supreme Court and the Idea of Progress* (New York: Harper & Row, 1970); Archibald Cox, *The Role of the Supreme Court in American Government* (New York: Oxford University Press, 1976), chaps. 2–3.

10. *Bowers* v. *Hardwick* (1986), 54 LW 4919.

11. Samuel P. Huntington, *American Politics: The Promise of Disharmony* (Cambridge: Harvard University Press, 1981).

12. For example: Sheldon S. Wolin, *Politics and Vision: Continuity and Innovation in Western Political Thought* (Boston: Little, Brown, 1960); Henry S. Kariel, *The Decline of American Pluralism* (Stanford: Stanford University Press, 1961); Robert Paul Wolff, *The Poverty of Liberalism* (Boston: Beacon Press, 1968); C. B. Macpherson, *The Life and Times of Liberal Democracy* (Oxford: Oxford University Press, 1977).

13. Ronald Reagan, *The Triumph of the American Spirit: The Presidential Speeches of Ronald Reagan*, ed. Emil Arca and Gregory J. Pamel (Detroit: National Reproductions Corp., 1984), p. 4.

14. Robert N. Bellah et al., *Habits of the Heart: Individualism and Commitment in American Life* (Berkeley: University of California Press, 1985).

GUIDE TO FURTHER READING

The sources on which the arguments of this book rely are fully indicated in the notes; specialists will have recourse to them. What follows is a deliberately selective, amateurs' guide to some of the most important interpretive works in the history of political argument in America since the Revolution. No reader whose curiosity has been touched by the themes explored in these pages will fail to come away from any of the following studies challenged and enlightened. But like *Contested Truths* itself, they are best read not straight but in conjunction with as much of the primary source material as the reader can find: a paperback copy of reprinted Revolutionary tracts, a workingman's manifesto, a brittling volume of moral and political philosophy, a compilation of presidential addresses, a campaign tract, or the day's newspaper.

WORDS. The study of language, having taken a back seat so long to the study of "harder" social facts, has been on the ascent in the 1980s. Talk of texts, readings, tropes, and discourse is ubiquitous in the humanities and the more adventurous parts of the social sciences—and with good reason. No social fact becomes a part of experience unmediated by words, unaffected by the need to comprehend and communicate it, untouched by the necessity of bending words around it and (equally) bending it to the stock of words at hand. Most of structuralist and poststructuralist language study, however, tends toward nouns: languages, sign systems, texts. A stronger, tougher study of language needs verbs. Among the best of the accounts of political language in this vein, as a set of tools and actions, are Quentin Skinner's "Meaning and Understanding in the History of Ideas," *History and Theory* (1969); Clifford Geertz's elegant and influential *The Interpretation of Cultures* (1973); Murray Edelman's caustic, wide-ranging *The Symbolic Uses of Politics* (1964); Raymond Williams's work, to which his *Keywords: A Vocabulary of Culture and Society* (1976) is only an introduction; and beyond them all, William James's *Pragmatism* (1907).

UTILITY. No one took the task of demonstrating the pragmatic, utilitarian, antimetaphysical character of the Americans more seriously during the post–World War II recoil from the specter of ideology than Daniel Boorstin. His *The Genius of American Politics* (1953) and his three-volume *The Americans* (1958–73) are monuments to a scholarly generation's faith in the unreflective character of American politics. Similar assumptions ran through Richard Hofstadter's powerfully influential *The American Political Tradition* (1948), through such key works in 1960s political sociology and political science as Seymour Martin Lipset's *The First New Nation* (1963) and Robert A. Dahl's *Pluralist Democracy in the United States* (1967), and in an odd, ironic way through what remains the single most important overall sketch of the character of American political argument: Louis Hartz's *The Liberal Tradition in America* (1955). Among the critical rebuttals, Michael Paul Rogin's *The Intellectuals and McCarthy* (1967) stands out.

Guide to Further Reading

The materials for a more complex and conflict-marked history of the relationship between economic calculation and ideological politics can be found in Morton J. Horwitz's *The Transformation of American Law, 1780–1860* (1977); Harry N. Scheiber's "Property Law, Expropriation, and Resource Allocation by Government," *Journal of Economic History* (1973); and Louis Hartz's own *Economic Policy and Democratic Thought: Pennsylvania, 1776–1860* (1948). For a demonstration of the sheer power of words in American political culture, on the other hand, Sacvan Bercovitch's work is important; a powerfully concentrated extract can be found in his "The Biblical Basis of the American Myth" in Giles B. Gunn, ed., *The Bible and American Arts and Letters* (1983).

In contrast to their American counterparts, British political historians have only recently begun to write in terms of "political culture" at all; but the work on Bentham is strong and controversial. On Bentham himself, the key introductory works are Mary P. Mack's admiring *Jeremy Bentham* (1963), James Steintrager's shorter but more comprehensive *Bentham* (1977), and H. L. A. Hart's acute *Essays on Bentham* (1982). The controversy over Bentham's influence can be gauged by the distance between Harold Perkin's claims in *The Origins of Modern English Society, 1770–1880* (1969) and the skepticism of William Thomas's *The Philosophical Radicals* (1979). On British political science the best, though episodic, survey is Stefan Collini, Donald Winch, and John Burrow, *That Noble Science of Politics* (1983). For the absorption of utilitarianism into the new, socialized Liberalism at the end of the nineteenth century Peter Clarke's *Liberals and Social Democrats* (1978) and Willard Wolfe's *From Radicalism to Socialism: Men and Ideas in the Formation of Fabian Socialist Doctrines, 1881–1889* (1975) are valuable guides.

NATURAL RIGHTS. In the beginning (more or less) was the American Revolution. For no other era of our history has political language attracted so powerful a set of historians—or controversies. Bernard Bailyn's *The Ideological Origins of the American Revolution* (1967), Gordon S. Wood's broader and still more ambitious *The Creation of the American Republic, 1776–1787* (1969), and J. G. A. Pocock's powerful and difficult *The Machiavellian Moment: Florentine Political Thought and the Atlantic Republican Tradition* (1975) are indispensable reading. So, too, are the best of the efforts to set the words of the Revolution in social context: Eric Foner's *Tom Paine and Revolutionary America* (1976), David Brion Davis's *The Problem of Slavery in the Age of Revolution, 1770–1823* (1975), and Henry F. May's *The Enlightenment in America* (1976). Too much of the recent work on the language of revolutionary republicanism, however, has tended to flatten out the countercurrents of the Revolution in such a way that the rhetoric of rights (wrongly pinned to Locke and liberalism) has all but disappeared. Staughton Lynd's *Intellectual Origins of American Radicalism* (1968) is a critically important corrective. The historiographical debate is sketched in a special issue of the *American Quarterly* (1986) devoted to "republicanism" edited by Joyce Appleby, in John P. Diggins's tortured *The Lost Soul of American Politics* (1984), and, most thoughtfully, in Robert E. Shalhope's "Republicanism and Early American Historiography," *William and Mary Quarterly* (1982).

The parallel developments in late eighteenth-century Britain are outlined in H. T. Dickinson, *Liberty and Property: Political Ideology in Eighteenth-Century Britain* (1977); John Brewer, *Party Ideology and Popular Politics at the Accession of George III* (1976); and E. P. Thompson's monumental *The Making of the English Working Class* (1963). For the relative currency of European political writings in America, Donald Lundberg and Henry F. May, "The Enlightened Reader in America," *American Quarterly* (1976), and Donald S. Lutz, "The Relative Influence of European Writers on Late Eighteenth-Century American Political Thought," *American Political Science Review* (1984) are both essential.

The story of the Declaration of Independence is traced in Garry Wills's brilliantly argumentative *Inventing America: Jefferson's Declaration of Independence* (1978), Michael Kammen's *A Season of Youth: The American Revolution and the American Historical Imagination* (1978), and Philip S. Foner's collection of alternative declarations of independence, *We, The Other People* (1976). On artisan radicalism, see Edward Pessen, *Most Uncommon Jacksonians: The Radical Leaders of the Early Labor Movement* (1967); Bruce Laurie, *Working People of Philadelphia, 1800–1850* (1980); and Sean Wilentz, *Chants Democratic: New York City and the Rise of the American Working Class, 1788–1850* (1984). On the rhetoric of rights in the abolitionist movement, Staughton Lynd's *Intellectual Origins of American Radicalism* and Aileen S. Kraditor's *Means and Ends in American Abolitionism* (1969) are important; for the rhetoric of early feminism, the best starting place remains Elizabeth Cady Stanton et al., *History of Woman Suffrage* (1881–1922).

THE PEOPLE. The language of mid-nineteenth-century popular democracy has yet to find its modern historian. John Ashworth's *"Agrarians" & "Aristocrats": Party Political Ideology in the United States, 1837–1846* (1983) is an effective corrective to Marvin Meyers's older, paradox-filled *The Jacksonian Persuasion* (1957). The paradoxes in democratic rhetoric cannot all be cast away, however, as Edmund S. Morgan's "Government by Fiction: The Idea of Representation," *Yale Review* (1983) makes clear. The links between democratic theory and the rhetoric of laissez-faire are explored in Yehoshua Arieli's profound and neglected *Individualism and Nationalism in American Ideology* (1964) and Rush Welter's *The Mind of America. 1820–1860* (1975). Jean H. Baker describes the marriage of oratory and ritual in the new mass politics in *Affairs of Party: The Political Culture of Northern Democrats in the Mid-Nineteenth Century* (1983). The Rhode Island controversy is given a social base in Marvin E. Gettleman's *The Dorr Rebellion* (1973). No one has yet tried to set the explosive popular political movements of Jacksonian America, Chartist Britain, and the Europe of 1848 in a common frame, but Gareth Stedman Jones's "Rethinking Chartism" in his *Languages of Class* (1983) makes clear the possibilities.

Too many of our assumptions about the frame of American political argument have been shaped by the debates peculiar to national politics, at the expense of the sort of political talk that flourished closer to home—and nowhere so freely as in the state constitutional conventions of the nineteenth century. A checklist of those debates (collected on microfilm in the Library of Congress's *Records of the States*) can be found in Cynthia E. Browne, *State Constitutional Conventions* (1973), and a guide to the conventions themselves in Walter F. Dodd's still useful *The Revision and Amendment of State Constitutions* (1910).

GOVERNMENT. The opponents of the rhetorical legacy of the Revolution have been better served by historians than the Jacksonians on the whole, perhaps because their work, bound and formidable, faithfully preserved in the college libraries they controlled, has endured so much better than the ephemeral, popular salvos of the people's partisans. Daniel W. Howe's *The Political Culture of the American Whigs* (1979) is a fine introduction to Whig thought and rhetoric. The social and political dimensions of the great revival are explored in Donald M. Scott, *From Office to Profession: The New England Ministry, 1750–1850* (1978); Paul E. Johnson, *A Shopkeeper's Millennium: Society and Revivals in Rochester, New York, 1815–1837* (1978); Clifford S. Griffin, *Their Brothers' Keepers: Moral Stewardship in the United States, 1800–1865* (1960); Donald G. Mathews, *Religion in the Old South* (1977); and Anne C. Loveland, *Southern Evangelicals and the Social Order, 1800–1860* (1980). On the antebellum colleges, see William Smith, *Professors and Public Ethics: A Study of Northern Moral Philosophers before the Civil War* (1956) and Daniel W. Howe, *The Unitarian Conscience: Harvard Moral Philosophy, 1805–1861* (1970). On the rhetoric of antebellum law, Perry Miller's *The Life of the Mind in America: From the Revolution to the Civil War* (1965) is learned and provocative. The tangles into which southern proslavery argument wound itself are described in William S. Jenkins, *Pro-Slavery Thought in the Old South* (1935) and Kenneth S. Greenberg, "Revolutionary Ideology and the Proslavery Argument," *Journal of Southern History* (1976).

The higher law strain in antislavery rhetoric has been oddly missing from much of recent work. In Eric Foner's pathbreaking study of the economic theme in antislavery thought, *Free Soil, Free Labor, Free Men: The Ideology of the Republican Party before the Civil War* (1970), the term does not so much as make an entry into the index. But the loss is critical. Lewis Perry's *Radical Abolitionism: Anarchy and the Government of God in Antislavery Thought* (1973) traces the theme of the "pre-emptive sovereignty of God" in the rhetoric of some of the most radical of the abolitionists. The war-fueled apotheosis of the divine and divinely guided nation during the

Guide to Further Reading

Civil War is described in George M. Fredrickson, *The Inner Civil War: Northern Intellectuals and the Crisis of the Union* (1965) and James H. Moorhead, *American Apocalypse: Yankee Protestants and the Civil War, 1860–1869* (1978).

THE STATE. In most western nations, the most visible agents of the state were its civil servants and bureaucrats; in late nineteenth-century America, the primary organ of state power was the courts. Among the best accounts of the judges' quest for power are Morton J. Horwitz, "The Rise of Legal Formalism," *American Journal of Legal History* (1975); William E. Nelson, "Changing Conceptions of Judicial Review: The Evolution of Constitutional Theory in the States, 1790–1860," *University of Pennsylvania Law Review* (1972); Arnold M. Paul, *Conservative Crisis and the Rule of Law: Attitudes of Bar and Bench, 1887–1895* (1960); and Morton Keller, *Affairs of State: Public Life in Late Nineteenth Century America* (1977). Robert Stevens's *Law School: Legal Education in America from the 1850s to the 1980s* (1983) is a magisterial history of legal education. On the rhetoric of the law, see Charles G. Haines, *The Revival of Natural Law Concepts* (1930), a critique of conservative jurisprudence filled with the sort of animus that inspired legal realism; William E. Nelson's somewhat overdrawn "The Impact of the Antislavery Movement upon Styles of Judicial Reasoning in Nineteenth Century America," *Harvard Law Review* (1974); and Robert W. Gordon's brilliant "Legal Thought and Legal Practice in the Age of American Enterprise, 1870–1920" in Gerald L. Geison, ed., *Professions and Professional Ideologies in America* (1983).

The story of late nineteenth-century American political science is told, essentially as the triumph of empiricism, in Bernard Crick, *The American Science of Politics* (1959) and Albert Somit and Joseph Tanenhaus, *The Development of American Political Science: From Burgess to Behavioralism* (1967). Dorothy Ross recognizes a more tangled trajectory in "Socialism and American Liberalism: Academic Social Thought in the 1880's," *Perspectives in American History* (1977–78) and "The Development of the Social Sciences" in Alexandra Oleson and John Voss, eds., *The Organization of Knowledge in Modern America, 1860–1920* (1979). Idealism is analyzed as a philosophy in Bruce Kuklick, *The Rise of American Philosophy: Cambridge, Massachusetts, 1860–1930* (1977), and as a culture of veils and obfuscations in Alan Trachtenberg, *The Incorporation of America: Culture and Society in the Gilded Age* (1982). For parallel developments in Britain, see Melvin Richter's fine biography of T. H. Green, *The Politics of Conscience* (1964), and Stefan Collini's "Hobhouse, Bosanquet and the State: Philosophical Idealism and Political Argument in England, 1880–1918," *Past and Present* (1976). Finally, for a sense of what men like Burgess were up against, David Montgomery's *Beyond Equality: Labor and the Radical Republicans, 1862–1872* (1967) and John L. Thomas's *Alternative America: Henry George, Edward Bellamy, Henry Demarest Lloyd, and the Adversary Tradition* (1983) are important beginning points.

INTERESTS. Partial and one-sided as Richard Hofstadter's *The Age of Reform* (1955) remains, no one has crystallized the Progressives' yearning for the social whole more clearly. Paul Boyer's *Urban Masses and Moral Order in America, 1820–1920* (1978) extends the theme. A more complicated sense of the intersection between interest politics and anti-Interest rhetoric is to be found in Richard L. McCormick's essays, collected under the title *The Party Period and Public Policy* (1986). The rise of the language of political realism is sketched in Stephen Skowronek's *Building a New American State: The Expansion of National Administrative Capacities, 1877–1920* (1982) and Robert H. Wiebe's enormously influential *The Search for Order, 1877–1920* (1967). On pragmatism, Morton White's *Social Thought in America: The Revolt against Formalism* (1957) and David A. Hollinger's "The Problem of Pragmatism in American History," *Journal of American History* (1980) are essential.

The beginnings of the idea of interest group pluralism are sketched in Douglass Adair, "The Tenth Federalist Revisited," *William and Mary Quarterly* (1951) and Paul F. Bourke, "The Pluralist Reading of James Madison's Tenth *Federalist,*" *Perspectives in American History* (1975). For the post–World War I currents in political science, Edward A. Purcell, Jr.'s *The Crisis of Democratic Theory: Scientific Naturalism and the Problem of Value* (1973), despite its strong bias against anything smacking of relativism, stands out for its breadth and vigor. Also valuable are David M. Ricci, *The Tragedy of Political Science* (1984) and Barry D. Karl, *Charles E. Merriam and the Study of Politics* (1974). The seeping of interest-group rhetoric into the vocabulary of the New Deal is traced in Ellis W. Hawley, *The New Deal and the Problem of Monopoly* (1966), and more generally in Hawley, "The Discovery and Study of a 'Corporate Liberalism,' " *Business History Review* (1978). When Alan Brinkley's work is done, it will be clearer how the thirties' straining for community, emphasized in Richard H. Pells's *Radical Visions and American Dreams: Culture and Social Thought in the Depression Years* (1973), eventuated in the piecemeal liberalism of the 1940s; but the deeper transformation of the term "public opinion" under the pressures of advertising and propaganda is still unexplored territory.

On the prehistory of the term "interest," Albert O. Hirschman's *The Passions and the Interests: Political Arguments for Capitalism before Its Triumph* (1977) is elegant and eye-opening.

FREEDOM. Historians have just begun to scratch the surface of political culture in post–World War II America. For the political rhetoric of the war and Cold War, Richard H. Pells's *The Liberal Mind in a Conservative Age: American Intellectuals in the 1940s and 1950s* (1985) and Robert Booth Fowler's *Believing Skeptics: American Political Intellectuals, 1945–1964* (1978) are valuable beginning places. The revival of rights talk is described critically by Alexander M. Bickel in *The Supreme Court and the Idea of Progress* (1970), sympathetically by Stuart A. Scheingold in *The Politics of Rights* (1974), and with dismay by Samuel P. Huntington in *American Politics: The Promise of Disharmony* (1981). The struggle to reestablish public talk about public ends has enlisted a powerful set of dissident writers; Sheldon S. Wolin's *Politics and Vision* (1960); Henry S. Kariel's *The Decline of American Pluralism* (1961); and C. B. Macpherson's *The Life and Times of Liberal Democracy* (1977) are tough-minded, historical, and rewarding.

INDEX

Index

Index

Index

Universal Declaration of Human Rights, 218
Upshur, Abel, 90, 126, 157
U'Ren, W. S., 184
Utilitarianism, 7, 11, 12, 224; American rejection of, 18–19, 30–44; Bentham's invention of, 18, 20–24; in Britain, 25–29; and property, 128; revival of, 19–20, 38, 177, 187–93
Utilitarianism (Mill), 29
Utility, 11, 12; and the Enlightenment, 17; language of, 15, 18, 20, 29, 30, 33–34

Van Buren, Martin, 89
Vattel, Emmerich de, 51
Veblen, Thorstein, 194
Verein für Sozialpolitik, 167
Vermont: bill of rights of, 233*n*22; constitution of, 61, 71
Virginia: constitutional conventions of, 36, 40, 81–83, 90–92, 95, 96, 126; Declaration of Rights of, 53–54, 58–61, 64–65, 69, 70, 85, 86, 233*n*22; judicial review in, 148; Reconstruction in, 139; during Revolution, 56; suffrage in, 236*n*12; University of, 68, 116
Virginia Company, 55
Virtual representation, 105, 107

Wage labor, 72–74
Walker, Francis A., 189
Walker, Timothy, 129
Wallace, Henry A., 206, 218
Walling, William E., 247*n*34
Ward, Lester F., 189
War Industries Board, 249*n*65
Warren, Earl, 221
Washington, George, 39, 68, 214
Watson, John B., 194

Wayland, Francis, 119
Webb, Beatrice, 37, 41, 42, 196
Webb, Sidney, 28
Webster, Daniel, 34, 40, 91–92, 104, 105, 124, 132, 135
Webster, Noah, 117
Wells, H. G., 176, 179
Westminster Review, 32
Whewell, William, 27
Whig party, 14, 89, 91, 99, 114, 126, 132, 152, 166, 169; and moral philosophy, 122; and popular sovereignty, 90, 98, 102; and property rights, 124; and religion, 117–18; and Rhode Island controversy, 104–5; and suffrage, 105, 107, 141
Whigs, English, 52, 54, 62, 119
White, Morton, 247*n*37
Wilkes affair, 233*n*30
William and Mary College, 126, 157
Williams, Raymond, 227*n*5
Williams College, 120
Willoughby, W. W., 158, 196, 243*n*29
Wilson, James, 35, 85
Wilson, Woodrow, 18, 42, 165, 170, 190, 199, 204, 245*n*8; and the common good, 178, 182, 186; on the Interests, 178, 181; on the People, 182, 184; as political scientist, 158, 159, 161–63, 166, 243*n*29
Wisconsin, constitution of, 234*n*42
Wise, Henry A., 91
Woman suffrage, 36, 107, 140–42, 153; and common good, 182; as Natural Right, 172
Wood, Gordon S., 233*n*25
Woods, Robert A., 171, 244*n*45
Woolsey, Theodore Dwight, 158–59
Wright, Carroll D., 189
Wright, Henry C., 134

Yale University, 128, 157, 158; Law School of, 205